Such a Lucky Lady

By Lady Donna Louise Wilder

Lady Donna Louise Wilder

Such a Lucky Lady

A true story of my sadness
And happiness

Lady Donna Louise Wilder

My Parents

This Book is Dedicated to the Memory of My Parents Daphne Christine O'Bryan and Roy William Pearce

Disclaimer

I am very aware that many of you will notice a lot of mistakes in this autobiography, like the lack of punctuations."!': Etc. I set this down to my lack of schooling.

I admit I could, and should have attended some form of further education course, in which to help me with my lack of this basic knowledge.
To be honest, I have managed to live my life so far without it, as I have a lot of confidence.
I am, who I am, and where I am today. which I put down to not ever allowing my lack of education to hold me back.

I don't wish to become a renowned author in the future, this is just me putting pen to paper so to speak, just telling it in my, own words, so I hope it makes some sort, of sense to you? As it does to me? You never know it may prove to be the most challenging book you have ever read.

Who knows, all the mistakes that I have created in this book may inspire you to write your very own autobiography.

At the end of the day, I am happy with all I have put into this book. Well, that is all that matters to me.

Acknowledgment

I first need to give a big thank you to my long suffering husband (Wally). Charles Walter Wilder, who has put up with me writing this book about my life, constantly spilling the beans about my past, day in and day out, plus throughout the night sometimes nonstop. He has catered for me literally, placing food in my mouth as I typed away on my keypad, well a piece of chocolate and a cup of coffee here and there. Joking apart, he has saved me from starving or dehydrating, as once I get my teeth into a project I don't let a little thing like food or drink get in my way. (Unless it's a drop of Famous Grouse Whiskey and American ginger ale). Plus, and more importantly for showing me that anyone can move on from their demons, helping me find a stable way of life.

And then my son (Mike). Michael Antony Wilder and my daughter-in-law Kelly Wilder, who have had the lovely job of correcting all my computer mistakes, I can tell you there were quite a few.

Also Greig Carlson, who explained to me that I was making silly mistakes like when you send a text and you miss out a letter, hence instead of its I had it or she, became he so my predicated text had taken over my writing.

Great thanks go out to my sister Jo-Ann Marie Davies and my two brothers Martin Roy O'Bryan and (Rick). Richard Thomas O'Bryan, who have helped me by reminding me of all the antics we got up to as children.

Lastly, My, beautiful Auntie Maureen & Uncle Barry, who I have always looked up to as my role model.

Such A Lucky Lady

Introduction

I am comfortable with who I am.

All through growing up I thought that I must have been adopted. Because I always felt like the black sheep of this family, I simply found it too hard to adapt to their dirty ways, I just knew I didn't belong,

I found it so very tough to manage with all the mess from the animals that were all over our house, plus being a very sociable person I found it so embarrassing having to tell my friends that they couldn't come to play at our house.

Even though I may look so much like My Mother and I definitely have My Father's sick sense of humour, I just felt this was not the life for me.

I am humble enough to know I am not better than anybody, also wise enough to recognise that I am different from the rest. I just longed to live a completely different way to them, maybe it was a dream, but it was one I was longing to have.

I don't judge anyone on how they live their life. It's up to them. Everyone has different standards.

If I could have picked out my ideal family throughout my childhood, it would have been with both parents in a loving.

and happy, clean house where I could have brought my friend's home to play and not feel ashamed.

As my life has gone by I now realise that their way of life is quite normal for lots of people, it simply wasn't the life for me.

Well, here it is my life story, it includes the good times along with some bad times, everything that I can think of, right up until this day.

Without all this going on in my life, I wouldn't be who, or where I am today.

I have decided to write this, as you never know as I'm growing older, I may not be able to remember it all, this is my way of having all my memories about me and my life at hand. I have noticed that as I have been writing this autobiography I was starting to forget things already, so I have had to write them down right away.

Throughout my life, I have come across some wonderful people that have helped me work out how to make the best of my life.

You will note that I address my parents, as My Mother and My Father throughout this book. It's because My Daddy/Dad, left when I was only six years and nine months old, and My Mummy/Mother had told us as we grew older that we were not allowed to call her MUM as it sounded too much like BUM.

Contents

		Page
Disclaimer		5
Acknowledgment		6
Introduction:		7

Chapter

1	Come Meet My Family	13
2	My Life Begins Here	33
3	My Father Left Us	45
4	Fond Memories	53
5	Running Errands	63
6	Unsafe House	75
7	The Eviction Order	83
8	Sibling Rivalry	95
9	My Best Intentions	107
10	Dicing With Death	113
11	Scarred For Life	123
12	The Real World	133
13	A Critical Time	141
14	Motherhood Begins	151
15	I Deserve Better	157
16	Haemorrhaging	167
17	Where Needs Must	177
18	Baby's Black Eye	189
19	Corrupt Solicitor	199
20	Stolen Heart	211
21	On My Own	219
22	Double Wedding	225
23	Homeward Bound	237

24 Together	245
25 Our Big Day	253
26 Test Tube	261
27 Friday 13th	271
28 From A Boy To A Man	281
29 Gods Garden	291
30 Time To Move On	307
31 Our Wilderness	315
32 Through The Pearly Gates	325
33 Jet Setting	341
34 Early Retirement	353
35 Family Meeting	361
36 Living The High Life	369
37 American Christmas	379
38 A Great Discovery	387
39 Claim To Fame	389

Letters And Poems

History O'Bryan, Brian Boru	17
BBC Letter	23
My Mothers Report	25
Newspaper Cutting	29
My Mother And My Father	31
The Letter From My Mother	311
Memory Letter	333
Poem I Did As You Told Me	335
Poem God Took You	337
A Massive Thank You	391
And Finally	393

Photos

		Page
1	My Parent's	4
2	Olden Day's	12
3	The Chart	22
4	Grandparents	24
5	Mother And Siblings	32
6	Me And My Siblings	44
7	Us All Grown Up	52
8	My Family	74
9	My Son Michael	82
10	Michael's Family	106
11	Step Children And Their Mother	122
12	My Step Grandchildren	132
13	Martin's Family	150
14	Martin's Grandchildren	156
15	Jo-Ann's Family	166
16	Jo-Ann's Grandchildren	198
17	Richard's Family	218
18	Richard's Grandchildren	236
19	Rebecca's Family	270
20	Rebecca's Grandchildren	280
21	My Half Brother's And Sister's	306
22	My Cousin's On The O'Bryan Side	310
23	My Cousin's On The Pearce Side	330
24	My Auntie's And Uncle's	334
25	My Sister-In-Law's	360
26	My Brother-In-Law's	386
27	Just Me	392
28	Just The Two Of Us	394

Lady Donna Louise Wilder

Olden Days

Large photo Pearce family
Martin, Donna, Daphne, Richard, Jo-Ann Rebecca on
My Mother's lap.
Bottom left to right
(1) Stephen, Josephine, Kingsley, Mandy, Paul Hone.
(2) James and Minnie Gardner
(3) Patricia and Charlie Stewart

Chapter 1

Come Meet My Family

Please feel free to check out the interesting information about my ancestry, including court cases at The Old Bailey, at this website. www.jacobstree.co.uk

Ancestors On My Grandmothers Side

My 4th Grandparents
Phillip Jacobs 1780-1862
A glass-cutter
Rosella Hyams 1788-1852
Married 12/02/1806
They had five children.

My 3rd Grandparents
Henry Jacobs 1815
A Glass cutter, carpenter joiner
Susanna Fisher 1816
Married 27/08/1836
They had eight children.

My 2nd Grandparents
Henry Jacobs 29/04/1839-31/03/1911
Glass/ China merchant, dealer/traveler salesman
Ellen Silverstone 1835-6/11/1913
Dressmaker
They had 11 children.

Henry then had a family with his mistress
Elizabeth Twine 23/06/1851-04/10/1890
They had seven children.

Henry's wife Ellen and his mistress Elizabeth both gave birth to their babies in 1897.
Henry passed away in Conley Hatch Asylum Barnet Middlesex,
It's not surprising Henry ended up in asylum having that many children 17 in total.

My Great Grandparents
Minnie Constance Jacobs 1879 tailors
Nov 1962 cause of death on death certificate, shock due to burns ignition of clothing Accident,
James Frederick Garden 1876 A Market Porter
Married 05/12/1901
They had 11 children.

My Grandmother Louise Constance Gardner
Born 06/07/1911 Died 20/10/1941
Married My Grandfather Thomas Albert O'Bryan
Born 15/11/1904 Died 15/09/1940
Married On 20th December 1930 at St Clement Church, St Martin London,
They had three Daughters
My two Aunties Patricia Josephine (Pat) Born Saturday 31/10/1931 Died 26/06/2006
Josephine Ruth (Jo) Born Thursday 08/02/1934
My Mother Daphne Christine Born Tuesday, 08/02/1938 Died 13/02/2005 born on her sisters Jo's 4th birthday.

Such A Lucky Lady

Ancestors On My Grandfathers Side

My 3rd Grandparents
James O'Bryan 1824
Married in Ireland
Mary? 1826

My 2nd Grandparents
James O'Bryan 1842 Ireland
Died 28/04/1909 Holborn Infirmary Cancer Pancreas
Married 21/01/1864 ST Aloysius Chapel Clarendon Square St Pancras
Margaret Greering 1841 Ireland
Died 21/06/1897 Bronchitis Pleural Effusion
They had 5 Children

My Great Grandparents
John Patrick O'Bryan Born 1868? 14 Wild Court Drury Lane Holborn
Died 11/10/1943 Eston Cleveland Cerebral Haemorrhage
Married 06/05/1890 Westminster Register Office
Annie Maria Heather Born 29/01/1872 at 3, Little Denmark Street
Died 13/09/1939 St Pancras Hospital Cancer Bladder
They Had 11 Children

My Grandfather Thomas Albert O'Bryan
Born 15/11/1904 at 4, Dunstable Court Died 15/09/1940
In the Second World War after a bombing raid.
Married My Grandmother Louie Constance Gardner
On Born 06/07/1911 Died 20/10/1941 Married on 20/12/1930 at St Clement Church St Martin London.

Lady Donna Louise Wilder

Ancestors On My Father's Side

My Great Grandparents,
Albert White
Married
Alice Rossana Maddox
They had 9 children, four sons and five daughters
My Grandmother Sarah-Ann 1912-2005

My Great Grandparents
George Pearce
Matilda Bailey
They had 3 children, two sons and one daughter
My Grandfather William John 1906-1983
Matilda remarried George Briggs, after her husband passed away

My Grandfather William John Pearce Born 1906-1983
Married
My Grandmother Sarah Anne White Born 1912
Died 18/06/2005
They had two Sons and a Daughter
My Father Roy William on Saturday born 25/08/1934
Died 25/12/2007
My Auntie Maureen Born Sunday 17th July 1938
And My Uncle Rodger Born Sunday 26th September 1948-24/01/2005

Surname History Of O'Bryan
(The following information I found on the internet).

O'Brien is in Irish Ó Briain, from the personal name Brian. The meaning of this is problematic. It may come from bran, meaning "raven", or, more likely, from Brion, a borrowing from the Celtic ancestor of Welsh which contains the element bre-, meaning "hill" or "high place". By association, the name would then mean "lofty" or "eminent".

Whatever the initial meaning of the word the historic origin of the surname containing it is clear. It simply denotes a descendant of BrianBorú, ("Brian of the Tributes"), High King of Ireland in 1002, and victor at the battle of Clontarf in 1014. He was a member of the relatively obscure Ui Toirdealbhaigh, part of the Dál gCais tribal grouping based in the Clare/Limerick area. Having secured control of the Dál gCais in 976, he defeated and killed the Eoghanacht king of Munster two years later, and proceeded to wage deadly war against the kingdoms of Connacht, Meath, Leinster and Breifne. Eventually he secured submission (and tributes) from all but the northern Uí Néill, the Leinsterman and the Vikings. His victory at Clontarf united all of Ireland, nominally at least, under a single leader, though Brian himself was slain. It is not surprising that Brian's harp became the model for the national emblem of Ireland.

The first individual clearly to use O'Brien as a genuinely hereditary surname was Donogh Cairbre O'Brien, son of the king of Munster, Donal Mor. His descendants spilt into a number of branches, including the O'Briens of Aherlow, the O'Briens of Waterford, the O'Briens of Arra in north Tipperary, and the O'Briens of Limerick, where the surname is perpetuated in the name of the barony of Pubblebrien. Today the name is the sixth most numerous in Ireland, widely scattered throughout the country, with particular concentrations in the above areas, as well as in the original homeland of Clare.

Unlike most other members of the native Irish ruling classes, the senior line of the O'Briens managed to retain a large part of their wealth and power, the English titles of Earls and Barons of Inchiquin, Earls and Barons of Thomond and Viscounts Clare. All the titles but the Barony of Inchiquin became extinct in 1855. The present, eighteenth Baron Inchiquin, a direct descendant of the first Baron, Murrough O'Brien, who acquired the title in 1543, is Conor O'Brien, still living in the ancestral territory of Co. Clare.

The O'Brien arms symbolise clearly the royal origins of the family with the lion the regal emblem par excellence. In the crest, the arm emerging from the clouds wielding a sword is to suggest the otherworldly source of their power.

The surname has been prominent in all spheres of Irish life. The novelist and dramatist Kate O'Brien (1897-1954) suffered, like most Irish novelists of worth, at the hands of the censors in the early years of the Irish Free State. William Smith O'Brien (1803-1864) was one of the founders of the Young Ireland movement, and took a prominent part in the rising on 1848. His grandson Dermod O'Brien (1865-1945) was a leading portrait painter in Dublin for almost forty years.

Lady Donna Louise Wilder

The Family Tree Of Her Majesty Queen Elizabeth The Queen Mother From Brian Boru King Of Ireland 1002 – 1014

The Lineage of the Queen Mother and that of her late husband King George VI can be traced back through twice-related families to Brian Boru, who was King of Ireland from 1002 to 1014.

Brian Boru was himself descended from the ancient Kings of Ulster and the present day O'Neill's are a branch of ancient family, taking their name from the Legendary Niall of the Hostages.

Irish tradition tells us of a Milesian prince, Nelius, who became Niul in the Irish records. This takes us back into BC era when he married Scota, one of the daughters of Zedekiah, the last king of Egypt under the protection of the Pharaoh of the time.

The prophet Jeremiah later left Egypt with Princess Tamar Tephi, the elder of the two daughters, and as such the heiress of the line of King David, and brought her to Ireland. Eochaidh, the reigning Heremon of the area married her, and their descendants may be traced through the Irish records. Tamar was buried in the Hill of Tara

Such A Lucky Lady

The chart reproduced on the following page is a version to show the lines of the families during the earliest times and then the more commonly known descendants from the time of King George I and Richard Wellesley.

Lady Donna Louise Wilder

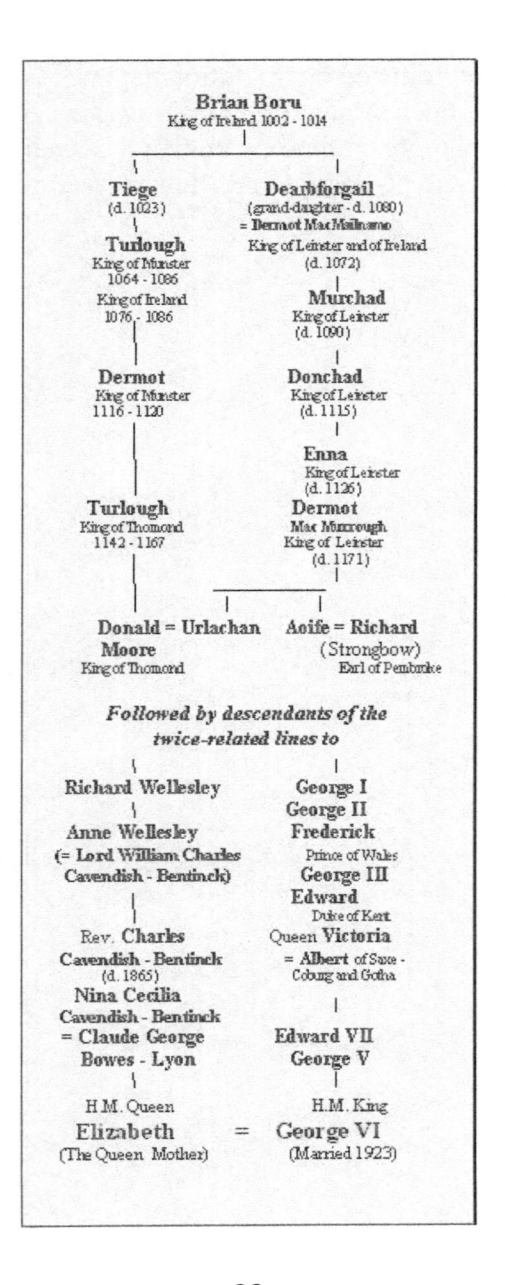

Brian Boru
King of Ireland 1002 - 1014

Tiege
(d. 1023)

Turlough
King of Munster
1064 - 1086
King of Ireland
1076 - 1086

Dermot
King of Munster
1116 - 1120

Turlough
King of Thomond
1142 - 1167

Donald = Urlachan Moore
King of Thomond

Dearbforgail
(grand-daughter - d. 1080)
= Dermot MacMailnamo
King of Leinster and of Ireland
(d. 1072)

Murchad
King of Leinster
(d. 1090)

Donchad
King of Leinster
(d. 1115)

Enna
King of Leinster
(d. 1126)

Dermot
Mac Murrough
King of Leinster
(d. 1171)

Aoife = Richard
(Strongbow)
Earl of Pembroke

Followed by descendants of the twice-related lines to

Richard Wellesley

Anne Wellesley
(= Lord William Charles
Cavendish - Bentinck)

Rev. **Charles**
Cavendish - Bentinck
(d. 1865)
Nina Cecilia
Cavendish - Bentinck
= Claude George
Bowes - Lyon

H.M. Queen
Elizabeth
(The Queen Mother)

George I
George II
Frederick
Prince of Wales
George III
Edward
Duke of Kent
Queen **Victoria**
= Albert of Saxe -
Coburg and Gotha

Edward VII
George V

H.M. King
George VI
(Married 1923)

=

Such A Lucky Lady

The following Information I Copied From A Letter My Auntie Josephine Hone Wrote To The BBC.

Thomas O'Bryan, My Grandfather, was killed on Monday 09/09/1940. It was after a bombing raid in London, as Lincoln House in High Holborn, had taken a direct hit. And many people were trapped inside. My Grandfather Thomas, who was a volunteer firefighter, went to help rescue the people. He left his wife and three girls in the Betterdon House shelter. In the morning as he hadn't arrived home. His wife, My Grandmother, took her daughter Josephine (Jo) with her leaving Patricia (Pat) and Daphne, My Mother in the shelter to try to find him, they went to the High Holborn station, the whole of High Holborn was ablaze.

My Grandmother started to cry as she had been, told. That the planes came back an hour later, and a lot of the rescuers were, killed. She was told to go, to the local mortuary because that was where the bodies had been, taken. When My Grandmother knocked at the door of the mortuary. A man opened the door and told her that she couldn't bring her daughter inside, so My Grandmother, took Josephine (Jo) to stay at a nearby school. She didn't find his body in there, but a part of his arm was found on the Sunday 15th September, his tattoo identified him.

Lady Donna Louise Wilder

My Grandparents And Great Grandparents

Left to right
(1) Louie Constance O'Bryan, (née) Gardner,
   Thomas Albert O'Bryan, My Grandparents.
(2) Sarah Anne Pearce, (née) White, My Grandmother.
(3) William John Pearce, My Grandfather.
(4) Annie Marie O'Bryan, (née) Heather,
John Patrick O'Bryan, My Great Grand Parents.
(5) James Gardner, Minnie Gardner, (née) Jacobs,
My Great Grandparents

Such A Lucky Lady

The following Information I Have Acquired From Reports I Have From The London Metropolitan Archives.

A year later their Mother, My Grandmother, died after an operation, her cause of death on the death certificate, Heart failure, rectal & vesicular fistula

So the girls were orphaned at a very early age. Patricia had been just ten years, Josephine 7 years, and Daphne 3 years old.
Soon after My Mother was evacuated to Seven Oaks, 17th November 1941.
She then returned to London on 3rd August 1942.
Then later re-evacuated to Private billet, 18th April 1943 but owing to allegations of a violent temper & bad language. She was then moved to a hostel.

Her guardian (grandmother) proposed allowing adoption by a Mr Hawkswell (family connections). 6th July 1943 But refused a Ministry's offer to accept guardianship. By 12th July 1943 her grandmother placed My Mother with Mr Hawkswell, but again My Mother at the request of Mr Hawkswell returned to her grandmother who still maintained refusal of ministry guardianship. She was placed in a Catholic foster home on the 25th July 1943.

My Mother and her sister Josephine were re-evacuated to Leicester by August 1944. Then Billetor asked for their removal due to Allegations of Josephine stealing. They placed them in another evacuation hostel, in Leicester.

Lady Donna Louise Wilder

October 1944, My Mother moved back to Billet (selected by R. C. Priest).
There was a home visit to see Guardian in London in February 1945.

Their grandmother refused any help, advice or homes for the children, By the 30th October 1945 My Mother was attending the St Clements Danes School (Non-Catholic). The Care Committee of L.C.C. Report on dirty and uncommon conditions 27th June 1946.

My Mothers guardian removed My Mother once again to Macklin St R.C School in February 1947. Less than a year later in January 1948, My Mother was admitted at the request of My Mothers guardian through the agency of the Crusade of Rescue to St Anthony's Home, Feltham and sanction given to the Ministry Officers to visit and keep in touch.

Then on the 8th September 1948, My Mother absconded from the home.

The N.S.P.C.C. Requested Crusade of Rescue to find other Convents for My Mother and her sister Josephine, 16th September 1949. A bad school report from Macklin Street R.C. School, about My Mother. (Daphne has a violent temper).

On the 1st November 1948, Crusade of Rescue refused further re-admission without legal protection, to give them authority and prevent children being removed.

Such A Lucky Lady

My Mother was taken into care by L.C.C. Section 1 of children act 1948. and placed in Convent of Sacred Heart Lewisham, on 7th January 1949, My Mother left the convent on 7th July 1950 at the request of her grandmother, (the convent report her as being very difficult). My Mother returned home and attended an Italian School. Where she was given an excellent report, but immediately there was trouble with her grandmother and sister at the home.

My Mother was then, placed in November 1950 by her guardian with her aunt. Mrs Wills in Kingsbury.
Because of friction with her aunt and cousin, she was once again removed in January 1951.
My Mother went back to the Italian School, where she received another good report.

On 6th January 1951, it was reported to the school by her grandmother, that, on the previous night My Mother had threatened her with a knife, and that she had sought advice from Bow Street Police Station. Then referred to the probation officer at Chelsea for advice.
My Mother was under supervision only, and was not in the care of the minister, as this course has always been refused by My Mothers guardian so there was no court order in operation.

My Mother was intelligent and in many ways gifted, and should benefit from a firm guidance and consistent help. All previous efforts had been ruined by her guardian's inability to leave My Mother alone.

Lady Donna Louise Wilder

Pushed, from, pillar to post throughout her childhood, being rejected by her grandmother, plus raised in an orphanage run by nuns, where she didn't receive any love or affection from any of them; consequently, she didn't know how to show or be affectionate with us.

My Mother may have been a very intelligent person, but she lacked the simplest tasks that we all face with running a home and taking care of our loved ones. (Your husband and children). As the everyday things were always just there in the orphanage, like soap, toilet paper, shoe polish, etc. so it never occurred to My Mother, to buy them. No doubt it didn't help that My Mother was in very ill health.

It was much later discovered that My Mother had a brain tumour today she would most probably be diagnosed with Depression as well as Chronic fatigue syndrome (CFS). CFS is also known as M.E. Which stands for myalgic encephalomyelitis. It causes persistent fatigue (exhaustion) that affects everyday life and doesn't go away with sleep or rest.

Such A Lucky Lady

This Is From A Newspaper Cutting, I Found About Minnie And James Gardner's Diamond Wedding Anniversary.

There will not be a party to celebrate the diamond wedding anniversary, of Mr. James Gardner and his wife Minnie for their home in Powis Buildings, Drury-Lane, W.C.2, is too small. Some members of the family went to tea last Sunday. On Tuesday, a daughter, her husband and several grandchildren called, and next Sunday. Other members of the family, scattered around London, will drop in. James is 85 and Minnie is in her 83rd year. Both have always lived in Holborn. Their parents were friends, and they were childhood sweethearts, attending the London Board School in Wild Street, W.C.2. James was born in what is now Kingsway. Where his father had a barber's shop and a side-line as a picture dealer. Minnie was born in Carter Street, Leicester-square, and as a tiny child was taken to live in Drury Lane, where her parents lived until their deaths.

Her father was a glass Traveller. Minnie became a tailor, and James, after working from the age of 11 as a shop boy for 3 shillings a week went to Covent Garden as a porter. James, now a frail man suffering from T.B. (contracted in the trenches of France during World War I), grinned when asked how he managed the baskets in the Garden. "Me?" he said. "I could carry 12 baskets with the best of them. But it was different in those days to what it is to-day. It was all chance work. I have gone out and been at Covent Garden at four in the morning and by noon I had earned only 6d." The couple had 11 children and have two sons and three daughters alive, 16 grandchildren, and 30 great-grandchildren. Both come from long-lived families. James' father lived to the age of 95 and his wife's father to the age of 84. James served with the 12th London Regiment, from the Tottenham Court Road Depot, where he was a Territorial. After his service he was not much use for the hard work at the "Garden," and later got a job as road sweeper with Holborn Borough Council, until illness made him unfit even for that. Minnie, who worked in Covent Garden shelling peas and topping and tailing beans until she was 80, was found at Holborn Darby and Joan Club at the Assembly Rooms. "We, were married at Clerkenwell 5,1901, and we have lived in our present flat for more than 40 years, so we can well be, described as 'dyed-in-the-wool' Holbornites," she said. "Coming to the club is my way of escaping old age.

My Mother And My Father

My Mother Daphne moved in to live with her sister Josephine and Brother-in-Law Kingsley Hone. In their new house at 28, South Park Way South Ruislip, Middlesex, HA4 6UL.
While My Father Roy was at home with his Parents, Sister and Brother at 144, Kingshill Avenue Northolt, Middlesex, UB5 6NY,

They both worked and met each other at J Lyons & Co. Tea factory in Greenford, West London. My Father's Mother & Sister Maureen worked there as well, as My Mother's Sister Josephine.

My Father Roy William Pearce, Married My Mother Daphne Christine O'Bryan, in March 1956 (My Mother was two months Pregnant with me at the time). After their Marriage, they lived with My Father's Family in Kingshill Avenue.

Lady Donna Louise Wilder

My Mother, Her Siblings And Their Mother. With Their Maiden Names

Maiden Names at time photos were taken.
Top left Patricia Josephine Stewart,
Middle Josephine Ruth Hone
Bottom Daphne Christine Pearce
Large photo Louis Constance O'Bryan

Chapter 2

My Life Begins Here

Well, this is where my life story begins; I was Born in Hillingdon Hospital, Middlesex The First Child to My Mother & My Father
Mrs Daphne Christine Pearce and Mr Roy William Pearce.
My Birth Name was Donna Louise Pearce,
I was born Thursday 18th October 1956.

My first Brother Martin Roy Pearce Born Friday 13th September 1957 He was born at home, in Kingshill Avenue.

My first Sister Jo-Ann Marie Pearce Born Friday 20th March 1959 In the Rustington Sussex Hospital.
My Father was in Prison at the time in Wormwood Scrubs; we were living in a caravan.

My second Brother Richard Thomas Pearce Born Saturday 2nd July 1960. He was born at home on Hayling Island. (I remember that day).

The last child My Mother had being Rebecca Christine Pearce Born Tuesday 20th November 1962 In St Mary's Hospital Portsmouth.
I find it strange that My Mother told me that she carried Rebecca for ten months.?

Lady Donna Louise Wilder

My Mother had 2 Miscarriages, I only recall the last one it was on Sunday 25th August 1963,
(That was on My Father's Birthday). It was after My Father had left us.

At one time, we lived upstairs in my Great Grandmothers House, (On My Father's side). At 21, Carlyle Road, Ealing, London W5 4BL
We only had gas lights, so My Father fitted new electricity.

My Mother did not get on with my Great Grandmother, so she would let us make as much noise as we liked. One time I can remember My Mother sitting us at the top of the stairs with pots pan lids and spoons to bang with, so we could make a lot of noise, this being before March 1959. as we had moved out and gone to live in Sussex, we stayed in a caravan that was where Jo-Ann was born Meanwhile My Father was sent to prison. (I was told it was because he took some money for a job and didn't do it) When My Father came out of Prison and saw Jo-Ann for the first time, she just screamed as she didn't know him.

(In 1959 My Mother's Sister Patricia and Husband Charlie along with their two children Colin & Elaine and baby Debra who was on the way, moved upstairs in my Great Grandmothers house when we moved out, later they bought the whole place).
We moved to Sussex, to stay for a short time on a house/canal-boat before moving into a house on Hayling Island.

Such A Lucky Lady

The day My Brother Richard was Born; My Father was watching us in the front room as we were playing. I had some transfers of Popeye that I had to place in a saucer of water; then I would put them in a scrapbook. Then I heard a Baby crying, the midwife came into the front room and said we could go and see our new Baby. Richard was placed in a drawer as they didn't have a cot for him; My Mother told me later that I wasn't happy about having a Baby Brother, as I said I wanted a new Dolly, so I closed the drawer with him in it.

The first house I remember living in the most was a prefabricated home (known as a prefab) at
20, Bursledon Place Purbrook, Waterlooville Hampshire PO7 5NL

I remember My Father and his friends, one called Eric, and the other one was Mick, taking me with them to the off-licence one night. It was a full moon, and My Father said when we reached the off-licence that the man in the moon had been following us. He told me to have a look outside the door and see if he was still there. I remember having a look, and the moon was right above. I could make out a face in it, I told My Father, and he said we would have to run home very quickly, he and Eric held my hand, and we ran, back home (my feet didn't even touch the ground).

Another time when My Father's friends were round, they were discussing how far it was to Lands' End in Cornwall. Then My Father Told My Mother to get us ready there and then. As we were going there to see how far it was. When we got there My Father turned on his torch as it was very dark, had a quick look at the sea, My Mother and us kids didn't get out as we were half asleep, he and his mates got back in the car, and we then turned straight around and came back home. He was crazy like that. Always taking us places at the drop of a hat. Once on one of our unexpected travels. We were walking along Brighton Pier when Jo-Ann noticed that she could see the sea between the planks of wood on the pier. She just froze and refused to walk on them, so afraid she was going to fall through. My Father just picked her up and held her over the side of the pier; he thought it was funny at the time. Poor Jo-Ann she must have been petrified. But that was My Father's sense of humour.

We were all going out one day, and My Mother was getting us all ready, as she finished each one of us. We were told to sit on one of the kitchen chairs; they were in a straight line. First me, then Martin, last was little Jo-Ann, the chairs were next to a bucket that was half full of soapy water with dirty Terry nappies in it, as My Mother was getting Baby Richard ready Jo-Ann fell head first into the bucket, My Mother was none too happy with her.

I remember My Father, making a chair with a tray on for Richard it had wheels on it as well, so we would push him all around the house, and a separate table that the chair sat on so it became a high chair; he even made a smaller one especially for my dolls.

Such A Lucky Lady

In September 1961, I started Purbrook Infant School. From this prefabricated home. On my first Day My Father came to pick me up, he was told by my teacher Mrs Ballinger that I was a very, loud little thing, and That they could of use me as a foghorn on the QE2. I had also told My Teacher that if she hit me with her cane, My Mother would be up the School to hit her.

(I had obviously overheard my parents talking).

We had loads of pink rose bushes in our garden, My Father cut a great big bunch and put them in the fridge until the morning for me to take to School and give to my Teacher Mrs Ballinger.

When it was half term, I volunteered to look after my Teacher's best plant, but we were going away. So My Father, placed the plant in the bath, and turned the tap on, just enough for a drip to fall now and then. But when we got back, the plant was enormous, he had to cut loads off before I could take it back to her, (she was very pleased).

I made Friends very easily at school. One Day in my class, it was a boy called Malcolm's Birthday, his parents owned a shop, that sold lots of things, including sweets. He gave every one of us in the class a traffic light Lolly and a balloon, when he had finished, he had one too many, so chose to give it to me, I think he was my first boyfriend.

Lady Donna Louise Wilder

For my 5th Birthday I got an enormous white cat/bear, it had a removable blue and white gingham skirt, but the top did not come of. My Uncle Rodger was down with my Nanny and Granddad, he was a teenager and just like My Father, he was teasing me by throwing my toy cat up at my glass wind chimes, and then he broke it.

The day Rebecca was born, I had been at School, when I came home My Mother was sitting by the fire, and she said what do you think we have. I said it's a Rebecca.

Soon after we moved across the road to a lovely three bedroomed house with a garden at number
4 Bursledon Place Purbrook, Waterlooville Hampshire, PO7 5NL

This house My Father decorated and furnished. We had Lino on the floors, but in the front / best room, we had a black & white carpet. It was not fitted right up to the walls. Therefore, the Lino went all around the edges. Plus, a sideboard. Table and chairs that my dad had made. A radiogram. A Three-piece suite, with wooden arms. A coffee table with a picture of the Taj Mahal under glass. TV in a cabinet with doors on and a big picture of a woman with a Green Face (Monika Sing-Lee) hung over the fireplace. An electric clock hung on the wall above the sideboard. In the back-room, we had a Formica table & 4 chairs. A unit in blue with cupboards top and bottom and a drop-down flap that you could use as a worktop, And a put-u-up sofa/bed. A black wood/coal burner. The room was divided up by three cupboards.

Such A Lucky Lady

My Father had removed the wall above the cupboards, so we had a tall shelf where the ornaments were placed. In the kitchen, the sink had a curtain around it, and our cooker was grey & white enamel. We had a single top loading washing machine, with a mangle that folded into the machine when not in use. Plus, a separate spin dryer, you had to pour water into it on top of the clothes, and then you had to place a bucket on the floor under the spout to catch the water while it was spinning the water out, and hopefully went into the bucket. A tall fridge with a small freezer on top. On the wall we had a can opener in blue & white and an electric blender.

We had a bathroom upstairs, which my dad decorated in a pastel mosaic pattern wallpaper. I shared my bedroom with Jo-Ann. We had bunk beds that were separated, and two bedside cabinets, a built-in wardrobe, and a chest-of-drawers, under the window. The box room was for Martin and Richard it had bunk beds, a built-in wardrobe and a chest-of-drawers My Mother and My Father had the front bedroom.

My Father was a carpenter, so he made lots of our furniture. I can still remember the headboard on my Parents bed. (It was black wood with white padded plastic that had a diamond Patten, divided into three panels by a thin gold strip, then on the top was a row of gold tubes spaced out). They had matching bedside cabinets plus a tall chest-of-drawers and a built-in wardrobe.

Lady Donna Louise Wilder

One day we were watching the TV when there was a knock at the front door My Father didn't want to open the front door to see them, so he closed the doors on the TV and told us all to be very very quiet. We were watching a series called Watch with Mother. It was on in the afternoon every day of the week. We would all sit down with a biscuit and a drink, to watch Bill and Ben the flower pot men with, little weed, or Andy Pandy, with Teddy and Looby Loo, the Wooden Tops, or Ragtag and Bob Tail.

My favourite TV Show's throughout growing up were Sara Brown and Hoppity, Charlie Drake, Twizzle, the Flintstones, Top Cat. We all looked forward to Lost in space. Then as I got a bit older, I liked to watch on the TV. The Harry Worth show, Crossroads, Take your pick, Opportunity Knocks. Along with The Golden Shot. The Avengers, the Saint, Randall and Hopkirk Deceased, and not forgetting Sunday Night at the London Palladium. If I had been good, I was allowed to stay up late to watch the TV with My Mother. I recall watching Peyton Place. After My Father had left us sometimes I was allowed to stay up very late with My Mother and watch Horrors and suspense programmes like Tales of the Unexpected and the Hammer House of Horror.

My Mother was out working Nights I think; at a Factory called Plisses (I remember her bringing home a wicker basket with blue plastic woven in it, that she had asked a Chinese woman to make for me).

Such A Lucky Lady

My Mother and My Father Were Friends with a couple, called Jack he was a Chief Petty Officer in the Royal Navy, I can't remember her name I think it was Barbara, they lived at no 8, I used to play with their daughter Linda, at school. She was a little older than me I think they had two boys as well one called Robert when the prefabs were all demolished. They built some new houses, then when they were all finished Linda, her brothers and Mum moved into one of them by that time Jack wasn't living with them.

When it was my 6th Birthday, I can remember my Birthday cake, it was round with white and pink icing, and a Ballerina in the middle, it was placed on the sideboard that My Father had made in the front room.

We would see My Nanny & Granddad Pearce, quite a lot. I loved her Ovaltine that she made me, (I called it omerlean). She used to make us dresses, on her sewing machine, and she was always knitting for us, I would love sitting and watching her. (I think it was My Nanny that I learned to do knitting from).

Richard had such little legs he would always step right in the middle of My Nanny's white & purple Alyssum flowers. (She had them as borders separating the grass from the path). One night we were staying, so My Nanny pushed two arm chairs together, so two of us could sleep top-to-toe. I can remember the orange street light right outside the front room window shining in. Over the road on the street corner was a shop, when it was closed they put a milk machine in front of the door, I would go with

My Father, to get some milk sometimes he also got a strawberry milkshake carton for me.

My Nanny gave my Father, a wooden cotton reel, he then went into my Granddads shed and found some nails, he then hammered them to the top to form a square. He gave it to me to take back into My Nanny, who sat me next to her, then with a ball of wool and a small needle, she showed me how to do French knitting. That kept me quiet for ages. She even showed me how to do finger knitting, which we all enjoyed doing, even My Brothers would try to outdo each other with the longest one.

One time we were driving home along some lanes and the bushes were full of thick Snow, another time while we were driving I asked My Father what was the lights in the middle of the road? He told me they were cats eyes. I felt upset until My Mother explained that it wasn't real cat's eyes.

When it was Christmas, My Father bought home a gigantic Christmas tree. It was so big that even after he had cut a big chunk off, it still touched the ceiling. Then the other half was put in the back room. He put crepe paper decorations up on the ceiling making a chessboard pattern, then in the middle of some of them he put Honeycomb decorations in the shape of bells, we had a Fairy on the top of the tree, some of the decorations were beautiful droplet ones made of silver glass with rainbow colours in stripes all around and silver glitter separating the colours, I remember getting School books, a pencil case and stationary that year.

Such A Lucky Lady

My Father used to work in London, so would leave for work early Monday morning, and return Friday afternoon. Most of the time he would pick me up from School when he got home lots of times, he would have to tidy up the house. My Mother would say she had been busy looking after us all. When the nappies weren't dry or she had run out of them, she would use towels, pillow cases, even My Father's vests, we would have empty, or part empty milk bottles all around the place. So one day in a temper My Father started to put them all unwashed on the front doorstep, but My Mother just shouted don't, don't let the neighbours see them, so he dug a big hole in the back garden and buried them all.

Once My Father was sitting in an armchair with his feet up on the fireplace, I was sitting on his lap. When My Mother came into the room, My Father, asked her to pass his cigarettes from the top of the fireplace, she shouted at him saying you're a lazy git, get them yourself, My Father, started to laugh at her, so she got mad, and shouted even louder. My Father just kept on laughing at her, and told me Mummy is being silly let's laugh at her;

Maybe Mother was mad because she was expecting another baby.

Lady Donna Louise Wilder

Me And My Siblings

At the time these photos were taken, we were all known as Pearce.
Top Left to right
(1) Donna (2) Martin
Center (3) Rebecca
Bottom Left to right
(4) Jo-Ann (5) Richard.

Such A Lucky Lady

CHAPTER 3

My Father Left Us

On Thursday, the 4th day of July 1963. My Father left us altogether. I have been told two stories as to why My Father left.

My Mother said that we had been away on a caravan holiday, and when we arrived back, My Father opened the mail and found that we were going to be, evicted as he hadn't paid the rent, so he just left.

My Father said that he came home unexpectedly from working in London. He came through the back door and went upstairs where he found My Mother with a man in bed he came downstairs, made them a cup of tea or coffee, took it up and said "you're welcome to her" and left.

The problem I have is that I can very clearly remember My Father coming in through the back door, I was playing in the back room on the floor with my dolls at the time, he put his finger to his lips telling me to be quiet. I don't remember him making any drinks, only him coming over to me rubbing my hair and saying "see you later".

My Mother had a Miscarriage on Sunday 25th August 1963, just after My Father had left. Her Sister Pat sent

Lady Donna Louise Wilder

her Daughter Elaine (my 9-year-old cousin) over to help look after us all. I showed Elaine my best dresses which were hanging in my wardrobe. My favourite dress was red with large white circles, each one with a monkey playing an instrument. I also had a pretty white one with block rows of poker dots in pale pink, yellow, green, lilac and blue. Elaine and I found that we could use our fingernails to pick them off leaving the coloured spot on the dress. Another dress I had was red and white with a matching coat; Elaine had the same one in blue.

I went back to School in the new term with My Brother Martin but as I was upset about My Father leaving I couldn't settle. So one day I went next door to play with the children, I told the lady (her name was Jane) that My Mother wasn't well and asked if she could please give us some breakfast; she gave us porridge. We then played with her children, Scott, Tracy and her Baby Clark. As I have a deafening voice, it wasn't long before My Mother heard me from the top bedroom window and ordered me to come home. My Mother wrote a note to my Teacher explaining that I was upset about My Father leaving and sent us back to School. We ran straight back to next door to play, I very boastfully showed the note to Jane, saying that I had written it myself, we were taken back home by Jane, who became My Mother's Friend.

My Mother took us all out to the shops one day, in our new raincoats, with matching rain hats. Martin and I had red ones while Jo-Ann and Richard had yellow, I can't remember what Rebecca had on. My Mother was pushing her in the pushchair. My Mother had on a beautiful lime green coat that was done up with one large black fancy button at the neck. With My Mothers very long, (at the time) dark, black hair, it, actually suited her.

We always looked immaculate and very tidy whenever we went out with My Mother. No one could have imagined the state of our house. A man and woman walked past us and said to My Mother how sweet and well behaved we all were. We were going to the barber shop for My Brothers to have their hair cut My Mother asked the barber to give them a crew cut, (a short back and sides). While we were in their My Headmaster, Mr Twig was sitting in a nice comfortable armchair, so I moved over to talk to him while I was talking to him I noticed that he had a bald patch on the top of his head. I told him that it looked like he had a hole in his head, Mr Twig laughed and said his hair fell away because of all the naughty boys and girls he had at his School.

One day at School I wet my knickers, My Teacher wrapped them in brown paper for me to bring home. When I got undressed at home, My Mother noticed that I had different ones on, and asked me where my ones were (As they matched the petticoat that I had). I told My Mother that I had thrown them in the bushes, My Mother told me to go and get them. But I couldn't reach them as the bushes were prickly but an old man got them out for me.

One day soon after it was one of Jane's children's birthdays and we were all invited to the party. My

Lady Donna Louise Wilder

Mother took Richard Rebecca and I round, but not Martin and Jo-Ann, who had done something wrong. (I guess they stole some luncheon meat). So were not allowed to go they were, left in the back bedroom, I could see them watching us having lots of fun in Jane's garden. Standing up at the window, they were dropping little pieces of yellow paper out the window.

My brother Martin, Sister Jo-Ann and I started playing truant from school. Most days we would leave as if going to school, but would go fishing for newts for hours. We would build dens or walk for miles. When we got hungry, we would wait for the bread man to come, to deliver to some of the houses. We would then go up to him, and say My Mummy said can you leave some jam donuts, cakes, sausage rolls, etc. Then off the milkman. We would ask for milk, orange juice, etc. So we run up a massive bill. Hence, we received a bashing from My Mother. Then we hit upon a brilliant idea! We would write notes and leave them on people's doorsteps, then wait until the baker or milkman had gone, then move and collect our goodies, and we even pinched milk off doorsteps. We always came home on time, so My Mother didn't know for a long time that we hadn't been to school.

In one case we were keeping a watch out laying on the grass in the park, we were looking through the hedge that separated Miss Browns house. (She was a very strict Teacher of our School). While Martin ran up her path to pinch her milk, well as her milk had been disappearing, she obviously decided to keep a watch and saw who it was, as she opened her front door Martin just ran for his life.

One day, Martin and I were called into the Headmasters office, for playing truant. We were ordered to go into the next room and choose a slipper/Plimsoll from his box. He was going to give us six of the best. We both went into the next room, where we opened the door that led into the hallway, and we just ran straight out the door, and out of the School. We ran home and told My Mother. Lucky for us she was in one of her better moods. She sent us back to School with a note, telling the headmaster that she didn't want him to punish us. As we had been finding it difficult, since My Father had gone away.

I remember playing ball games along the brick walls of the school, especially with the ball in the stocking, singing a little rhyme.

Have a cigarette Sir
No Sir,
Why Sir Cos I've got a cold Sir
Where'd you get the cold Sir
From the North Pole, Sir,
What you doing there, Sir
Catching Polar Bears Sir
How many did you catch, Sir?
One Sir Two Sir and so on,

Then we had the jumping games with the rope. Plus, the French skipping with the elastic, handstands up the ramparts. Jo-Ann had once done one showing everything she had for breakfast. (She had no knickers on). The boys at school would run about the playground singing,

We won the war in 1964. Another song I can remember us singing in the playground was this one.

I'm Kathy Kerby
I'm a movie star
I've got a real, good figure
when I drive in my car
I've got the hips the lips the legsssssssssssss
I'm a star.

We would do all the moves to the song, and then at the end, we would do a star jump.

When Jo-Ann started school, she was still sucking her middle two fingers, plus as she was so tiny, the teachers would carry her around the Playground. I suppose they were frightened she would get knocked over.

In the School playing field were some air raid shelters covered with grass, we would try and climb to the top when we did, we would shout out, I'm the King of the castle. We managed to go inside one of them once, but we were caught, and told off by the dinner ladies.

At junior school, we started having swimming lessons. We were all taken by coach to the swimming baths. One day, a floater, was discovered floating on the top of the pool. We were all ordered to get out of the pool. As the girls all had swimming costumes on, the teachers decided to have a look at the boys first. (No way could they do this today). They had a look at all the boys one by one until they found the dirty little sod.

Another time we had a school trip to see a Pantomime at Christmas, in Southampton. We travelled by coach and were all given a bag of mixed sweets and a carton of orange, in the intermission, we were, given an ice cream.

At lunchtime, we all would have to go to the dining hall, where we all sat at a long table. The dinner Ladies would bring us our meal it was always nice, and we would all clear our plates. There would be jugs of water on the table as well. When we had finished our dinner, we would be given a dessert, most of the time it would have custard to go with it. The dinner Ladies would ask if you wanted custard then you were offered more if there was any left. Very soon Martin got the nickname more custard.

At one time throughout my schooling in infants, Martin and I were in the same art class, as there was less than a year between us. Well, in this lesson, we had to draw our favourite pet. I drew a little kitten, my friend next to me drew a little puppy, along with nearly everyone else in the class. But for Martin, who drew a parrot, I must say it was lovely and colourful, but then the teacher had us all draw parrots in every art lesson, as he wanted to put them all around the walls in his class.

Lady Donna Louise Wilder

Us All Grown Up

(1) Donna Louise Wilder, (née) Farrant, O'Bryan, Pearce,
(2) Martin Roy O'Bryan, (née) Pearce,
(3) Jo-Ann Marie Davies, (née) Rigg, O'Bryan, Pearce,
(4) Richard Thomas O'Bryan, (née) Pearce,
(5) Rebecca Christine Webster, (née) O'Bryan, Pearce

Chapter 4

Fond Memories

As a child, right up until My Father left, my childhood was a very happy one, full of fun and laughter. One day he bought some Hovis mini rolls, and cut them into slices and made jam sandwiches, and helped me create a tea party for my dolls, with little cakes, ice gems, and dolly mixtures the lot. With all my dolls and My Father all sitting in the front room, holding a lovely tea party. My Father suddenly said what is that horrible smell? I think your Baby Angela, has done a Pooh. Well, knowing that it couldn't do a Pooh I just said no she hasn't, but he insisted I had a look, and to my horror, there was a lot of poo in her nappy, you should have seen my face. My Father had put piccalilli in my dolly's nappy. I had a beautiful silver cross coach built pram, in turquoise, white and silver chrome with a matching bag attached, for Christmas when I was five years old, I was a proper little girl, I loved to play Mummy's with my dollies.

My Father was always teasing and joking around with us, if we asked where something was he would say "upstairs Behind Nanny's wallpaper" or he would send us to get his hat with the feather in it from the hallway. (He never wore a hat).

Lady Donna Louise Wilder

My Father got some Matey bubble bath and filled the bathtub up with a little water, but emptied the whole bottle into the bath. Swishing the water around, and making the Bubbles go up really high, he then got, and dropped poor Richard in it; he disappeared under all the bubbles telling me that the bubbles had eaten him all up, I didn't want to get in after that.

'We had some lovely toys I always remember my little cooker it had some small firelighter cubes (roughly the size of a sugar cube, it must have been, impregnated with a flammable liquid,). (Health and safety non-existent in them days). My Father would light it with a match, and you could then boil a little tin kettle, on it, and prepare a cup of tea. My Mother wouldn't join in as she said she couldn't drink from a tin cup. I also received a lovely trolley like a hostess trolley with lots of different coloured glass's but made from Perspex.

At one time we had been out to the fair, and we all had little white Skeletons with a sucker to stick to the windows, so we stuck them on the back window of the car, and I remember the people laughing and waving to us, as they passed our car.

I survived on a ride with My Father at Battersea Fun Fair it was called the Rotor. You went in through a doorway and stood with your back to the wall, and then they closed the door, and the ride started to spin round, faster and faster, than the floor would drop away and you would be, stuck against the wall. I have to say I, absolutely loved it.

Such A Lucky Lady

I remember going with my parents to London zoo and seeing Guy the Gorilla; he looked massive to me. I liked him and the funny monkeys, and then the Polar Bears as they looked very cuddly.

We always seemed to do a great deal more things when My Father was around, as he was a lot of fun,

My Mother would say he was just like a big kid. He would get down on the floor and play with the boy's train set or their racing car track; he would colour in my colouring books with me. I remember him colouring in a Fairy for me He was telling me all the wrong colours, I was getting, really mad at him.

Once and only the one time, as I can only remember it happening the one time. I didn't recognize who it was, but whoever it was I wasn't afraid of them. They pulled my pants down to my ankles, then laid me on the end of My Mother and My Father's bed. (I guess I was still playing with a toy or something at the time). Then, without hurting me in any way they satisfied them self, they must have made a mess of my pants as they were cleaning them, saying, I had better clean this up we don't want Mummy to see do we? It wasn't until I was older that I realised it wasn't right, Thank God nothing ever happened like that again to me, that I can remember. Perhaps the guilty conscience of what they had done made them feel ashamed. I will never know.

My Brother Richard and I missed My Father the most as Richard and I started wetting the bed, and Richard seemed to stop growing, My Mother said it was the shock of My Father leaving as we were his favourites.

One time My Mother told me to unplug the electric fire that was high up on the wall between Jo-Ann and My beds. Well, remembering what I had always been told, that I was never to touch the plugs. I thought I would use a dinner knife it had a bone handle I pushed it down the back of the plug to remove it. There was a big bang and the fuses blew. I suffered a bit of a shock, and the knife didn't survive, it had a big chunk taken out of it.

The first time I saw My Father after he had left was when he turned up at our House. And My Mother wouldn't let him in to visit us; we had to talk to him at the backroom window, it was in October for My 7th Birthday, he had brought me a red Timex watch. I felt so grown up.

He then turned up again at the back window another time and gave us each a ten bob note (50p), and he tried to give My Mother a £20 note. But she said as she was on Social Security she wasn't allowed to take it, and then he gave it to me. After he had gone My Mother took all the money from us and said that we needed a fridge hence, that is what our money went on.

The next time he came round My Mother said she would see him next door at her friends Jane's house we all went round. I remember sitting on My Father's lap at her back door; he was crying, and asking My Mother if he could come back saying he had nothing to live for, and he may as well end it all. But My Mother was with her Friend joking and laughing saying have you got enough pills do you want some more? We were allowed to walk him to his car it was a Dark Green Morris Minor Traveller.

I can remember My Father coming down and taking Martin and me to the cinema, and then to a Wimpy Bar in North end, I recall being able to choose some sweets in the foyer, then having an Ice Lolly in the intermission. I had on a red and white frock that had a red coat that matched, My Father came down a few times to take us out. I liked it when he took us to the fun fair. I always wanted to go with him, and I often went with him on my own, I recall him coming down in a removal van, he took me with him, and we went round to see a lady, who had a little girl, I'm sure her name was Karen.

My Father used to send us now and then a shoe box full of sweets; inside was five of everything, milky-ways, Smarties, Fruit polo's, milky bar's the lot, plus he still got some Bournville plain dark chocolate, Fry's chocolate cream & Turkish Delight for My Mother.

My Mother and My Fathers Friend, Jack Kitchen started coming round on a Friday eve, and he would stay until Sunday late afternoon. When he was coming, us three older ones had to tidy up. We used to begin at the top and sweep anything and everything, from each of the bedrooms and the bathroom, onto the landing, and then sweep it all down the stairs. Then at the bottom, we would sit and sort it all out. When Jack came round us older three were sent upstairs to play. But Richard &

Rebecca were allowed to stay downstairs with them; we would stand on the landing asking if we could come down, but My Mother or Jack would tell us to go away and play upstairs or go to bed. When we heard anyone coming, we moved away from the stairs and kept quiet, if it were Jack that left the front room to go to the kitchen, Martin and I would try to spit on his bold head. (I didn't like him being around as I was missing My Father). We would sing the nursery rhyme.

Jack Sprat could eat no fat
his wife could eat no lean
and so between them two
they licked their platters clean.

Then in the morning we would have breakfast, Jack used to give us a Weetabix with corn flakes on top, something we had never experienced before.

One-day Jack took My Mother and us all in his car to Portsmouth town, when he parked up, they left us three locked in the car, and they went shopping. I think they must have been, gone for a very long time? (I believe the car was an Austin) Because we must have been, really board as we had removed most of the dashboard and the indicators from the side of the car.

My Mother said that Jack stopped coming round as he had asked My Mother to place us older ones in care. As he had wanted to marry My Mother and bring up Richard & Rebecca, but she had refused.

(We were always, reminded of the fact that she would have had a lovely life in Gibraltar if she had done that).

I never remember My Mother cuddling me or even sitting me on her lap, and never do I remember a goodnight kiss from her. I reckon that she never had anyone show her any affection, so she didn't know how to be affectionate.

After My Father had left us, My Auntie Pat invited us all to come and stay for a little break with them just for a few days in Carlyle Road. Well as there were so many of us eight children and three adults, eleven in total it was, decided they would get sausage and chips from the local chip shop for all the children and fish for the adults. (My Mother always had Haddock). We were all gathered around the table, I was sitting next to my cousin Elaine, I then began to use my fork to pick up as many chips as my fork could carry, saying "Elaine, look what I can do". As I proceeded to ram them all into my (really, little) mouth, all at once. My Auntie Pat, who witnessed this grabbed my arm and started to slap my hand, really hard a few times, I never liked her from then on.

While we were away someone, (My Mother said it was My Father) had been staying in our house, as My Mother said she found lipstick on her pillow case. And she also found a little girl's pinafore dress that wasn't mine. The pinafore dress My Mother placed in a draw in the back room. I liked it, but My Mother wouldn't let me have it, but in the end, I got it.

Lady Donna Louise Wilder

One day My Mother said to me to help her move Rebecca's cot into my bedroom, she said you can have Rebecca and look after her I can't do it any longer. (I was just seven years old). As I was, a very dolly loving child I was in my element. I have done everything for her. I remember Rebecca calling me Mummy. She and I were, really close, I remember one day when it was Rebecca's Birthday I think, My Mother had got her a Teddy bear from her green shield stamps. We would get them from Participating stores. You would have to lick them and stick them in a book which you would then exchange for goods from a catalogue. When she went to give it to Rebecca who was sitting in a chair as she had just wet on the floor, I stood in front of her and told My Mother that Rebecca wasn't allowed to have it now as she had been naughty.

We had a lovely white cat called Jinxes, well one day I found some scissors and became scissor happy by cutting the cat's whiskers off, and the ringlets on Jo-Ann's hair, and the sausage looking curl on the top of Rebecca's head. (probably I was jealous as my hair was straight). As I was the eldest and thinking, I was the boss of the house that meant My Brothers and Sisters had to do as I said. We like most children used to slide down the banisters, but as I was getting brave I found that I could climb over the banister railing's at the top, then hold on to the upper part of the top stair, and drop down. Maybe about a 3ft drop well before long I got the rest to have a go first Martin no problem, and then Jo-Ann, a bit frightened, then following my orders dear Richard.

(I think I told him he had to if he wanted to be in our gang).

Well, we helped him over, only he just froze stiff, so as it was my go next and he was in my way he just wouldn't let go, I got the poker from the fire I got it red and warned him, what I would do if he didn't drop down, it was probably about 4ft, time was running out, I needed my go, so I touch his foot that made him jump higher??? (I think in all likelihood that must have made he jumped up a bit higher?). My Mother bandaged his foot up, and she kept him away from us he would sleep in her room in a camp bed, from then on. We were finding lots of daredevil things to do, like in my bedroom we had a window that had two side openings plus a smaller one at the top in the middle. We would open all three windows then one of us would walk out one window, hold on to the smaller opened window from outside, and then back in through the other open one, we all had to have a go. We would wait until they were outside holding on then we would close the two end ones, leaving them outside holding onto the middle window. (Children can be so very cruel).

I used to have to go to the shops for My Mother and get her sanitary wear they were Dr White's. Not knowing what I was getting I asked her one day what they were for, so she told me but as I was only seven years old, and I obviously didn't understand. I thought that if you wore one, you would bleed, and then you got a Baby, so I took one, placed it in my knickers then spent all day back and forth checking to see if I had a Baby on the way.

Lady Donna Louise Wilder

(You guessed! It didn't work).

Linda Kitchen and I were playing outside by my house, just across the street where there had been a fire in one of the Prefabs. It had burnt down a few days ago. We were climbing over piles of ashes, when we found some make-up, lipstick, powder compact with a mirror in the lid, when you opened it, a comb, plus a necklace with some beads on it, they were shiny with lots of colours in them, I thought they were diamonds. I put some of the makeup On Linda, and she put some on me when I went home My Mother told me to wash it off at once, and because I had put a dead old lady's makeup on my face, that one day I would wake up with a wrinkled old face.

We would climb out the bathroom window and play on the flat roof that ran over the coal shed, the outdoor toilet and shed. And so many times one of us would quickly close the window, leaving whoever we had persuaded to climb out stranded on the roof. At one time it backfired on me as I was rushing to close the window, I caught my thumb and had to go to the hospital, as I had broken it. They had to put on a herringbone bandage.

Chapter 5

Running Errands

I would go to the shops for some of the neighbours, most of the time I would get a three pence piece for going. On the way I sometimes passed a clothes shop, one time in the window was a purple and white gingham dress, and the price was 10s /11d. I asked the lady in the shop if I could pay her my 3d until I had paid for it. She said yes and took my order and put it in her book. I would go into her shop and pay her every time I got any money, as my dream was to invite my friends round to play and wear it standing next to my curtains in my bedroom as it was the same.

I would go to the local sweet shop and make the man a cup of tea, (as he was on his own). He would let me read the comics. I liked reading Nurse Susan & Doctor David in the look and learn comic. They were a brother and sister who looked after all the Brocken toys, and, of course, The Numskulls another comic strip in The Beezer, the strip is about a team of tiny human-like technicians who live inside the heads of various people, running and maintaining their bodies and minds. Beano, Dandy, and the Topper. I remember the day his ice cream freezer broke down, and he let me have loads of ice cream. I was riding my bike home, and a neighbour saw me, she then asked My Mother if I had an illness that meant I had to eat ice cream as she had seen me with one in each hand.

Once, I was sent to get a bag of coal from the hardware shop one cold, dark December night. Rebecca's pushchair was Broken, so I had to carry it, My Mother had given me a ten bob note. When I got to the shop to order the coal, the shopkeeper was just about to go out the back to get it. When a man came in, so he served him first. The man bought some raffle tickets from a display in the shop and gave one of them to me, as he saw me looking lovingly at a big teddy that was one of the prizes. Saying I hope you win, I went home with the bag of coal, which was hefty for me to carry. (It weighed 28lb, that is over 12kg in today's money as us older ones would say).

When I got home, My Mother asks me for her change. I didn't have any. She started screaming at me saying you are a thieving little bitch, what did you spend it on, I told her I hadn't, but she just hit, and kept hitting me, screaming with every slap thief, thief, thief. Then she said get out and don't come back till you get my money. I worked out that the man must have forgotten to give me the change, or I had left it on the counter. I ran back, but I was too late, as the shop had closed. So I started walking and walking, I ended up in Waterlooville where the shops were still open (as it was the main town, Fridays was a late night shopping). A lady saw me on my own and asked me where is your Mummy? I was crying and told her that I couldn't go home until I had My Mother's money. Then the kind lady took my hand (her hands were nice and warm as she had some furry gloves on). She took me into Woolworth and brought me a big bag of sweets then the lady walked me all the way back home, she let me wear her gloves. When we reached my house, she knocked on the door Martin opened the door. The lady shouted to My Mother and told her to come to the door. When she did, the lady then threw some money at her and gave her a big piece of her mind. Telling her how wicked she was for letting me out late at night on my own. As soon as the lady left My Mother not satisfied that she had her money and her daughter back safe and sound. Started interrogating me, wanting to know what I had spent it on, in the end. I owned up to buying some sweets, so I got another good hiding. She worked out I must have bought something else, so I said I bought a box of chocolates, after that bashing she then wanted to know where they were. As there were no chocolates, I told My Mother that I ate them all so another beating for being a pig.

I would sometimes pass an elderly couple on my way to the shops, who would see me going past on the other side of the road while they were doing their garden, and would always say hello to me. One day they waited for me to go by and called me over, they offered me a drink and a biscuit. The lady said how much I reminded her of her granddaughter who lived in Australia. And that they didn't see her much, I would stop off at their house on the way to the shops for a little chat, (and drink and biscuits). When it was near to Christmas, they gave me a gift; it was a knitted scarf, gloves and a whole tray of toffee with a little hammer.

Lady Donna Louise Wilder

Sometimes when I went up to the shops, I would see this little old man, who would walk all hunched over with one arm round his back, the hand was closed. Well, someone told me that he walked up and down the street every day and that in his hand was his eye that had been blown out during the War. Whenever he was in front of me, I would run past him like Greece lightning. Not once was I brave enough to turn around and look to see if he had an eye missing, and neither did I cross to the other side of the road which would have been the most sensible thing to do I think.

I get my social skills from My Mother as whenever we were out with her even at bus stops she always started talking to complete strangers she came across as a very sophisticated and highly intelligent lady.

One day My Mother took only me out with her, it was a warm and sunny day, I had a navy blue and white summer suit on, it was navy crop trousers with a white crop top that had a seaside scene on the front and rope ties around the sleeves.

One time I think My Mother was going to see someone for a job, as she had a couple of little cleaning jobs. One job was to clean an empty house; we all went round to help clean it. It was a large house with a large conservatory that went right across the back and one side of the house. My Mother gave us all jobs to do in the house we had a great time working together. When we had finished, we walked home stopping off at the shops where My Mother bought some nice tasty things for us to

Such A Lucky Lady

have a tea party when we got home. We could all choose one thing each, so we got two bottles of fizzy pop, 2 Swiss rolls, some biscuits and crisps then we all walked home with an orange ice lolly My Mother had a choc ice.

I always remember the Apostle teaspoons in our house that we called Jesus spoons, I would always hide one as I liked them. I still have one that I use in my coffee jar.

Once in a while, My Mother would seem to have a new lease of life, and she would even stay up all night spring cleaning the place. It would be spotless when we got up, sometimes we would come home from school, and she would have been up the shops. She had bought everything to make a beef stew for us all. (Tined meat, tin potatoes, and a tin of mixed vegetables). Jelly and even some sweets usually dolly mixtures. My Mother would share them out making sure we all had the same, even down to the colour, as many a time I would be the one thinking I wasn't getting my fair share. I would, and still do take the middle slices from a loaf of bread, as I had noticed that it was raised up in the middle, so that would give me an extra mouthful and I would measure the oranges until I found out that the thicker the peel, the smaller the orange. We all tried to be the last to finish our food then we would tell the others that we had more than them. When we used to have Lincoln biscuits they had little spots on the top so we would nibble them off first trying to make them last longer.

One time My Mother must have been feeling really sad. As she called us all into her bedroom, where she handed us each a handful of painkillers like Panadol/ paracetamol. They came from a bottle that contained 100 tablets. She then said that I've had enough of life so you can all help to kill me. She then told me to hand my handful to her. But I was crying and said No she then raised her voice and turned to Martin, and told him to give them to her, as he went to give her them he was crying, she shouted that's it, so you want to kill me.

Another time My Mother had decided that she had enough of life. So made us all lay down in the back room on the studio couch, which was a sofa that went into bed, the legs to it were zipped in the top at the back. My Mother and the younger two Richard and Rebecca were up the window end, and us older three were at the bottom in front of the gas pipe in the fireplace. I was told to turn the gas on as we were all going to die. (not before the yellow budgie was, put in the front room in its cage). Us older three were all thinking the same thing, which as we were right next to the gas, we would die first, then My Mother would turn the gas off and save herself and the younger two. We were all screaming please Mummy don't. We will be good please Mummy we all love you. Please, we will be good. We promise. We were making so much noise that in the end, My Mother told me to turn off the gas.

A few days later there was a knock on the door, and My Mother asked me to go and see who it was. I went to the front door and asked who is it? A man said I'm Mr. Leach from the NSPCC. I need to speak to your Mummy can you get her for me. I went and said to My Mother that a man wanted to see her. She told me to tell him to come around to the back door. He told My Mother that he came as a neighbour, had made a complaint, about My Mother beating us. He said that we were heard screaming for mercy. My Mother just laughed and told him that we wouldn't even know the word mercy yet alone know what it meant. He looked at us all, and we didn't have any signs of being unhappy or ill-treated. The place was a mess with clothes toys and rubbish all over the place. I don't know exactly, what My Mother said to him but in the end, it was us kids who were the ones being told off by him for making a mess. My Mother told him that having five children in the house, running around all the time there would be times that she would shout at us and get cross, as we had made a mess. My Mother told him she had gotten cross with us because we had pulled the top covers off the top bunk, to make a Den on the bottom bunk. So she had shouted at us for that, I had a whitlow on my finger so he said he would go and get something magical to make it better. He came back a little while later with some treatment to help make my finger better, and I remember having to put my finger into this smelly hot stuff, a few days later it was much better.

I think it was at this point that we were all placed under the welfare care of the social services. They would then be classed as our family's next of kin, but we would still stay with My Mother, but they would work with My Mother. to help her bring us all up.

Lady Donna Louise Wilder

My Mother told us that at any time, we did anything wrong we could be taken away and put into care, (One thing I will say about My Mother was she always stood by us whenever the authorities got involved with us, she did her best trying to keep us all together). I would pray that I was taken and put into care as I believed my life would be a lot happier, even after listening to the horror stories My Mother had told us about her time in care. I just thought I would be happier.

My Auntie Pat came all the way down from Somerset once, to bring us some food and things. But My Mother wouldn't open the door, so I had to talk to her out the bedroom window, with My Mother telling me what to say. I had to say that My Mother was out, to which Auntie Pat said, I'm your Auntie Pat just open the door, so I can bring all this in for you all. Put the kettle on I'm dying for a cup of tea. (she loved her tea) I was told to say just leave it on the doorstep, after a long while she did leave the parcels on the doorstep. As soon as the coast was clear, we went out and got the parcels. (as Auntie Pat had a catering business). She had left us a gigantic box of cornflakes, giant cans of jam we just ate it with spoons, some dried prunes, custard powder that we ate as sherbet and a load more things.

My Mother would travel to London by coach to see her Sister Jo, she would take with her Rebecca and mostly Richard, as she knew we would pick on him. We would all walk to the church where she would catch the coach. Because it was very early in the morning, My Mother would give us some money to buy a traffic light lolly from the shop at the top of the hill. We were told to eat it before we got to school so walk very slowly as to waste some time.

(I remember going one time with My Mother to London). I loved going on the underground; I had new clothes and a lovely new pair of sling back white sandals with a little heel.

This one time when My Mother had gone to London, we had come home from school and were trying to be quiet. (but remember we were all under ten years old). When someone knocked on the front door, we all kept very quiet, and then we heard them come round the back, and they knocked on the backroom window. I straight away thought it was My Father. so I opened the window, but there were lots of people, one said where is your Mummy we're from social services. We need to talk to your Mummy, we all screamed, and I closed the window, we ran upstairs to hide in the box room. Then we could hear dogs barking; our imaginations were going haywire. We thought that the dogs were going to eat us all. When My Mother got back it was early in the morning around 1 am, she told them that her neighbour was supposed to be watching us?

Auntie Jo bought me a Sindy doll for Christmas. I can remember knitting it a blue dress; I would cast on 32 stitches and knit until I reached the dolls arms. Then I would knit 7, cast off 2, knit 14, cast of 2, knit 7, the next row I would knit and then add two stitches at each place where the arm holes would be, back on making the 32 stitches back again. I then would cast the stitches off and stitched it up then I made a finger knitting belt for it. My Mother would only show you once how to do anything so you had to work thing out for yourself if you had forgotten what she had said or shown you.

We were all playing hide and seek one day in the house except for Richard, who was downstairs with My Mother laying on the mattress in the front room. We couldn't find Rebecca; we had looked everywhere, the police were called and had to meet My Mother at a friend's house just across the road. Because My Mother didn't want the police to come into the house, as she knew it was in a state. Eventually, Rebecca was found, she had hidden under a bed amongst everything imaginable that was under there and fallen asleep.

On the way to school I would pass this boy he was a bit bigger than me (but then most kids were) he had ginger hair and wore a very posh uniform probably going to a private school, I would shout at him.

"Ginger you're barmy
you went to join the army
you got knocked out with a bottle of stout
Ginger your barmy."

Then one day he turned and said very politely, "you're not very lady like are you" Well I can tell you, that stopped me in my tracks, I never said it to him again.

Such A Lucky Lady

I remember getting a bike when I was about ten years old it had been given to me by my Auntie. It was a Raleigh RSW in red when we moved from Purbrook. It got left behind like most things.

Being a very dolly kind of child, imagine my horror when one of my baby's eyes got pushed in. I was horrified. My Mother told Auntie Jo how upset I was, she told My Mother to remove the head (without me seeing it of course), and sent it to her. So she could take it to a dolls hospital, where they will mend it. (Auntie Jo came to the rescue).

One school trip I liked was the one to Carisbrooke Castle on the Isle of White. My Mother was washing my hair the night before when I began to start to scream as some water had got in my ear, so I had to go to the hospital, My Mother. While we were there my uncle Roger turned up out of the blue; he had gone to our house first, and Martin had told him where we were. When My Mother saw him, she first, thought it was Roy, My Father, she said to Uncle Roger I assumed you were Roy; I was thinking how brave to turning up at a Hospital emergency department. When we got back home I helped My Mother get my packed lunch together; I had a new lunch box, a bit like the Tupperware ones, I had boiled egg, ham, cheese and salad very posh it looked. My lunch was very nice and health, My Mother gave me one shilling to spend then my uncle Roger gave me half a crown that was two shilling and sixpence. I think I had the best lunch and the most money than everyone that day.

Lady Donna Louise Wilder

My Family

Top left to right
(1) Charles Walter Wilder, (Wally) (2) Michael Antony Wilder, née O'Bryan, (3) Clive Graham Farrant, (My Ex-husband)
Large Photo
Donna Louise Wilder, née Farrant, O'Bryan, Pearce,

Chapter 6

Unsafe House

By now our home was in such a mess that we all started sleeping in the front room, all on one double mattress, three up the top and three down the bottom. One night very late, we were all asleep when there was an almighty crash. My Mother told My Brother Martin and me to find out what it was. We opened the front room door to the hall, and then we crept along to the kitchen door. Upon opening it, we saw that the whole ceiling had fallen, in the back room. We were so scared to tell My Mother that we went back and said it was the cat jumping onto the Formica table. With that we all went back to bed, I just lay there waiting, simply waiting for the whole house to fall on top of us all.

My Mother could have quite easily just opened the doorway leading into the back room and inspected for herself! The next morning, we were to go to school, but we were so afraid that the house was going to come down and kill Rebecca. (We had decided that we didn't care about My Mother, or Richard, as he was the only one of us to generate any attention from My Mother). We climbed onto the window sill at the rear of the house, just watching and waiting for it to happen, (it never did). I suppose this happened because My Brother Martin would play in the bath with his soldiers on bits of wood, and he left the taps running. When My Mother eventually found out, she must have known that we would have to be re-housed. My Mother told us that if we tidied up the outside shed, we could have rabbits and guinea pigs with a couch and TV. In other words, she promised our very own little den. We were so excited as we ran outside so full of determination, we were going to do the impossible. The shed was about 6ft square x 7ft high with a window on the back wall. When we opened the door, it was as if a compressor had been used, as it was full to about 5ft high. But nothing could put us off. We climbed in and sat on top of everything, simply picking up bits and bobs and deciding if it was any good to keep. All the time we had fleas jumping all over the place, and a robin in a nest by the cracked window. We slowly realised that this was one task that was just impossible for us to do.

My Mother would punish us for tons of things, if she didn't know who had done a particular thing, we would all have to line up in descending age, (starting with the eldest one, me) asking if we have done it? If I said no she would strike me with a flip flop on both of our hands as hard as she could, (I can tell you they were made off much stronger stuff in those days). Even if we had done it, we would never own up until she had hit Richard, and then merely as she would finish hitting him whoever had actually done it would own up just in time just so Rebecca never got hit. Then My Mother worked out what we were doing, so she set off with the youngest so we would own up straight away. Whoever had done it, had to go without their tea, a sandwich with either, mixed fruit jam, Lemon curd, salmon & shrimp paste, or

Such A Lucky Lady

Marmite. And whoever had done anything against Richard, would have to make their own sandwich, and before they began to eat it, My Mother would make them hand it over to Richard, and tell him they were sorry (for whatever they had said or done to him). No wonder he always looked healthier than us.

Because My Mother hit us so often, I decided that I was going to kill myself the very next time she laid a finger on me. I found a length of silver colour twisted wire, (I believe it to be bell wire). I tied a noose at one end, (well, I tied it my way) and I tied the other end to the landing balustrade. I told myself that the next time she hit me, I would hang myself, and then she will be sorry. Well, I was hit again, but I chickened out because I got a picture in my head of Rebecca crying at my graveside. And then my next plan was to fill the coach built pram that was in the hallway with any clean clothes I could find. I took My Mother's Social Security/Family Allowance books, intending to get some money to survive on. Then, with Martin, Jo-Ann and little Rebecca. (Whom I managed to force into the hood of the pram). I very quietly pushed the pram down the three front door steps, and away we went- leaving, My Mother and Richard behind. We walked all the way to Waterlooville and to the end of the town where there was a big Supermarket. It was a Sunday, so everything was shut. We were going to sleep in the cardboard boxes around the back, but a Police car came over and took us all back home. My Mother didn't even know we had all gone.

Lady Donna Louise Wilder

There was a Tallyman/lady from Blundells, who used to come round every week. My Mother would buy us clothes and shoes, etc. from her. When she knocked on the front door, I would shout for her to go around to the side window, (which was in the hallway) and I'd give her some money. Then she would pass me something to show My Mother. The lady had good taste and would bring something that was just right for me. Once she brought a lovely pale blue jumper with a white diamond shape on the front, they went from a big one going right down to a small one in the middle. I told My Mother I would love it for my 10th birthday. (I got it). As I was the eldest, if I liked something, I would bribe My Mother by telling her how well I'd look after it, so it can be passed down to Jo-Ann when I grew out of it. Jo-Ann and Rebecca always got this pack of Two Cotton dresses when she came round.

Someone came round from the British Legion one day and asked if we all wanted to go to a Christmas party. My Mother said we could go so we were all picked up in a big minibus. We went to a hall in Waterlooville, where we had a smashing time playing with all the other children. We had tons of food, jelly, and loads of sweets, party hats, and crackers, we got to play games and sing funny songs, I always remember the elephant song. I could just picture elephants coming out to play on a spider's web.

Then Father Christmas gave us all a present, and we were then taken back home with a carrier bag full of sweets, fruit and some small toys. I got a beaded

Such A Lucky Lady

necklace set from Father Christmas, which started me off on my bead collecting. When I went back to school, I would swap beads with my friends (although I was only interested in the rainbow coloured diamond shaped ones). Anyone who had them was my best friend! We were also, given a Christmas hamper, it was full of lovely things. My Mother had the tin salmon, the nuts, dates, and the tin of mandarin oranges, but some not so nice things, like a tin of tongue, that would follow us to every house we moved into for years to come.

On my 10th birthday, My Mother had to take me to Waterlooville by bus to see the dentist. They gave me gas and air, and then they removed three teeth. Two were baby teeth so that my second teeth had room to come through properly, but I still don't know why they took away one of my second back teeth… as I still have the gap!

Our local shops used to close on a Sunday, so we sometimes went to one that was open on the next Estate. To get to it, we had to go down the next street it was called Days London Road, and then through an alleyway.

One Sunday, Martin and I went with the pram to the bubble-gum machine around the side of the shop. We found a way to get the bubble gums out and swiftly, we emptied the contents into the pram, finishing with, the machine itself. As we needed some tools from home to get the money. Soon after, when we got home the police came and asked to speak to My Mother, but she told them it wasn't us as we had been at home all day. Just then Martin came downstairs with his mouth full of bubblegum blowing a big bubble, giving us a way. Thankfully, we were underage, so we just got a telling off from them.

I remember one Saturday we went to a jumble sale in Deverell hall. That was on in the morning, about 10:00 am. We then took what we had bought back home before going to another one in the afternoon. At St John the Baptist Church, London Road, in this one there were Nun's. I found a box with lots of jewellery in, (well, I now know its called fashion jewellery). The Nun said I could buy it for a penny, I went over to My Mother and asked her for some money. She gave me a threepenny bit, I went back and got my gems. When we got home, I was playing with my new jewellery and found that one ring was far too big for me. So I showed it to My Mother and asked her if she wanted to buy it off me. (Even at this age, I had a passion for making money to better myself). My Mother noted that it was gold straight away, and agreed to buy it from me for one penny. The ring was gold with a topaz stone in, My Mother then began to tell me about a ring that her mother had, with a topaz in it and that one of her sisters had the ring, but it was supposed to have been her's.

At the jumble sales, My Mother always looked for books for herself. She liked books by Dennis Wheatley, we had loads of Readers Digest books in the home, along with piles of master detective and true detective; she was always reading. I can recall her watching university challenge on the TV, and she would get most of the questions right. Once when she answered a question wrong, it was (where was a place). She shouted they must have moved it.

There was this house near Devrall Hall, it was empty, and the garden was very overgrown. We sneaked into the front garden, and went and looked through the windows, it looked very ancient inside and was empty, apart from piles of paintings piled up against the walls. It reminded us of the Addams family house in the Munster's, so we were too scared to go in.

Once when we were all walking to the park with My Mother after school, I was pretending I was really tired of walking up the little hill, by bending over as I was walking. My Mother kicked me from behind with her pointed shoes and caught me right where it hurts right between my legs, saying in a stern voice to walk properly.

My Mother started meeting us all near the School and taking us to the park we loved it as we could play till it started getting dark. But every so often we were told to go over to a clearing and have a look to see if there was a car outside our house. It wasn't long before we worked out that someone was coming that My Mother didn't want to see (So low and behold every time we looked there was a car outside). I found out later that it was the Council they were coming round to evict us.

Lady Donna Louise Wilder

My Son Michael

2 weeks old to 16 Years old

Chapter 7

The Eviction Order

My Mother gave in, these men came in with white suits on and big tanks on their back, what they were doing was fumigating the whole house, and moving us to a two bedroom two up two down house, at number 10 Selbourne Road, Havant. It had a dark Black door. I remember thinking it was very posh and saying we lived at Number 10, Down in the Street. (You get it Downing Street). We were given a grant to get new bedding and curtains etc. plus we were given some furniture, beds, sofa, etc. My Mother took me with her to Portsmouth to a store called Brentford Nylons, where we got orange & purple nylon sheets, and some wallpaper to decorate the place.

Well, this was the first time in ages I saw My Mother working to make a decent home for us all. I helped My Mother with wallpapering the house; we had a brick effect paper to put on the chimney breast, but we were one drop too short, so we left the right-hand side undone. My Mother said if anyone was to come round we were not to let them sit that side. My Auntie Pat and Uncle Charlie gave us some curtains as Uncle Charlie worked for a Fiberglass manufacturing plant that made them. They gave us a purple pair and a gold pair very modern. The house had sash windows. I was sitting on the

Lady Donna Louise Wilder

window sill upstairs one day, leaning out cleaning them while My Mother was holding my legs so as I didn't fall. My dear Brother Richard came by outside and shouted up "Donna I can see the hairs under your arms". I got down and said that I could never go out of the house again. Everything was going great for the first three months, My Mother was cooking stews for us, and the place was quite respectable.

The Tally lady still used to come round with new things for us all. My Mother bought all our Christmas presents from her. One day My Mother said that when each of us reached 11 years old and left to go up to secondary school, she had decided that she was going to get them an extra grown-up present. So as I was the first I got a Petite Typewriter. Near Christmas, My Mother was showing me all the presents that she had purchased and hidden in a high cupboard. She was sorting them out into piles when she showed me a doll that she had got for Rebecca. It was a walking, talking doll called Chatty Kathy, My Mother got it to talk, but then I believed I heard someone coming down the stairs, so I put my hand over the doll's mouth to keep it quiet.

We had some lovely toys. I had things like beads, knitting, French knitting and a sewing machine. Jo-Ann had Spirograph and a kit called dip a flower; it's where you dipped wire into some liquid and made flowers, etch-a-sketch. The boys had the batman and robin cars James Bond car. Martin loved the Cowboys and Indian's with the towns, the soldiers with all the tanks plus his fort, a rifle and guns and holster. Richard had a garage

Such A Lucky Lady

plus he was following in My Mothers footsteps with his love of books. Rebecca had tiny tears and dolly things, fuzzy felts, plus we had games like, mouse trap, buckaroo, frustration, ker plunk, building bricks, Lego, marbles, books with a paper doll and clothes, one of us would always get a compendium of games also colouring books and pencils and then felt tipped pens, etc.

Every Christmas, My Mother would buy a hamper from Blundell's. She also had to purchase a new set of saucepans, cutlery, and a dinner set every year. So as we could have our Christmas dinner. We used to have a Capon with all the trimmings, and then on Boxing Day, we would have the other half, by this time I was old enough to cook it.

Most of our clothes came from jumble sales. Once in a while, My Mother would go and talk nicely to the ladies behind the stools, saying how many children she had, and not much money, they would help her fill big bags with clothes that would be suitable for us all and would only charge her a little. When we got back home, all the clothes were tipped on the floor, and I would get first pick. This one time there were lots, of quite new dresses that were my size, but no way was I going to wear them. One, in particular, was a pink and white striped dress. In the white stripes was Sooty and Sweep dancing around. It had been handmade from a lovely cotton material, very sweet for a baby or toddler but defiantly not for a young lady as I thought I was. I gave the dress to a lady down the street who had twin girls who were about two years old, and she made them dresses out of it.

Lady Donna Louise Wilder

My Brother Martin found a scrap yard, which you could take bags of clothes to and they gave you money for the weight per bag. So Martin gathered all and any of our clothes, including my very new midi black skirt, and my long cardigan with the tie belt and pockets, (my pride and joy). These were in a drawer with my favourite clothes plus an old singer sewing machine, of course, they were happy to pay him as the sewing machine was worth a lot more.

At one jumble sale, I got a gold Masonic ball, and it opened up into a cross, but one of the clasps was missing. My Mother said I couldn't have it as it was only for men who belonged to an exclusive club. My Mother took it from me and hid it but I found it one day and took it to a second-hand shop where the man gave me 50p for it, he made a good bargain, as now I know it was worth a lot more.

I was in my new Secondary School Warblington; it was a Comprehensive School. And very modern, I liked the uniform, maroon and light blue, as I got a grant for my uniform and My Mother didn't take me to get it from McIlroy's in Havant, I was made to go with the truant officer.

She was a Miss, just like Miss Trunchbull in Matilda. I was given a choice in the overcoat either the old flasher-a-Mac one or the new modern one without the belt. Naturally I choose the modern one, but Miss Trunchbull said I couldn't have it, so I dragged the flasher-a-Mac all along the shop floor and all along the street I never wore it. We all had free school uniform and free school dinners.

I found it hard, at first, to fit in as everyone knew each other, I was, and felt like an outsider. This one girl Amanda took an instant dislike to me and tried to start a fight with me in the playground. There was a big circle with her and me in the middle, she was pushing me saying go on hit me, but I didn't want to. Then she hit me, and I don't know what happened, but I just went for her, she came off worst. We were both taken to the Headmasters office, where we were told that the School would not tolerate trouble makers. So from then on I got a reputation for being a hard fighter. I landed up with lots of Friends.

One frosty October morning our first lesson was hockey, it was so cold, and there was frost on the grass and there we were dressed in our light blue air text short sleeve tops and maroon knickers freezing. But our PE teacher was in her royal blue Tracksuit. (you know the ones? the ones with the go fast stripes on). She was all nice and warm. Well after sitting down with my arms and legs folded for so long trying to keep warm. I refused to move and said to the teacher that if she were to wear the same as us, she would know how we felt. My friends were all with me until the head came out to get us all moving then they left me. I stuck to my guns and was carried off to the headmaster's office still with my arms & legs crossed, this time, I was told that if I were sent to the office again, then I would be excluded from the school.

Lady Donna Louise Wilder

I only ever once tried to get out of having a shower at school, as I looked forward to having them. I would take my own soap and shampoo to school as I could have a nice shower and have my hair washed in nice hot clean water. One day at School, our last lesson was tennis, as I didn't have to play in this lesson, I went to school in my P.E skirt, it was a wraparound pleated one. I thought I looked the bee's knees. I was going to meet my new boyfriend as soon as school was over. I said to the Teacher, "I'm sorry miss, but I can't have a shower, as I'm on my period" but as she was fed up with lots of girls making excuses, she decided to make an example of me, and told me, she wasn't having any excuses. As I hadn't brought a towel or a change of clothes. I insisted I couldn't have a shower, but she wasn't having any of it and said: "just get in the shower now". I replied if you want me in the shower you will have to put me in there; hence, she did, fully clothed, and then after a bit, she told me to hurry up.

By this time, everyone had finished in the shower apart from me, so she came in and said "come on get out," I said "you put me in here you take me out" so she did, saying get dry and hurry up, I'm waiting to lock up. I just stood dripping, when she came back, shouting will you hurry up. I said, "Miss I told you that I couldn't have a shower today, so I don't have a towel or dry clothes". She then threw a towel at me to use. I told her I wouldn't use it as I don't know where it had been so I just stayed there until I was dry. She was furious as she needed to lock up before she went to meet her boyfriend, who just happened to be the male P.E Teacher, so he wasn't happy with me either. It was gone 7 pm. Before I decided, I was dry enough to make my way home.

At school, we had domestic science. Once the teacher told us to bring in a handkerchief to wash as we were going to do some hand washing. When I told My Mother, she said that I had to cut a pillow case up into a handkerchief size, as we didn't have one. But when I got to school a friend had brought in more than one, so I asked if I could wash one of hers as I was embarrassed with my bits of rags. I liked this lesson. In the next lesson, we were going to make a jam tart, so the teacher told us to bring in some jam and 10p to cover the pastry.

I asked My Mother how to make the pastry, obviously not listening I thought I heard her say it was just flour and water with some jam. So I decided to make some, I rolled my very own special recipe pastry out with a clean milk bottle, I filled it with mixed fruit jam and baked it. It looked lovely, and I was very proud of myself. I showed My Mother and she even said it looked lovely, I got back to the kitchen to cut it but I couldn't. I then started crying. My Mother asked me what was wrong. I told her the knife wasn't any good It won't cut it; she asked me to tell her how I made the pastry. When I told her she began to laugh and said I had made and cooked glue, but My Brother Martin ate some, he said it was nice....

We had to come home straight from school to do any jobs My Mother wanted doing, like shopping, tidying up or picking up the dog and cat mess, and going to the launderette. One day I was given a letter to take home from school saying that we were going to be sent home early, as they had a Teachers meeting on the following Tuesday. I didn't show My Mother the letter as I was going to go round a Friend's house for the first time. Her name was Sally, she had a pony in her garden, and her Mum made us some lunch while we were playing lovely together. Her home was so very posh and was all nice and neat and tidy. Her Dad popped in for lunch, we all sat at the kitchen table to eat and then her dad said would we like to go back to work with him, (he went to various places emptying the fruit machines). He was going to Butlins, and we could get in for free.

We had our swimming costumes with us, as we had done swimming at school. Sally's Mum sent us upstairs to wash our hands and face before we went, that was when I saw Sally clean her teeth as well. (as I didn't have a toothbrush I put some paste on my finger). I thought I would be back home in time so it would look like I had been to school. How very wrong I was. Sally's Dad dropped me off at the corner of our road at about 7 pm. But as I walked across our street, precisely at that moment, My Mother looked out of the window and saw me. She had been waiting for me to go up the shops, so now she was mad, really mad. She was waiting for me to go in to have a go at me, but I didn't come in, I was too scared so I went into the empty house next door and sat on the toilet, in the yard trying to come up with a believable story. I must have been shattered as I fell asleep. Meanwhile, My Mother sent my Brother Martin to go and get me, but he couldn't find me. Eventually,

Such A Lucky Lady

My Mother got in touch with the Police, who came and searched for me. My Mother told them that she knew I was by water and told them to go and search there. (she was right as there was water in the toilet). They were looking for me all night. When I woke up, I decided to walk the 1.5miles to school as normal and when nearly there I was stopped by a policeman in his car. It was only 6:30 am, he asked me my name, then took me back home. I begged him not to, and I told him that My Mother would beat me as soon as he left. He said no she won't she would be so happy that I was safe, and that she wouldn't be angry. Well, at our front door My Mother greeted me with open arms, and with a big smile and a very tight cuddle, it was lovely. Alas not for long, as soon as the door closed I had it from every direction. (the policeman lied to me).

One day soon after, My Mother Told My Brother Martin and I to bring her mattress downstairs and put it on the floor in the front room, as she felt too ill to go upstairs to bed. (That is where she stayed until we were evicted once again in 1972)

My Mother was still having her periods so her sanitary towels were all just thrown into the fireplace and once in a while they would get burnt in the fire hearth.

Sometimes on Sunday evenings, we would have to bring My Mother a bowl of hot water, a flannel and a bar of Lux or Camay soap and My Mother washed us one at a time starting with the cleanest one. I came out as number one, followed by Richard and Rebecca Jo-Ann then lastly Martin. My Mother would store all her anger up for this time as we were all told to strip and stand in a line if we had done anything wrong in the week this was her time to get her hands on us. She would rub the face cloth with lots of soap and then slap it on our backs, and as she rubbed and scrubbed us clean, she would remind us of anything we had done wrong in her eyes. Plus, My Mother would wash our mouths out with soap if we ever used bad language, and then she would attack our hair and if we dare to move you got a wallop with the wooden brush on the head.

If My Mother ever heard us swearing or talking dirty, it was the bar of soap straight in the mouth. I remember finding out that I could say bloody, as long as I added tower straight away and I would say you a basket meaning b-----d.

My Mother would also get one of us to bring her a bowl of hot water and she would attempt to have a strip wash, with a flannel smothered with Lux soap she would have one of us to wash her neck, it didn't take long before the house was a tip.

If My Mother needed to use the toilet she would call one of us to bring her the bucket, (somehow that job always went to my sister Jo-Ann). We only had the one toilet in the house, and it was in the bathroom, which was downstairs at the back of the house, in a very badly built extension. Well, one day the whole toilet bowl got broken into about five jagged pieces, so you had to hold it together while someone flushed it for you. The bath

Such A Lucky Lady

used to be full of washing that had been soaking in Bio-Tex, we would have to empty the whole packet into the bathtub of water and then put the clothes into soak. They would be in there for weeks and weeks, and then we were supposed to rinse them and put them on the line to dry, but then they would stay out on the line for ages.

I remember My Mother coming to the back door as I was hanging some of the washing out on the line, she started talking to me about the stars as it was a very clear sky, (it must have been one of her good days).

Then one day as the house next door was empty Martin, Jo-Ann and I agreed we would go inside and see what we could find. We started exploring, and we found a new floorboard had been newly laid so we decided that it must be hiding some treasure. We pulled most off the floorboards up, but hence no treasure. Then we thought that they must have hidden it in the attic, so somehow we climbed in there. Then we found that we could walk right the way through to the end of the terrace, and we could lift up people's loft hatches and look inside. We would lay there for ages listening to our neighbors talking. (In other words, we were peeping toms).

My Brother Martin was still very obsessed with newts and frogspawn, so filled the next doors bath with water, and kept his catch in there. Until one day the Council came round and boarded the empty house up. At the back of our house was an alley with a high wall, (all kinds of work building and factories were there). We would walk along it and jump down the other side into the yards and play and explore. We found loads of empty Corona bottles. We would take as many as we could and take them back to the shops where they gave you some money for every returned bottle. (It was even better if they still had some pop in, as we would drink it first). Then we noticed that the pub at the top of the road had some beer bottles in its yard. So we would sneak in and grab a crate, and then take them round to the front door and get the money on them.

I think I must have inherited My Father's sticking out ear along with his sick sense of humour, it's only my left one, but I became very conscious of it. I would always want my hair down so as to cover it. One time at the doctors My Mother mentioned it to the doctor, along with Jo-Ann having a small bit of skin on one of her ear lobes. The doctor made an appointment for us both to get them sorted. Jo-Ann's appointment came through first as hers was easier to do. Just after she had hers done, I hit, pushed, slapped or something to her, obviously for something she had done or not, so she dramatized it like she did whenever she had a nose bleed, which she used to have quite a lot (without any of us touching her).

Once when her nose started bleeding she went and leaned over the sink and squeezed her nose to make more blood come out and added a little water, so It looked really bad. Then she told My Mother that I had done it, so as to get me into trouble. Well, after Jo-Ann's Drama Queen act My Mother never chased up my appointment, and I never got my plastic surgery done, I have just had to live with it

Chapter 8

Sibling Rivalry

We didn't involve My Brother Richard in anything we were doing, as we had grown up to believe that he was My Mother's favourite. He was the only one of us that she had any time for, he would be told to go and see what we were up to all the time. So he would creep up on us, have a look, then go back to My Mother and grass us up. Then we would hear My Mother shout out, Donna, Martin, Jo-Ann get down here now. Then we would all get into trouble, My Mother would hit us, so we didn't like him at all. One time when we were making our sandwiches after school for us all, we had creamy cheese and watercress. I suppose one of us had grown the watercress at school, (it may even have been Richard). Well, one of us thought it an excellent idea to cut up some bugs. (Ants spiders alike) And put them into Richard's sandwich. (Thinking they would look like the seeds from the watercress). We all had great pleasure in watching him enjoying his tea.

The house started getting in a mess My Mother headaches a lot, so she wasn't very happy and used to have us bring her food to her in bed.

One day My Mother was treating herself to pork chops chips, mushrooms and tomatoes. I had to prepare and

Lady Donna Louise Wilder

cook it all for her, I hadn't tasted a mushroom before, so I ate one, not for one minute thinking My Mother would have noticed. Well, when I took My Mothers dinner into her, she saw at once that one was missing, My Mother told me that I was wicked, and how could I begrudge her, her dinner. She said that I had taken the food from her mouth, and I may as well have it all and that I was a thieving little bitch.

At school, we all had free school meals that would be when My Mother sent us to school to have them. But as My Mother would keep one of us home with her all the time, that one would have something special for their tea instead of merely a sandwich. The choice was
1) A large family tin of creamed rice pudding.
2) Lardy cake.
3) A box of sugar puffs with a pint of milk.
4) A packet of cream crackers and creamy cheese.

Martin would have the sugar puffs and milk, but as you couldn't always find a cereal bowl, he would use the washing up bowl or a saucepan. At the top of every shopping list was dog food and cat food, then anchor butter, ham on the bone, Edam cheese, cream crackers. Jo-Ann would eat the red wax off the cheese, and the fat from the ham. Pots of jelly with fruit at the bottom, shredded wheat, that My Mother would have with tea on top as she didn't like milk. She would have roughly a teaspoon full of milk in her tea. Bottles of Coke a cola, cream soda and orange juice. Dark McVities chocolate biscuits, all this for My Mother. Then for us, children were echo or stork margarine, Marmite, cream cheese triangles, spam with the red wax band around it. Lemon curd, salmon & shrimp or pilchards & tomato fish paste, mixed fruit jam, for our sandwiches. Bread, two tins of baked beans between the five of us children. Until one of us decided to tell My Mother, that we didn't like baked beans so hoping that she would still get the two tins of baked beans plus a tin of spaghetti in tomato sauce, that way we would have three tins' between us five children, but it didn't work. We had to share one tin of each, so one of us had to have half of each. Weetabix that we sometimes had to eat with water as we had no milk Lincoln biscuits and pink waffle biscuits.

In the supermarket, they would have baskets where any dented cans or out of date and broken packets would be placed. They then would be reduced in price. My Mother told us to look in the basket first. Some of the tins had lost their labels, so it was like a lucky dip, you never knew what it was inside the tins, it could be peas beans or even peaches it was fun guessing.

Jo-Ann used to collect bugs in match boxes, one day our cat had caught a bird, so Jo-Ann got the baby birdie from the cat, and put it into our big display cabinet. It was about 6ft long x 4ft high with glass sliding doors up the top in the middle. She put twigs & leafs in it then she went out to collect worms so she could feed her new pet. (She would chew them up for the bird yuck). Behind the cupboard was a large carpet folded up, we heard a squeaking noise one day. When we looked, it was one of our cats that had its kittens behind the cupboard on the carpet. So, Jo-Ann had another little family to care for;

she loved taking care of all the pets. Once she pinched a hamster from the pet shop at the top of the road, by putting it in her anorak pocket, she had a hole in her pocket, so the hamster ran around the back of her coat. It was Jo-Ann's job to take care of all the pets that we owned. We had a Dog called Sindy, she was a golden retriever cross, she was a very shy and nervous dog. Who also had mange, so she would always chew her back until it bled. Jo-Ann was always putting flea powder on the animals.

My Brother Richard would always snitch on us he was by far My Mother's favourite. My nickname for him was, A Spastic Shrimp from a Reject Machine, I was never close enough for My Mother to hear me say it. I knew that if ever she heard me call him it I would get a bashing. If and when he told My Mother. I always denied I said it.
(you see I had to tell a little white lie, as I would have gotten a beating).

My Mother had told the boys that no matter what, they were never to hit girls, as boys were stronger than girls. Then one day after I had been my usual bossy self, My Mother saw me hit Martin, and he just stood there and did nothing. So My Mother said to him hit her back, Martin said no I'm not allowed to hit girls, with that My Mother said just hit her go on. Well with that he pulled my head down at the same time he brought his knee up and well you can imagine what happened. Yes, you're right a nose bleed, well then Martin was in trouble as My

Such A Lucky Lady

Mother didn't mean him to do that, so Martin got a bashing from My Mother.

The inside of all our houses were the same it's like they say what happens in Vegas. Stays in Vegas. Well, what came into our house stayed in our house. And that goes for everything and I mean everything. The dustbin men never emptied our bins, as there was never any rubbish in them. All the rubbish that a typical family would put out in the rubbish bins. We'll all of ours like the cat and dog cans, glass bottles, and paper was scattered all around the house. Along with any cutlery and crockery, pots and pans, clothes, books, and toys. Nothing had a place it all went where you left it. (Even the pets thought it was ok to do their business anywhere and everywhere).

As we didn't own a washing machine, any clothes, that we needed washing (like our school uniform) had to be taken to the local launderette, we used Daz or OMO soap powder. So we would attempt to put as much as we could into the machines so we could spend some of the money. We even used to pinch some things out of some of the machines, if no one was about, one day when we were there this one dryer had a pile of towels in it, they were all black and white striped hand towels. When we finished ours, we emptied the towels into the bag, that had been, left in the basket in front of the machine and took them home. My Mother never said anything, (they probably belonged to some hairdressers).

Some other time when Richard was with us, we got him to climb into the dryer, and then we put a coin in, and then we held the door shut. He was going bright red in the face, and he seemed quite mad. So Jo-Ann and I held the shop door open while Martin held the dryer closed, and then Martin, Jo-Ann and I ran home laughing all the way. When Richard came home he was extremely upset, so much so he said that he was going to kill himself, by putting a plastic bag over his head. (Thank God he didn't do it).

One day after school I and some friends were walking home just playing about pushing each other when I got pushed into a bush, as I fell my hand landed on something hard. It was a large Grundig radio; we decided to take it and hand it over to the police station. (Probably if I had been on my own I would have just fetched it home). The Officer said that we had to wait for six weeks to see if anyone claimed it if no one did we would be able to keep it. Well after the six weeks was up no one did claim it, so we each took it in turns to have it for a week each.

I don't know what happened to it in the end. We probably just got bored with passing it around. I guess that was when I started being interested in pop music, one song I liked listening to was Grocer Jack, by Keith West, Excerpt from A Teenage Opera. I would wait to hear it played on the Tony Blackburn show on Radio One before I left for school. And also Ernie the fastest milkman in the West by Benny Hill, there was many a time I would have to run to school as it came on too late. I started buying a monthly record song book called

Such A Lucky Lady

Words for 7s.5d it was good as it had all the lyrics to the songs.

When the summer holidays came, we would try to get out of the house as much as possible. My Mother would be sleeping most of the time, so we would just go out exploring. We would go to the dump looking for anything that could be used we found some old bikes so one day we got on the bikes and went to Hayling Island. On our way, we went through a field and found a derelict barn, inside was a batted caravan. We were in heaven; we were going to clean it up and move into it. So we set to work each of us with great intentions, so all of that summer holiday was spent packing it out. We would go and play bingo down on the beach front.

As we had soon found out from previous experiences, that some strangers were a soft touch for a hard luck story. We would go up to complete strangers and ask them how far it was to Portsmouth, as we had to walk there to see our mother, who was in the hospital and we had lost our bus fare. Many times they would give us the fair, and then we would wait at the bus stop for the bus if they were still around we would get on the bus but get off the next stop.

If and when we won at playing bingo we would choose things that we could use in our new home/caravan. Like pots, pans, mugs, cutlery, and a very posh rack with a tea set on. We got dozens of tins of food and packets and placed them under the seats. How we obtained most of the food was, When My Mother sent us shopping Martin,

Lady Donna Louise Wilder

worked out that. If he picked up a receipt from the pavement of the supermarket. (Fine Fare) In those days it only had the price of the item on it, so he would get a shopping trolley, then put a box inside it. We would then walk around the supermarket looking for something that we could match up with what My Mother wanted on her list. For example, if she wanted five tins of cat food, we would go to the shelf and look for tins that were the same price. We would go down My Mothers list and get as much as we could. Then we would just walk out the supermarket; we would then cross reference what we had with mothers list in the Chinese restaurant. Where we would order egg fried rice that was wrapped up in tin foil. Plus, a milkshake drink. We would sit down at a table and start counting out our money. As for bedding, we had to have sleeping bags we all decided. We were down the seafront and at a gift shop, that had hung up outside, buckets, spades, rubber rings, etc. at the end of the display was a sleeping bag, without knowing at the time Martin had pinched one of them. It was all rolled up, so it didn't look massive. But I remember him holding it up and thinking how brave my little brother was, (he was my real hero). Then one day when we went back to our beautiful home/Caravan we were heartbroken to find it had gone!!!
The barn had been, demolished, and our home had been, nicked.

Another one of our adventures to Hayling Island we trespassed into a field where we found a gigantic tent that had been, erected it was huge. We climbed on to the

Such A Lucky Lady

top and were running around until we tired ourselves out and continued with our exploring.

My Mother said one day that she was going to read us a story every night and that we could choose a book, she would read it to us all, we all would have to sit and listen to it. Well, Richard's choice was the first one (no surprise there). It was the Borrowers; I can only ever remember her reading that one.

As we had stopped using the front door to come in, we always came in through the back door, so when Martin got hold of some boxes of puffs from the school. After he accidentally kicked a football at the windowpane, (so he said? He got in and decided to take some of the boxes, but not wanting to get found out by My Mother, he tied some string to the boxes and heaved them up to the bedroom. Where all the boxes, were emptied, and the contents hid all on the bedroom floor, as you couldn't see the carpet for clothes, pots and bottles anything and everything was on the floor in every room even on the stairs. Hence, everywhere we walked all you could hear was a CRUNCH, CRUNCH, CRUNCH.

I lost count on how many times I ran away to see My Father, but every time I had to go back as My Mother had full custody of us all, My Father tried for custody a few times but back in them days it wasn't heard of for a father to have full custody. One time when he picked me up from Waterloo train station My Father was doing some work in a boutique; He had to take me there while he was finishing the job. He asked the owner if she could help me with some new clothes, she helped me pick out two outfits, My Father told the young lady, that he would take it off her bill; I felt so grown up. Another time, he took me to a job he was doing in London, in an enormous Victorian townhouse. The houses were exactly like the ones in the film Oliver when he is singing the song. Who will buy?

At school, we were all asked to bring things to school, that we no longer wanted, as the school was going to be holding a jumble sale. So Martin, Jo-Ann & I decided we would go knocking on houses asking for any jumble. We then brought it all home and went through it holding back anything that we wanted. On one of our collections, we had far too much to carry, so as we had seen a pushchair parked outside one of the flats, we decided just to borrow it and return it after. Only when we went back to get it, I noticed two gorgeous blouses hanging on the washing line, thinking how beautiful they would look on me, I asked Martin to swipe them for me, so he did. We ran home with all our goodies, guess what we didn't take the pushchair back. A few days later the police arrived at our door, as we had been, seen with it. My Mother told Jo-Ann that she had to take the blame, as she was under ten years old, and she wouldn't get into as much trouble as us older ones. By the way, the blouses fitted me just fine, and I thought I looked like the bee's knees.

I went past a house just down the road one day, when the little dog in the garden ran out and bit me on my hand, it was a Jack Russell. It simply wouldn't let go of me, even with my screams. The lady came out and got the dog off me, she took me to her house and cleaned me up. She gave me some chocolate and some money it was a note, but I can't remember how much it was. She also said that she would take me to the circus if My Mother would let me go. As I was leaving to go home, she gave me a little tin box with some antiseptic wipes inside. A few days later she took me to the circus with her granddaughter. I had lots to eat and drink (I think she was just trying to bribe me not to tell). But not long after, the dog died.

My Mother took us with her to court; I imagine it was for her divorce from My Father. After they had finished at the Court, My Father took us all including My Mother out to dinner to a Wimpy Bar, and then we went to the cinema with him to see Carry on up the Khyber.

Lady Donna Louise Wilder

Michael's Family

Large photo:
Kelly Wilder, née Bingham Michael Wilder, née O'Bryan,
Bottom left to right:
(1) Ben Wilder, née Bingham, (2) Kelly Wilder, née Bingham, Michael Wilder, née O'Bryan, (3) Angie Wilder, née Manning, (Michael's Ex-wife).

106

Chapter 9

My Best Intentions

At school one day we had a fire drill, as I was taking it all in, I began to question how we would escape a fire in our house. So I decided to do my, own fire drill with my brother Martin and sister Jo-Ann; first, we got the mattresses from the bunk beds, then threw them out the bedroom window on top of each other. First, Martin was brave enough to volunteer and go first; he then came back up wanting another go, but it was Jo-Ann's turn. She was a bit scared, I'm not sure who it was, Martin or I knew, she needed a little push, she went a bit too far and landed on the extension guttering, hanging by her knickers, (she wasn't hurt).

One day at lunch time I went out of school with a friend of mine at the time called Doreen, we went to her house for our lunch. We took a shortcut over an old discontinued railway line, known as the Puffing Billy line. As we were walking along someone shouted to us, get out of here, we looked up to see an old man, all in rags he was dirty and was surrounded by cardboard boxes, of course, and he was a tramp. We just run away laughing, but when we reached Doreen's house we were feeling sorry for him, so after finishing eating our lunch we decided to make him an excellent sandwich. It started off like any other sandwich, bread butter, ham, cheese, a bit of salad then some salt pepper, and a squeeze of toothpaste to clean his teeth, a squeeze of washing up liquid to wash himself and a sprinkle of vim as he was so dirty. Cut into triangles and wrapped in tin foil, perfect. We couldn't wait to give it to him we were laughing and giggling all the way, but when we got there. Lucky for him, he had moved on, (I like to think that we would have changed our minds had he still been there).

At school when it was lunchtime if you didn't get in at the first sitting, you had to line up and wait until someone had finished. Then the dinner lady would let some more go in. Well not wanting to stand in the line for the whole lunch time, my friends and I would jump the queue. When the dinner lady wasn't looking, if she saw you then you would be sent to the back of the queue. This one time when we pushed in, this one girl wasn't having any of it, and told, on us. We were told to go to the back of the queue, well on our way to the back of the queue, my right leg must have had a spasm, as it kicked the said girls wicker basket, well on impact my foot went straight through and made a hole. I tried to tell the headmaster that I tripped, but he didn't believe me. I was then, told that I had to buy her a new basket, which I did not do. As My Mother wouldn't give me the money and I wasn't going to give her any of mine, as they say, boys will be boys, and girls will be right little madams.

I joined Guides it was fun until Brown Owl gave me a uniform for free as My Mother couldn't afford to buy me one, the skirt was so long that I took it to school, and the needlework teacher helped me take it up. I merrily went along to the next Guide meeting with it on, and Brown

Such A Lucky Lady

Owl had a go at me for making it too short it was above the knee, so I soon left.

I used to get chilblains lots of times as a child, it is very painful, probably because I would put my cold feet as near as I could to the heat from the oven. I would light the stove to warm my clothes and sit as close as I could to get dressed.

One time for the run up to bonfire night, Richard was put into a pushchair by us with a mask on, so we could beg for money. Someone once gave us a half a crown; I think maybe by mistake as it was the same size as a penny.

Plus, we used to go round carol singing not one of us could sing so it must have sounded like strangled cats, with the money we made, believe it or not, a tidy sum. We would go to the chip shop and buy us all sausage in batter with chips and haddock and chips for My Mother and bring them home, and then with the rest of the money, we gave it to My Mother to help with our Christmas.

One Christmas Richard got a projector called Flashy Flickers, it was a magic picture gun, that you had to put a roll of film into to make it work. It had a small touch light bulb, and you shone it on the ceiling or a plain wall, then when you pulled the trigger it would show the film, he had Wonder Woman, Aqua-Man or Tomahawk. The next day being Boxing Day we decided we would go around and shine it through people's windows, and then when they came to the front door, we would ask them if they wanted a movie show, some of then would give us some money.

My Mother would get Bronchitis a lot, and she also suffered from asthma, a few times we had to get the Doctor to come to the house when she was very ill. Because she would refuse to go into hospital, the doctor would give her an adrenaline injection, and tell me to look after her, and he would leave medication for her to take.

Auntie Jo went on holiday and asked My Mother and us to house sit her animals. She had a ginger cat that had a very furry tail; My Mother got me to put a ginger fox tail that Auntie Jo had, under a suitcase. So it looked like the case had fallen onto the cat, we then called Jo-Ann in to see. It was very hard to keep a straight face, as Jo-Ann was such an animal lover, she went white as a ghost, and didn't want to lift the case off, then the cat just walked into the room. (a sick joke I know).

There was a toy shop in Havant precinct that caught fire, one evening we soon found out and went and rumbled through the ashes and came home with lots of string puppets.

Auntie Jo brought me a Ben Sherman shirt one Christmas; it was light blue and white check, so I was able to wear it for school. My friends all liked it. As we were living far from London, it would take a while before we got the up to date fashion out in our town. I got on well with the needlework teacher so when our school agreed that girls could wear trousers as part of the school uniform. I asked her if she could help me make some trousers in our lesson, she said could I wait until the end of the lesson, and she would cut a pair out for me. I could choose to have Black, Grey or Burgundy; I went for Burgundy. So she helped me cut them out. Then when we had the next lesson, she said Donna we need to cut your trousers out first don't we, I know I should have told her that she did it last week. But I didn't so I went ahead and made two pairs. (naughty I know, But I was a kid).

My sister Jo-Ann was sent up the shops one day to get something for My Mother. she was, given a ten bob note, on her way she stopped to play with some friends. So places the note under a brick, when she went back to get it, she couldn't find it. When she told My Mother, she's gone mad. Grabbing Jo-Ann by her hair bunch, and pulling her down, onto the mattress. My Mother was still laying on; then she called me to get the scissors, as she was going to cut her hair. (none of us girls ever had our hair cut up until then) I came back and said I couldn't find them, and she screamed at me saying find them or I'll cut yours too. With that I ran to a neighbour crying, very soon Martin came to tell me that My Mother said, I was to get back. I was hiding on the neighbours stair. After a little while, I went back to find poor Jo-Ann with one of her bunches missing and, a massive hand print on her face. My Mother had used a bread knife to hack one off her bunches off only on one side. Jo-Ann couldn't go to school for a while. Eventually, My Mother tidied Jo-Ann's hair up.

Lady Donna Louise Wilder

My Father went on to marry twice more. 1st to a lady named Jenny with whom they had two girls (my half Sisters). Karen Pearce & Kelly Pearce.

Then his 2nd to a lady named Jane, with whom they had A Daughter & 2 sons (my half Sister and Brothers). Nicola Pearce, Robert Pearce, & Jordan Pearce.
Jane was younger than me.

Once my parents got divorced around the late 1960s, early 1970s My Mother went back to using her maiden name O'Bryan, and then we all were told to use that name from then on.

Chapter 10

Dicing With Death

Then not long after that, I had asked My Mother, for some money for a cookery class as she begrudgingly handed it over to me she said as God is my witness you will be paid back for taking my money, well it went in one ear and out the other. I was running across the road at the zebra crossing as the lights had just changed, but a car travelling way too fast from Hayling Island hit me. I was laying on the road, lots of people came from the bus stop and piled their coats on top of me to keep me warm until the Ambulance came. I kept on going in and out of consciousness all the time. They were asking me for my name, and where I lived, I managed to get Donna out, but then went unconscious again; eventually I gave my full name Donna Louise O'Bryan. Not Pearce as My Mother had said, not long before, that our name was no longer Pearce.

So when the police went to our house My Mother, as usual, wouldn't open the door, everyone in the house just kept quiet until they went away. My Brother Martin was told to look carefully out the window to see who it was. Well, after telling My Mother it was the police, she began hitting him. He was being, battered black & blue as he owned up to everything he had done; even telling about fighting a boy at school and not doing his homework, even that he pinched a slice of bread, the lot.

But My Mother said. It wasn't severe enough to bring the police to her door. The police then came back, but still My Mother didn't answer the front door. A neighbour came out, and when the police said they were looking for a Mrs O'Bryan, the neighbour said that the family that lived in that house was called Pearce. So they went away again, In the hospital, I was found to have broken my knee & ankle. I had my leg put in a plaster cast right up to the top of my leg. Then, as no one had come to find me, I was placed in a ward with a lot of elderly ladies, it was very nice as they all started fussing around me, giving me some of their fruit and sweets.

Eventually, My Mother found out about my accident around 7 pm; she came up the hospital with a box of Smarties, then she said I told you that something would happen because I took her last bit of money. She also said that It was a bit drastic getting run over just to get a new pair of tights. When she went home, I was taken care of by all the elderly ladies in the ward. (I loved all the attention I was getting). The next day, a Health visitor came to see me. I was then taken home by ambulance, but when we arrived back home, there was another, health visitor waiting outside our house. She told My Mother that the hospital was concerned, as I looked like I was undernourished, she said to My Mother that we needed to be given glucose with raw egg in milk, to fatten us up.

Because My Mother would keep one of us from school to stay with her at all times plus including us playing truant, we had fallen behind with our schooling.

Such A Lucky Lady

My Mother had been, threatened with court action. So the next day after I had been, run over, I got my crutches and set off for school, trying to get on the back of the bus was hard, but I got to school in one piece. Only to be told that I shouldn't have come in, but I was allowed to choose two friends to wait on me hand and foot. With my feet up, and my dinner brought to me on a tray, (like lady muck) I remember thinking this is the life. The truant officer wasn't happy at all, so she tried to arrange for a taxi, but It would have cost too much.

After six weeks I had to go back to the hospital, but on the day I went into a sweet shop with Rebecca, we were looking in the window as the lady owner was busy serving a customer. When she had finished, she obviously recognised me and shouted at me making me jump, that made me bang my leg down on the shop floor. She said it was a shame my husband didn't kill you. I quickly worked out that her husband was the man that had hit me with his car, so must be being done for running me over. So later when I reached the hospital, and they took the plaster off, they found that my ankle was still, broken. So I had to be plastered up to my knee, that meant another six weeks in plaster. When that six-week was up the plaster was removed. So I was free, to come and go as I liked.

The first mad and stupid thing I did was to sit on the handlebars of a lad's bike, he was showing off and was swerving in and out of some young trees, which were being, supported by a bit of wood with a leather strap around them, held together with two nails. I thought we were going to crash into the little stream.

So I grabbed hold of a tree. Unfortunately, the leather strap was broken, and the two nail heads stuck into my left wrist, ripping a large bit off my skin of, and scratching my vein. I honestly thought I was going to die, and so did my friend at the time, as we had been talking about your veins at school. I ran home screaming; I went indoors and My Mother without even having a look, said go to the hospital. I ran out into the alleyway in a big panic screaming. An old lady that lived a few doors down our alley. Came out and took me to her house, where she bandaged me up. (She said she was a nurse in the war). I went to the hospital, and a very young nurse stitch my wrist up, by a running stitch all around the edges, and pulling it together then cutting the frayed edges of skin off.

As I was leaving the hospital a doctor asked if he could have a look at my wound, he removed the dressing and gave me an injection in the wound first, and then he took out the stitch and re-stitch my wrist with five stitches. (I was lucky he saw me as my wrist would have healed all deformed).

At school, I tried to convince my teachers that I was left handed so wouldn't be able to do any written work. (but no joy they weren't having any of it).

Every household appliance that used gas had to be, adapted to North Sea gas. But when they arrived at our house, to do the conversion My Mother wouldn't let them in. They tried lots of times, but she just wouldn't let them in to do their job. So they cut off our gas supply from outside, My Mother, who liked her cup of nearly black tea, sent me out to buy one small pan and a camping stove with Butane/Propane gas. She was trying to put it together, but she had threaded it wrong, so some of the gas began escaping. So she told Martin to watch outside that no one walked by with a lighted cigarette. Then one day after the workmen had finished all the other houses on the street. They had to get an order to break into our house, so they knocked the door in and just came in and adapted all the gas in the house. My Brother Richard was off school that day so was in the front room with My Mother.

Walking to the shops one day, this young boy started talking to me, and he asked if he could take me to the cinema to see The Railway Children. I said I didn't have any money to go, but he said he would pay for me, so we arrange to meet the next afternoon. He even paid for sweets and ice creams, and then he walked me to the top of our street. His plans for our next date the next day was to go to the cinema. So we met the next day and went to see The Railway Children again. (he paid for everything once again). He then walked me back to our street saying see you again tomorrow? We met, and he suggested we go to the cinema, once again, we went to see The Railway Children. When he walked me back and asked to meet the next day again, I thought he must know somewhere else to take me, but no, The Railway Children it was again. So after the film, and Before he could ask me again, I said I couldn't come out tomorrow. I can't remember what excuse I gave him; it could have been I had to wash my hair.

I was invited to be a bridesmaid with my cousin Mandy for her Auntie Judy & Uncle Jack, we both wore white embroidery Anglaise trouser suits. I thought we both looked very grown up and very sophisticated. It was a lovely day; after the wedding, my Auntie Jo & Uncle Ken took me on holiday with them to Spain. We went on the hovercraft from Dover to Calais, and then my Uncle Ken, who done all the driving, drove over the Pyrenees Mountains, after a long while we stopped at a campsite for the night. Then bright and early the next morning we were on our way, when we were nearly there my cousins Paul and Stephen got out of the car and sneaked into the camp site, the campsite was on the Costa Brava.

There were some shops on the site, a fishing/boating lake, that flowed out to sea, lovely yellow soft sand, and a bridge that went over to a night club/disco. After we were all set up with the caravan & awning, all us kids went down to the beach we all had a great time. After a little while, I got out of the sea and went and laid down on my towel, but I soon fell fast asleep, I think it was only for about 45 minutes or so. Then when I got back to the caravan, my cousin slapped me jokingly on my back. I started crying because my back was sore as I had got sunburnt because I hadn't put any sun cream on myself. Mandy and I liked the disco we would hang around there most of the time; it was free to go. But one time we went to go over the bridge, this time, we had been told that we

Such A Lucky Lady

had to pay. I didn't want too so we started arguing, in the end, Mandy, who had my money on her, dropped my money down my top and walked off. (it all fell into the sand). I bent down to find it all; then I went off to the beach on my own.

Meanwhile, Mandy had gone back to the caravan without me, (she told whatever story naturally to make me look like I was the bad one) so there was a manhunt for me, (well a kid hunt). When they found me, I was told off as we had been told to stay together. (plus not forgetting they didn't want to draw attention to the fact that they hadn't paid for us all to be on the site). My cousins were in the blow-up boat that my Uncle had got from the petrol station, with the saving stamps he had been getting along the journey. It would only take two passengers at a time. So two of us would wait our turn at the water's edge trying to catch fish. You could easily see them, I noticed a fish coming downstream and thought I would try and catch it with my bare hands. (and so I did) only to find it was half of a fish, it was dead.

One day I was sitting on a neighbour's fence just talking to the little children in the garden. When Martin came along and jokingly pushed me off. A bit of the fence splintered off and stuck in the cheek of my bum. I tried to get it out but I couldn't so I eventually had to show my bum to My Mother. she couldn't get it out as every time She tried with a sewing needle it just broke into little bits. I had no choice but to go up the hospital to see if they could remove it. (as by now I hadn't sat down for a week). I was so, embarrassed. But even they couldn't remove the splinter from my bum. They gave me something to put on my bum so it would help to draw it out, a couple of days later I was on a train going to London, to see my dad. I had phoned him up and asked if I could come and see him; he said to get on the train to Waterloo, and he would meet me at the other end, then pay for my ticket. When I was having a bath a few days later, the splinter came out in the bathtub, it was the size of a matchstick in length, and as thick as two matches.

While I was staying at My Fathers, he took me to see My Auntie Jo and told me to tell her why I kept running away. I told her that My Mother was in bed all the time and didn't do anything but read books, or sleep and that she didn't even leave the room to go to the toilet. My Auntie Jo told My Father that I was just exaggerating and demanding attention. She said that he shouldn't listen to my lies.

A fun crazy, I just had to have, that was going around, was the Clackers. They were two balls on a piece of string that you held in the middle between your finger and thumb. And by raising your hand up and down slowly, you made the balls hit each other until you got the rhythm. Then you went faster and faster, so the balls touched at the top as well as the bottom. It really, hurt when you missed when it hit you on your wrist. I had so many bruises on my wrists that it even hurt to write. Well, that's what I told my teacher.

I got myself a paper round to earn some money than a Saturday job filling shelves in a supermarket.

Such A Lucky Lady

We didn't have a set bedtime so one day at school in a history lesson, the teacher was talking about Henry VIII. Which I was very interested in, but I had fallen asleep. So when he noticed he shouted Donna. I woke up shouting "I found it, I found it," he said what have you found Donna? I said "the head I've found the head" everyone fell about laughing.

One evening Janice and I was playing badminton at the Youth Centre. When two lads asked if they could join us, in playing doubles. Well, we agreed and were having a good game, I think us girls were winning at one point. Then I slide my racket across the floor that had old wooden floor boards when a splinter when up my nail and out through the back of my finger. I then was taken to the hospital where they had to remove my fingernail, to be able to get it out, so that put me of badminton.

When Martin was small he was circumcised, so while growing up and seeing both brother's bits and bobs were different, it was easy for me to assume that Richard had the wrong one, as not liking him everything about him was wrong. I believed that all men's bits and bobs would be like Martins. So the first time I saw one the same as Richards was when we were in an art lesson and some girls when the teacher had left the class got this lad to get his out, and they painted it with red paint. Well after seeing his I was completely shocked and very confused.

Lady Donna Louise Wilder

Step Children And Their Mother

Top left to right
(1) Audrey Wilder, née Reed. (Wally's Ex-wife). (2) Natasha Wilder, my stepdaughter. (3) Dave Lawrence, Natasha's Ex-partner.
Bottom Left to right
(4) Justin Wilder my step-son, (5) Samantha Wilder, née Hogan, My Ex-daughter-in-law, (6) Katrina Hunt, Justin's partner,

Such A Lucky Lady

Chapter 11

Scarred For Life

There was this very popular boy called Kevin who came over to me after school one day and asked if I wanted to go to a party with him on Friday night. First, I said My Mother wouldn't let me go, so he said ok I'll ask someone else, not wanting to miss my chance to go out with the number one boy in the school. I quickly said ok, but only if you get me my drinks, (My Mother had told me that at parties they get you drunk and rape you). So on Friday I finished school and went home and put on a pair of lee cooper jeans. I placed a nappy type safety pin, (they have a head on that you pushed down to lock it). So from the inside of the jeans over the zip then back through to the inside, that way no one can take your jeans off. When we arrived the place was very busy, Kevin got me a coke in a glass, and he had a beer from a bottle.

I sat down on the sofa the party was at an elderly lady's house, whose husband had not long passed away, her eldest son was taking charge of her and his younger brother. The front room had been, knocked into the back room, so it made the room much bigger. There was a table down the end of the room where a lot of people were all gathered around. A young girl came up and asked to fill my glass up, I said no thanks, I was ok, she said what are you drinking, coke? I said yes, she then took my glass and came back with another one with what look like coke and gave it to me, Kevin by now was on his 3rd bottle, talking to his mates. I finished my drink and started to wander down to the table to see what was going on. Well, this older guy about 25 years old, was dipping a sewing needle that had sewing thread wrapped around it into a pot, of Indian ink. Then he started sticking it in this other, guy's arm. I could see little bits of blood coming out; the guy was biting on a pencil. I walked away as I didn't like it. I went upstairs to the loo I felt a bit funny, but I put it down to the smelly sticks that were scattered, about the place, (Joss sticks).

When I went to go downstairs, I fell and got my foot stuck underneath the front room door. I don't remember anything until I woke up at home in my bed. I panicked but was quickly relieved to find that my jeans were still on with the pin still in place, but my arms felt strange. First, I thought I had some blue felt tip pen on my arms. I went to wash it off, but the soap and water wouldn't shift it, then panic set in, I tried using a scrubbing brush until my arms were bleeding,

(What had been, put on my arms was my name Donna with a row of small dots underneath on my right arm, and a swastika about ¾" of an inch in size on my left arm). I needed to tell someone, so I went and told Martin and Jo-Ann. I was unaware Richard had been listening, he went straight to My Mother and said mummy have you seen what Donnas' got on her arms, with that My Mother screamed come here now, she pulled my sleeve up and then started thumping, punching, slapping me the lot until she ran out of energy. Well, that's what I got from My Mother when she saw that I had my name, DONNA underlined with dots on my right arm. Then my dear brother said have you seen her other arm mummy. With that My Mother grabbed my arm and pulled my sleeve up, I knew that was it, I was dead. As on my left arm was a very crooked swastika, well that was it. My Mother just broke down, saying you had better get out of her sight as when she got her strength back she was going to kill me. And she never wanted to see me again, I just went upstairs and stayed out of her way, I didn't come down until Monday morning when my brothers & sisters had gone to school.

I bucked up the courage and went and knocked on the front room door. When My Mother said what do you want, I opened the door and stood in the doorway, too scared to go in, crying and saying I'm sorry. After a bit My Mother told me to tell her the truth as to what had happened after I told her she said right were going to the police station, she got dressed and took me to see the police at the station. I had to tell them what had happened and where the house was. They wrote it all down, and then they took us in the police car, so I could show them where the party was. They left us in the car and went to speak to the lad that lived there. When they came back, they said that he had insisted that he never saw anything. Then they said that without any witnesses, there was nothing they could do.

They told My Mother that I was lucky, as a young couple over the weekend had been tattooed, with each other's names on their chest's, in 2inch letters. When we were going back, My Mother asked the police if they would drop us at our doctors. We got in to see the doctor quite quickly; My Mother told me to show the doctor my arms. He suggested that I when to see a plastic surgeon and have surgery on them. We got an appointment very quickly; My Mother took me to see the surgeon/doctor. Then after he had a look, his exact words were. If she is silly enough to inflict them on herself, then she can keep them. I would cover them up all the time with long sleeves or sweat bands.

I needed a coat, but the only one I liked was the one in a shop window by the bus stop. I would see it every day it was £8.00 I begged and pleaded with My Mother for ages. Eventually, she gave in, and I got the coat of my dreams. It was very smart, black with a shiny red lining. Well, one day Janice and I were with a group that we sometimes hung around with, we all decided to go to a pub on the way to Horndean, called the G.I. (The Good Intent). I very gracefully hung my coat up on a coat hook, because it was a Crombie. (a mod's coat) Some hells angels that were in the pub got my coat and tipped beer over it, and then they chucked it on the floor and stood on it. I had to get it dry cleaned. One of our friends had a bubble car he would give us both a lift home. Only if Janice gave him some money for petrol.it was a bit tight; I would have to sit on Janice's lap. I then fell in love with the two-tone tonic skirt suits, I only wore the jackets with my lee cooper jeans, as I believed my legs were too thin.

Such A Lucky Lady

When we played truant from school, Janice and I (sometimes Jo-Ann and Martin would come with us). We would go to this house known as the drop in house. It was where lots of kids would go and hang out. We would go shoplifting for our lunch. We would get a Fray Bentos steak and kidney pie in a tin, a tin of potatoes and a tin of mixed veg. Then on the way out we would pick up a packet of Mars bars and run like hell. We would take it all and cook our dinner in the drop in house. I would do the cooking but get my sister Jo-Ann to do the washing-up.

Once one late afternoon round the drop in house, the lads got together and for a joke told all their girlfriends that they didn't want to go out with them anymore. They wanted to see their reaction, well there were five girls Janice and me, Janice wasn't bothered one way or another so just accepted it, the other girls were crying and even pleading with their boyfriends/ex-boyfriends. I just said that's fine which wasn't the response Kevin expected. He said what do you mean it's fine? So I said there are plenty more fish in the sea. Well, that didn't go down very well. Because his mates started laughing at him. and by now they had told the girls it was only a joke. So all six were hugging and kissing each other. Kevin came over and said, come on give us a kiss; I said no sorry were finished remember.

I walked past him and went upstairs to use the bathroom when I had finished I opened the door, and Kevin was standing there. He was mad, he pushed me back into the toilet and said don't you ever show me up in front of my mates again. I told him I wouldn't as were finished. With that he slapped my face, I just hit him back but as I had rings on one must have cut his cheek, I left the bathroom and the house never to see Kevin again.

I started going to a youth Centre with my friend Janice as she was her parents only daughter, she had two much older brothers, so was spoilt by them all, so she paid for me to get in, and then one day Janice got a bottle of cider. And we would drink it as fast as we could, so we felt drunk. I think I must have been the dominant one. As I told Janice to drink the first half, I don't think she worked out that I had a little bit more than her, as she had less because of the neck of the bottle. She wasn't able to get any money once for the cider, so she decided to pinch some of her dad's pills. (I don't know what they were).

She met me on the corner and gave me one saying that it would make us feel like we were drunk. I thought one couldn't hurt, well I was fine, but she wasn't, as it turns out she had taken one before she met up with me. At the Youth Centre Janice started falling over and couldn't walk very well, one of the youth workers thought she was drunk. She was told to leave; the Youth Centre told her she couldn't come back ever again. So we had to find somewhere else to go. We decided that all the fun would be at the fair. So we started hitchhiking to Southsea. We both agreed that we would only get into a car that had just the driver in it. I would always get into the back, and Janice would willingly get in the front, I carried a hairspray in my bag, as I had heard that It would blind an

attacker long enough for you to get away. Well if the driver thought he was in for a good time I would always say that I wasn't interested, but Janice would volunteer every time. So they would pull over, I would wait on the pathway until they had finished, and then we would go on our way, after having fun at the fair we would then make our way back home, by hitchhiking again. Janice didn't do anything on the way back home, as many times it would be getting late and she had a set time to be home.
(thinking back I have a lot to thank Janice for).

As I was leaving school soon, I decided to find out what I was good at and then concentrate on that subject. I had already crossed out religious education and P.E. So the first lesson was science, I was sitting next to my mate Janice concentrating. When Janice started talking to me, I turned to say be quite, but the teacher caught me talking and hit me with a ruler across my knuckles, so that was the end of my concentrating I just gave up.

Our deputy head arranged for all the school leavers that hadn't arranged a job to go for a day in an egg factory, it was, I think to show us what we would end up doing if we didn't find work ourselves. (it was smelly and horrible). it worked as we soon found our, own jobs.

I started smoking, along with everyone else at the time. I didn't enjoy it but thought for, a little bit I was a real grown-up. After about three months I still didn't like it. Then one day I asked My Mother for some money for a pair of tights, (as mine had a few ladders in them, but as it was fashionable to wear white knee socks over your tights I could hide them most of the time). She said no I couldn't, then a few minutes later I asked My Mother for some money to buy some cigarettes. This time, she gave me some money, so I brought the cigarettes and sold them to my friends, for profit, so I was able to buy my tights and some more cigarettes.

As we had all been off school either playing truant or because My Mother had kept one of us of school to stay at home with her, the authorities decided to make an example of Martin and sent him away.

I had an evening job in the fish & chip shop. One night on the way home through Havant Park, I went into use the toilet (as our toilet at home, was, still broken). While sitting on the throne as you do, I just happened to look up to see a face looking over the divided wall, I just screamed, then heard them run out, so waited a bit then I just ran all the way home,

At the fair one evening in 1972 Janice and I made a record, the only song we knew the words to at the time Was Blue is the colour the Chelsea football song.

(By the way, I don't support any football teams).

I met a lad called Kevin, one Friday evening while I was working as a waitress in the fish and chip shop in Havant. He was 17 and working. Janice and I both got our first job in Wingard's a factory in Chichester on the assembly line putting together seat belts; I wanted to work there as that was where Kevin was already working. I later found out he was seeing someone else. As I was walking through the park one evening when a group of seven girls all came over to me; one said are you going out with Kevin? When I said yes she started punching me in the face saying well you better not be, I didn't even try to defend myself, as thought the others would just join in. A couple walking their dog shouted out, so they all ran off. When she had finished with me, I was bleeding from my cheek.

The couple walked me to the police station and gave me a white cotton handkerchief. (they said I could keep it). At the police station they had a look and cleaned me up, I told them what had happened and that I had seen the girl at my school. I gave them her name. They knew her so they took me to her house to see her parents, when they knocked on the door, it was a little while before the dad opened the door, (he was in his dressing-gown and not very happy).

The police man told him what had happened then his wife came downstairs (in her dressing-gown). They were very apologetic saying that they will be dealing with her when she came in. The police man said that I could prosecute her for actually bodily harm (ABH). Just then their daughter came in. Well after her parents had finished shouting at her saying that she was grounded, for a month, with no makeup, and only her school uniform to wear. And her month's pocket money was to be given to me, along with a written apology. I thought she was being, punished enough, so I just let it drop.

Lady Donna Louise Wilder

My Step Grand Children

Top photo:
Mason Wilder, Harley Wilder,
Bottom Left to right
Aaliyah Sharnell, Lawrence, or Wilder, Ben Wilder, née Bingham,

Chapter 12

THE REAL WORLD

Janice and I got our first job together, it was in a factory assembling seat belts, we took home £8.00 a week I had to give My Mother £5.00 per week. Well, that left me with not much, so I made sure I got something back for my lunch at work and my bus fares. We were only at Wingard's for six days, because the bench where we worked on was old and made of wood, so every night it would be, covered before we started working with a strong white tape, this young lady named Kathy would come in first and start writing on it. KATHY LOVES, KEITH LOVES, KATHY LOVES, and so on right along the bench. So there was no space for me to write, DONNA LOVES, KEVIN LOVES, DONNA LOVES, and so on. I would have been quite happy if I could have had my, own little bit of space to write on; Kathy was a very respectful young lady.

Not at all like Janice and I who were fun, chatty and very fashionable, (in other words right little madams). When Kathy came into work after the weekend showing and boasting about getting engaged. I just couldn't resist; Announcing that I knew her Keith, she said no you don't, so telling her that he has dark, brownish, blonde hair and greenish, brownie, blue eyes, trying to convince her that I knew him. I said, I was just going into a sweet shop, when I saw Kevin, he was just coming out. He had a Jamboree bag/lucky bag. He put his hand inside the bag and pulled out a ring, and he said Wow. Look a ring, just right for Kathy. Well, she screamed, and then slapped me right across my ear. (it was so very painful). She ran into the toilet's crying. Well, then Janice and I were given just 10 minutes to get off the premises. Well, we had to make our, own way home, we were both afraid to tell our parents. So we went to Farlington industrial estate to get jobs. The first place we had an interview, they said that I had the job but not Janice. She said that I shouldn't take it without her, but I needed the job as My Mother would go mad at me. So I said yes, Janice wasn't happy with me, but she did get a job somewhere else.

I remember with my first wages. I bought myself one bar off every chocolate in the local sweet shop. I then proceeded to eat a square of each. (How sad was I). I was on my way to the bus stop one day going to work. If you looked down the road you could see when the bus was coming, so I reached the bus stop, and the bus was not in sight, so I started walking to the next one. On the way, a car slowed down and offered me a lift. As I was on my own, I said no thank you without even looking at the car or the driver. Then the driver said, you don't remember me do you? I looked and said no, he said, I gave you and your friend a lift a few weeks ago to Southsea. Then my bus went by, and I missed it, he said, let me give you a lift as I've made you miss your bus. I then noticed that he had his leg in plaster, so thinking I would be safe I agreed. He dropped me at work, then when work finished, he was waiting outside the factory. He offered me a lift home; I asked him if he would drop my new friend of as well, he said yes, we both got in his car. He dropped my friend off first, and then he dropped me at the top of my road, I didn't want anyone knowing where I lived. He would take me to work, then meet me for lunch, and even take me home for the next few weeks. (I saved all my bus fair money up, and brought myself a new pair of boots, they were knee length lace–up in a blue denim). Then one day he came to take me home, I took one look at his leg without his plaster on and just couldn't get in his car. (you see I felt in complete control and safe all the time he had his leg in the plaster). I never saw him after that.

My Mother gathered us all around one day to say she had received a letter telling her that the whole street was going to be demolished, as a new development, was being built. So My Mother told us all that we had to gather anything worth taking with us, well, there wasn't much I can tell you. As with the last house, My Mother told us to tidy up the place, as deep down My Mother knew how we were living was not acceptable. As I've already said, nothing left our house, not even the rubbish. So black bags were filled up with whatever there was laying around our house. Everything was just shovelled up and put into the bags, tied up and then put into the attic. (I suppose you could say we had our very own private dump). I remember thinking what a shock the workmen are going to get when they find it all up there, opening the bags to see if they had found anything valuable. Every bag was just full of dirty clothes, odd shoes, newspapers, tin cans, glass, plastic bottles, crockery, cutlery, pots, pans, broken toys the lot along with any cat or dog mess even an occasional dead bird or mouse the cats brought in. Not long after we were being, evicted again, the men with the tanks arrived to fumigate the house again. (surprisingly, none of us ever got ill or got head lice). We were moved, to Morley Crescent Cowplain My Mother was given a voucher to get some furniture, as you have guessed nothing was worth taking from our house. Well, we were sent to a warehouse run by some charity. My Mother then told them what we needed. We got a cooker, a fridge with a small freezer compartment. A sofa and a put you up, a table and four chairs, three chests of draws. And all our kitchenware and bedding. We got two double Beds, one for My Mother, and one for the two girls, and a set of bunk beds for the two boys. As they didn't have a bed for me, I was given a camping bed a bit like a sun lounger I was happy with that as I was going to have my very own room so I could keep it all neat and tidy.

I travelled to work from there, but It became a little too much as it was further, so most of my wages got spent on bus fares. So I got a job in Woolworth's in Waterlooville at first. I was just filling the shelves, and then I went for an interview for the manager's job, in the new record/toy department, as they had knocked into the empty shop next door. I was lucky enough to get the job I was enjoying it, but a young girl who had been working there as a Saturday girl, she was now staying on at schools to further her education made a bad atmosphere, so I went looking for another job. I landed up working in Tesco's in the butchery department, with a lovely old man named

Such A Lucky Lady

Joe. He took me under his wing; I was doing well there. Then one day at lunchtime My Mother turned up at the store, she was waiting for me to come back from lunch. When I saw her, she said that she had enough and was leaving, I had no choice but to stay and help My Mother sort things out, so we went into a café for a cup of tea and we were talking until I persuaded her not to leave. When I went into work the next day, Joe was furious with me. As it had been a busy Friday, that meant we would have had lots on with orders to be ready for the morning. So poor Joe had to stay late to finish. He wasn't interested in my excuse, so like a spoilt child, I walked out. In those days, you could easily get a job. So I went for a job at Waitrose working in the delicatessen department. Again I was working well, and then after just over two weeks I was called into the office, to be told that they had found out that I had been sacked, from my first job at Wingard's, so out the door I went. So I decided that shop work wasn't for me. By the way, the money wasn't much and the hours were too long.

I got a job working in a factory on an assembly line that did a part for TVs. I had just to twist four wires onto a part, and then pass it on to the next person who had to do a different thing to it, and so on. (It was piece work). I would work through my lunch and tea breaks; I would start at the beginning of the assembly line doing all the stages up to mine, where I had them all piled up. Then on the next break, I would continue till the end, so at the end of the week, I had extra wages, I wasn't very popular as it didn't look good for the other workers. (But I was greedy and needed the extra money). As I had something very exciting going on in my life at the time. I got a second part-time job working in the local fish & chip shop. Then when this shop closed at the end of the evening, I would go to their next one that was up the end of the street which stayed open longer, and worked out there. I stayed in these jobs until I had to leave in August 1973. As I didn't know anyone in the area, I decided to go to the local youth club I was only 15 years old. Well, the first young lad that asked me out in the club, I said yes, as thought I would go out with him thinking that I would meet his friends and so on. (I had no intention of staying with him as he just wasn't my type). But before the night was over I had dumped him, as another young lad asked me out who looked more handsome. So I told the first one that we were over before it even began.

So the second one's name was Jonathan, who's nickname was (Blackie). He seemed nice at the time and invited me round to meet his family for tea. They put on an excellent spread and made me feel very welcome. But it wasn't too long before he began to get very possessive, and wanted to meet and see me all the time. So I finished with him. Then his mum & dad came round to see My Mother telling her that he is not eating and is very upset. So My Mother should talk to me and tell me to go out with him again. I still wasn't interested, so I said no. Then I started seeing another young lad also named Jonathan; he was in college. One day we were in town when this group of men around 20 years old. Came over to us and said to me, "you're supposed to be going out with Blackie" when I told him I wasn't, he said "it's either him or me, make your mind up" Meanwhile the

Such A Lucky Lady

other men were pushing and knocking Jonathan around. Not wanting to get involved, we went our separate ways. (I don't know what happened to either Jonathan's). I then meet a lad called Marcel; he was half Spanish again, I met and got on with his parents. After seeing him for about three weeks, he said he was going to his mate's house one Saturday afternoon, and he asked if I wanted to go, as I had no other plans I said, I would go with him. I went into the kitchen where some girls were making some food, sandwich, cakes, etc. Unbeknown to me they contained an extra ingredient. As when I walked home that evening, I looked up at a tree and started laughing hysterically, as I thought I saw Basil Brush sitting in the tree. I must have been hallucinating.

I saw Marcel for a couple more weeks then we were invited to a housewarming party, where the parents had gone away on holiday and left their daughter home alone. We went round with a bottle of vodka; I had heard that vodka and lime was a drink. So I picked a tall glass filled it to within 2in from the top with the vodka, and as they didn't have any lime, someone ran down to the off-licence to get some. While I was waiting for them to come back I started to drink it neat, when the doorbell went I went to open it, well the fresh air hit me, my hand went straight through the glass window, next to the door and smashed. I cut my hand (not too bad). Marcel took me home, when he knocked, at our door he asked to see My Mother, I just started walking upstairs, but My Mother was so fascinated with Marcel's hair, (you see he had a gigantic afro like Michael Jackson). My Mother hadn't even noticed that I was swaying from side to side.

Marcel kept saying "you had better watch her" well after he had gone and My Mother had closed the front door. She yelled for me to get down the stairs. She had got either Martin or Jo-Ann to fill the bath up with just cold water. As I stumbled down the stairs, My Mother grabbed me just as I reached the last couple of steps, and dragged me into the bathroom, where My Mother pushed me into the bath of cold water, fully clothed, with my hair wrapped around My Mothers' hand she pushed me under the water. Shouting I'll teach you to get drunk you little bitch, as she pulled me back up by my hair, I would be gasping for breath. Then as soon as I got some and could breathe, My Mother just pushed me back under again, she continued this until she was exhausted, lucky for me she got tired very quickly. (well it didn't stop me from drinking). I would go into the spotted cow pub in Cowplain and ask for a pint glass of Cresta. It was a soft drink (advertised by a polar bear). I thought I was cool, sometimes the men in the pub would offer to pay for my drink. They would even sometimes buy me a packet of crisps or a chocolate bar as well, (Looking back now I now realise how lucky I was, not to have been groomed or assaulted).

One day Jo-Ann was going to her first school disco, as I was a dab hand at make-up and fashion, (well I thought I was). I was kind enough to allow her to borrow some of my clothes, but not my best ones. And then I put her hair up and some of my make-up on her, I think I did an excellent job. But as soon as she was out of site of the house she told me later that she wiped it all off. (I bet she looked a right state, with it all smudge around her face).

Chapter 13

A Critical Time

My Mother and I started going to see the all night horror movies at the cinema in North End. We would take a bag of goodies to eat and drink with us; you would get to watch five full-length horror films, along with cartoons in the intermission. On one of our visits, they were showing what was coming up in the following weeks. The one that we both thought was funny was a little old lady walking through a museum, looking at statues of nude men, with a small toffee hammer in her hand. She was knocking off all the men's private bits; My Mother said this looks funny we should come and see this. So we came to see it during the week, with our bag of goodies. We sat down ready for the film to start, My Mother looked around and said it's not that busy in here. There were about 25-30 or so people, but they were all men on their own. The film started the first bit was the old lady again, and then things got very blue. (Obviously, this was the only decent bit of the movie they could show in the advert). My Mother said come on let's go; we did laugh at the Thought of a mother taking her daughter to see a blue movie.

My Mother began allowing us to bring friends back to the house. Some of our mates would bring some pop, bread, and even potatoes round as we would get Jo-Ann to cook us all some chips. One day a young lad called

Lady Donna Louise Wilder

Monty said that he would get My Mother some potatoes.
Well, Monty did turn up so excited one evening.
With these six sacks. When he opened them, they were
all full of oranges. He tipped them all on the front room
floor.

One day My Mother and I were upstairs in My Mother's
bedroom sorting out some toiletries. Monty and one
other mate knocked at our house; I shouted out were up
here you can come up. Monty got on with My Mother,
really well; he was very intelligent. He had been adopted
by a very wealthy family and had been to grammar
school. When they came up, as I was passing the
toiletries to My Mother reading what they were. Monty
started opening them and smelling them, adding a little
bit behind his ears or on his wrist, then just as I had read
out hair removal cream he put some on his head. (By the
way, his hair was his pride and joy as he had a Mohican
hairstyle). I hadn't passed that one over at that time, we
didn't tell him, so he thought his hair was going to fall
out.

One time I opened a bedside cabinet in my sisters and
My Mother's bedroom that was next to My Mother's
bed. It had a pile of maggots in it, on the windowsill,
there was, dog and cat food tins, plus milk bottles full of
urine.

Janice and I would go to the Mecca on a Saturday night.
We didn't have the money to get in, so we would stand
looking around. As if we were waiting, for our
boyfriends to come. Then pretend that we had been stood

up. So then hopefully, a young lad would ask if you wanted to date them. We would say yes ok then, only to get them to pay for us to get in. Then when they had paid for us to get in and after they had brought us both a drink. We then would look around the room and then announce that our boyfriends, (who would be someone we knew) were over there. So we had better go, as they would be so mad if they were to see us with anyone else.

One time Janice and I had an argument about something and nothing, she stormed off. So I missed the last bus back home, and the late bus from the Mecca was fully booked, so I went and stayed at a young lad's place until the buses started in the morning. So around 6 am I got the bus home, only to find my Auntie Jo had arrived unexpectedly, My Mother was doing a fantastic job as the worried and upset loving, caring and doting Mother. Telling Auntie Jo how worried she was that I hadn't come home and had been missing all night. So Auntie Jo started having a go at me saying "there's a name for girls like you" my reply was "will you should know" I then turned and walked out until Auntie Jo had left. Martin then walked in with a cigarette in his hand, when Auntie Jo saw it, she said to him "what's that in your hand, Martin? He told her it was a cigarette, and that it was something to do with his hands, she told him, "try picking your nose."

Another time Janice and I were on the train going to Portsmouth from Havant. I had a pair of lee cooper jeans on; I was sewing flower patches in a very artistic way onto them as we were on our journey. I was still finishing them off when we were standing in the queue waiting to get into the Mecca. When the doors opened the doorman said that I couldn't go in with them on. So, I then stood outside removing them all, (I thought I looked so cool). Still, I was allowed in with the 4in tassels I had sewn on my long black tie belt cardigan.

I would do babysitting for some neighbours one family would leave me some cheese & biscuits; that's the first time I had eaten cheddar cheese. I have been hooked on cheese ever since. Then when they came, in they would cook for us all a Vesta curry, I liked the chow mien one, and then they would pay me....

I was having a little bit of a disagreement with My Mother on Friday 11th August. Because I didn't get my, own way about something, I stormed out of the house in a huff. As I reached the garden gate, some mates had just pulled up in their van, saying they were going to the Reading Pop Festival, and did I want to go with them. I said yes, so off we went. It wasn't until I heard them talking about sleeping out under the stars that I realised we would be away until Sunday. Not wanting to upset anyone I just went along with them. I had no clean clothes with me nothing, when we got back My Mother asked where I had been. Lucky I told the truth to My Mother, as I, was seen the next day on the 6 o'clock news. I was Laying my afghan coat out on the ground to lay on. (my afghan coat came from a store called C&A, Martin and I stole it, we put it into a bag on wheels and just walked out the store).

Such A Lucky Lady

The house we had moved into at Morley Crescent had three bedrooms, my brothers were in one, with bunk beds, My Mother & my sisters in the larger one with two double beds. Then I had the small box room with a camp bed and a chest of drawers, and my full-size poster of Elvis. It had been, decided that no one was allowed in anyone's room without being, invited. One day I came home from work intending to go straight out with my friends, so I took my white short sleeve jacket off, put it on the back of the armchair, then went and had a wash and changed, when I had finished I went to get my jacket, and it was gone. My Mother was in the front room laying on the sofa, and Jo-Ann had been told to tidy up. I called to her and asked her if she had seen it, and where it was, she started swearing, so I raised my hand and slapped her across her face, saying don't swear at me. With that, she ran off,

So I went hunting for my jacket, after looking everywhere else, I went to open my sister's bedroom door. But it would only open a little bit as there was something behind the door stopping it from opening. So I put my hand around and lifted it up, it was a drawer from the chest of drawers. On entering the room, I had to step up onto the piles of everything; that was just dumped on the floor. It must have been at least 1-foot-high; I saw my white jacket in the middle of the floor. As I picked it up, I was horrified to find it had been, put on top of some dog poo. So I couldn't wear it, the mattress from one bed had been placed on top of the other one, as it was being used by the dogs and cats, some of the poo had turned white. My sisters were sleeping on the springs of the bed covering them self with some of the clothes. All the things on the floor were as high as the beds so you couldn't see any of the floors. On the window sill, was tin cans and milk bottles full of urine, I left the house in discussed,

I had just left, and I was walking across the green when I heard a neighbour shouting to me, to come over saying, you have smoke coming out the back of your house. I ran around the back, and you could see that smoke was coming out of the keyhole and under the door. I ran indoors shouting to, My Mother to get out (she was in the front room) of the house as the house was on fire. She got up and opened the kitchen door; she then told me to get a blanket, so I ran upstairs and got one. When I got downstairs with it and gave it to My Mother she took it and chucked it over the chip pan to put the flames out, meanwhile the flames had reached the ceiling which had those polystyrene tiles on, they had been, painted, so they were dripping. My Mothers hands and eyebrows were burned, along with the knobs on the cooker that had melted. And the water pipe had burst, so we had water going everywhere. The fire brigade came and knocked on the door, but My Mother wouldn't let them in, she sent them away, (Jo-Ann had left the chip pan on when she ran off). So Jo-Ann had to scoop the water up every morning before she went to school, and when she came home. Until Martin came up with a brilliant idea, he made a hole in the threshold at the back door so the water could run out the back into the garden.

Such A Lucky Lady

On Sunday 12th August 1973, I came home from work to find My Mother lying on the sofa as usual. But as she turned around I noticed that her face was not right, (My Mother had a stroke). When the doctor came, he took one look at My Mother from the doorway and called an Ambulance at once. My Mother was taken to St Mary's Hospital in Portsmouth, where she stayed for two days. (they didn't think she would make the journey to Southampton). After two days they moved her to Southampton hospital. They discovered that My Mother had been born with a Brain Tumour. Which lead to her going Parshly blind in one eye. That was, of course, all the years of suffering she had from her headaches. She needed to have brain surgery very soon. (My goodness it must have been an absolute nightmare having to bring up five young children, all running and screaming around like children do?).

My Aunties (both My Mother's elder Sisters Jo and Pat). Were contacted and both came down at once. When my Aunties Jo and Pat came down, they took My Brothers and Sisters back with them. Aunty Jo took Jo-Ann and Rebecca to stay with her in London, and Aunty Pat had Martin and Richard to stay with her in Dorset. As I was eight months Pregnant with My Mother's first Grandchild, I was left to defend for myself. They didn't want to take me with them.

Auntie Jo also took our two dogs, Sindy and Jason with her. (Nice to know that the dogs came before my baby and me). Sindy still had her mange, and Jason, who was across German Shepard/ Irish wolfhound. So he was a huge dog, he was also very free spirited, and would just roam around the village. He had a great character as well. He would bury his bones on the green, this one day we watched as he befriended an Alsatian, by digging up his bones and letting the other dog choose one, and then he buried the rest again. When the ice cream van came around, it would stop a few doors down. Jason would sit and wait for him to come as he would give Jason an ice cream. While he ate it, the van moved to the other side of the green. So Jason would run over and get another ice cream, he soon worked out that he could run to the entrance of the green and would sit in the road to get another one.

When the baker van arrived the man would put a sausage roll in his pocket, and Jason would retrieve it. But one day a different man came and wasn't told, about Jason, so when Jason ran up, he just jumped into his van until one of the customers told him just to give him a sausage roll. He would wander up the shops and come back with a box from KFC, with chicken in it. They gave it to him at the end of the evening. Then at the paper shop, they would leave a biscuit behind the counter so he would just go round and get it. Everyone knew and liked Jason. But at Auntie Jo's house, he was locked in her kitchen while everyone went out, so desperate to be free. He smashed through the louver windows and got out when Auntie Jo found him she took him and had him put to sleep; I don't know what happened to Sindy.

Such A Lucky Lady

My Mother refused to sign to have her operation until she had seen her first Grandchild, so she was kept in Southampton neurological Hospital until I had my baby.

Lady Donna Louise Wilder

Martin's Family

Left to right
(1) Martin O'Bryan, née Pearce (2) Lisa Stanley, Caroline O'Bryan, née Stutz, (3) Vicky O'Bryan, née Baker, (4) Liam O'Bryan, Laura O'Bryan, née Elliott, (5) Annie O'Bryan, Steve Atherton, (6) Cheryl Wilson, née O'Bryan, Tony Wilson, (7) Holly Cummins, Brady O'Bryan, (8) Charlie O'Bryan, (9) Josh O'Bryan,

Chapter 14

Motherhood Begins

I came into Labour on Wednesday 12th September; I was taken by ambulance, to St Mary's Hospital in Portsmouth on my own. They were very unkind to me, as I was young and unmarried; it didn't help that I had no one with me. One young nurse (not much older than me, seemed to like telling me how much it was going to hurt). I was determined not to show how much it hurt. I wasn't offered anything no kind of pain relief, not even the Gas & Air, not anything, I eventually gave birth naturally, I had to have some stitches that's all. And yes, it was very painful, but well and truly worth the pain.

My Son, Michael was Born on Friday 14th September 1973 at 13:26. My baby was taken straight away from me, as in those days' babies were put in the nursery at night so that you could get some sleep. Then your baby was brought to you to look after in the morning. (I had been, told that I had just given birth to a little girl with curly hair). I had to have stitches and then I was put right down the end of the ward, in a side room on my own. I called many times to see my baby but was, told that I had to rest. Meanwhile, the social services were trying to persuade me to have my baby adopted, I was told that they had a lovely family in the next room who would be able to give my baby everything that I couldn't. But I knew I would do my best so refused, I eventually got to meet my baby on Saturday morning just after 6 am as the staff changed over, they just brought your baby's to you from the nursery. My baby didn't have curly hair and wasn't a girl). As I held my baby, I just knew he was mine, Poor little thing was the spitting image of my younger brother Richard. (My Mother said it was God's way of punishing me, he was paying me back for all the horrible things I had ever done to Richard). I just removed his clothes, and that is when I found out that I had a beautiful little boy.

You stayed in the hospital for one week in those days. So as soon as I could, I let My Mother know she was a Nanny, (My Mother had already told me that no way was she going to be, referred to as a grandmother or grandma. My Mother was brought by ambulance from Southampton to Portsmouth to see her 1st grandchild. After My Mothers visit, she agreed and signed to have her operation the following Wednesday. They had to cut her wedding ring off as it was so tight, she gave the ring to me and said to get it mended and that I was to wear it. (As with anything that had a value Mick pawned it). As luck would have it, they had to shave all of My Mothers' hair off. (her hair, was so matted as she hadn't washed or brushed it for years, plus it had fluff from the blankets in it and was full of knots. (Sometimes My Mother would use a fork to try and untangle her hair). My Mother told them it was like it because Martin had split air fix glue in her hair. (When My Mothers hair grew back it wasn't as straight as before it had a slight wave to it).
After feeding and changing your baby for the night, you would have to take your baby back to the nursery, where

they were, looked after so you could get some sleep. Well, I was on my way down the corridor with Michael in the see through cot that was on wheels. When I passed a nurse who said, your baby looks like A little Chinese baby. Not understanding what she meant, I thought she was just unkind to me, (like the other nurse was to me when I was having my baby). So I said nothing. Then, as I pushed the cot into the nursery another nurse said your baby is jaundice, I had never heard of this and didn't know what she meant. So I just carried on pushing the cot into an available space right by a large internal window.

When I had finished saying Goodnight to Michael, I went to walk out, when the nurse said don't worry, we will look after him for you just go and get some rest. Easier said than done when you're worried that the social services were trying to take your baby away from you. So I hurriedly went to the toilet had a shower, and rushed back to see Michael through the large window. When I arrived I couldn't see him I was panic-stricken and rushed in shouting where's my baby. I was very quickly told not to panic, by a nurse, who said we've had to move him over to the lights. On looking to where the nurse was pointing, I could see him. All his covers and nightgown had been. removed. All he had on was a nappy and his identification band around his wrist, and a bright light shining down on him. I then was told it was quite common for new-born babies, and that he had to have phototherapy a particular type of light, that shines on the skin, which alters the bilirubin into a form that can be more easily broken down by the liver. This nurse was very friendly and reassured me he would be okay. I told her that I don't want to lose him, she then said don't worry love you won't, I'll take care of him for you. After a couple of days, Michaels jaundice went.

After a week. On 21st September, My Father came to the hospital and picked Michael and me up and took us to visit My Mother, at Southampton Hospital she was very drowsy and sleeping a lot, I wasn't allowed to take Michael, in to see My Mother in the case of any infection to them both. My Father took some photo's of Michael and me. his first Grandchild, and he gave me some money. Saying to hide it and use it if ever I needed to. (I hid it in the hem of the curtain thinking it was a safe place, but Mick found it). I would go and visit My Mother as much as I could. Otherwise, she wouldn't have had any visitors; I was her only family left in Hampshire. As My Mother was going to need help with her recovery the council had her tenancy moved near to her sister Jo in Ruislip, So I had to get out and find somewhere else to live. When I left the hospital with Michael as I didn't have a pram or pushchair I had to use the carrycot that had been given by a lady across the green where we lived. It was navy blue, and it came with a stand plus a set of wheels. I couldn't afford to buy a pram or pushchair, so I would carry Michael everywhere I went. When the health visitor came round one day Michael was nearly four months old, I was holding Michael on my lap facing me; he was pulling himself up to standing then bouncing. The health visitor said that I shouldn't let him stand as he was far too young. And it would make him bandy, but anytime he felt his feet on something he

Such A Lucky Lady

would try and stand up. It didn't matter how many times I put him down he just would try and get up.

As I was quite small, 5ft 1.5in and only weighed 7st 7lb. It wasn't long before Michael began to get very heavy for me to carry everywhere. I was standing at a bus stop one day talking to a lady; she was complimenting me on how nicely dressed Michael was, in his sweet hat and a warm coat. Saying what a big lad he was and that he looked too heavy for me to carry when I told her I didn't have a pushchair The lady very kindly said to meet her at the bus stop the next day. As she had a pushchair, I could have.

When I met her the next day she gave me the pushchair plus she even gave me some covers a few nice toys, plus a baby bouncer that went over a door frame, Michael loved it. Down at the shops one day, I parked the pushchair outside the supermarket and put Michael into a shopping trolley. I had done my shopping and went outside to load up the pushchair, but I was struggling with the shopping bags plus Michael. As Michael had rains on, I was able to slip the strap over my arm and stand him next to the pushchair, while I hung the shopping bags onto the handle of the pushchair. But then all of a sudden I felt a tug on my arm, thinking Michael was falling over. I quickly turned around to see Michael taking his first steps. Backwards I, mite add. But never the less he was walking. He was just over six months old at this time; he carried on walking backwards for the next two and a half months, By the time Michael was nine months old he mastered walking forwards.

Lady Donna Louise Wilder

Martin's Grandchildren

1st Column;
Harper-Nellie O'Bryan, TJ Wilson, Luisa-Jane Wilson.
2nd Column;
Lacey O'Bryan, Oliver Mack.
3rd Column;
Summer Atherton, Stephen Atherton, Riley O'Bryan.

Chapter 15

I Deserve Better

Now here is where I explain my relationship with my Son's so-called Farther, Mick....

When I was at the Mecca on 21st October 1972, it was a Saturday night with My Friend at the time, we decided to get the last bus back home. Janice had both Bus tickets with her in her bag, so she had my bus ticket as well. She disappeared with a chap she had just met. So as I couldn't find her I then asked another friend if she knew anyone that lived my way, and could give me a lift home. She introduced me to this man who was in his early twenties; he was more than willing to drop me home along with a couple he was with. after dropping them off he took me home. Then outside my home, he asked if he could meet me tomorrow and take me to the pictures, not wanting to upset him or put myself in an awkward situation, I said yes but with no intention whatsoever of going.

When I went in the house My Sister Jo-Ann, who had run away on Wednesday 18th October (My Birthday) for a few days had returned, so we were all up late that night talking to her about where she had been, so we didn't get to bed till about 5 am. At around 1:30 pm this car pulls up, and this bloke knocks at our door. My brother Richard looks out the window and seeing him wearing a leather coat, says to My Mother, that Donnas' going out with a hells angel, (which My Mother had banned me from having anything to do with). I said no I'm not, it's a leather coat, and he wasn't a hells angel or a biker. I said to, my Brother go and tell him that I didn't want to go out with him. But My Mother insisted I went, as she put it if he were kind enough to bring you home safely, then the least you can do is go out with him. So I was made to go to the pictures with him (we saw on the buses). He brought me back home safe and sound. Later that night he came back and said that his dad had kicked him out for coming in late, My Mother stated that he could stay on the sofa. Well, that is where he stayed, he soon made himself at home. He got a phone line put in the house and a new colour TV. (from Rumbelows) So everyone in the house thought he was a nice bloke.

He then started planning what Christmas gifts we could get for my brothers & sisters, so they were all getting very excited, looking through the catalogues. My Mother and siblings all got on well with Mick, He then started turning up at my workplace at lunchtimes, and he would be outside my works, to give me a lift home at the end of the day. As time went on we were seen as a couple, and that is how we ended up together. I had started losing contact with most of my friends from school as we had moved to Complain from Havant in the summer.

As I had made it to the age of 16 years old, without doing the grownup thing like having sex, unlike most girls I knew. Plus, I didn't think it would happen to me, especially my first time. I gave in and then found out how, and where babies, really do come from, I didn't know at first that I was pregnant, but my mum did. One day My Mother said, "you think you're pregnant, don't you", I said, "I don't know" She then said, "what do you want a boy or a girl what colour should I start knitting". (it was not the response I was expecting).

My Mother took me to the doctors to have a pregnancy test done, and yes, My Mother was right, I was expecting her first Grandchild. When I told Mick he was very excited and told My Mother that he would take care of the baby and me, he started to talk about what we needed to get for the Baby, saying that we needed to get three off everything, vests, baby grows, etc. Saying one on, one in the wash and one airing, plus three dozen nappies the lot, by the way, Mick wasn't working. It didn't take long before My Mother had put two and two together and worked out that he already had a child, as he knew too much. When she confronted him and told him he should tell me, Mick pushed/hit her. So he came up with a sob story as to how he wasn't allowed to see his son, and how the mother wasn't a nice person, I didn't care as I knew I would never settle down with him.

I decided that I was going to have my baby, and he or she would be my priority, they will be coming first I may not be able to provide the best materialistically. But I would give them whatever I could, including every bit of my love.

My Mother said that she would buy and pay for a new pram for her grandchild, so My Mother and I went to choose a pram for my baby. I decided with the help and advice from My Mother to go for a navy blue and white pram, and a beautiful pram blanket. My Mother was going to buy it for her first grandchild. In them days you were able to pay what you could until you had paid for it in full. So My Mother would send me to the shop to pay a little every week, I also chose for my baby, there first Teddy bear from this shop. As on the counter were little music boxes with a string, that you pulled to make it play I brought them both home and undone the back of the bear and placed the music box inside and stitched it up.

I spent all my wages on baby things. (so I had to cut down buying new socks, knickers, etc. For Rebecca). She still stayed in my camp bed with me; My Mother had told Mick that she wouldn't have any going's on in her house, so he still stayed sleeping downstairs on the sofa, while My Mother slept on the put-you-up/sofa-bed in the same room. My Mother said that I needed to start eating healthily from now on, so I would take to work two ham and cheese salad crispy rolls, a whole cucumber that I ate on its own, and then when My craving kicked in, it was shellfish. As I was working at the fish and chip, shop at the time. I would eat jars of cockles and mussels, and then scampi and chips nearly every day. Then when I got home, I would have a block off Neapolitan ice cream, which I ate while Jo-Ann was busy cooking, my six bird's eye's fish fingers along with my four slices of white bread and butter, (well I was eating for two now). (I later found out that they bought cheaper fish fingers, and they used to put them in the bird's eye box).

Such A Lucky Lady

I had a very easy pregnancy, I was only sick the once, and fainted one time, after getting out of the bath, I went from 7 stone to 8 stone, so only gained one stone, my doctor gave me iron tablets to take.

I brought a toy monkey for my baby from Woolworth; its name was Jacko. He had on a red pair of trousers and a striped top in blue and white, his arms were up so you could hang him up by his hands, I showed him to My Mother and said I think I will call my baby Jacko if I have a boy. My Mother said no Grandchild of mine is going to be called Jacko so being me I kept it going saying I liked the name, but, really liked Michael for short Mickey, and if I had a girl Michaela as liked Kayla for short. Mick asked My Mother if he could marry me, but I think My Mother knew he was not any good for me. Also, I wasn't showing any signs of being in love with him. She said I was too young and to wait until I had the baby, and she would see them.

While I was expecting my baby, Mick was sent to prison for stealing a young mother's purse, he denied it but was found guilty and got nine months. (He didn't do all that time). I didn't care as I only had one thing on my mind. (My baby). I knew I would be alright; it was all so natural to me, I was quite prepared to have and bring up my baby on my own. While Mick was in prison, My Mother would send him letters, (as she put it prisoners looked forward to receiving their mail). I never sent him any. So she would tell him that I didn't like writing, (which was true as I didn't as I had no confidence having missed so much schooling).

Lady Donna Louise Wilder

When he came out of Prison, he returned to My Mothers house. He started begging me to Ask My Mother to let us get Married, saying that he wanted us to be Married before his baby was born. I just kept saying no. I'm not ready to get Married yet and that I didn't want to get Married now, he told me that I had to as he was the father, he went on and on about it.

One day after My Mother had gone into Hospital, I couldn't find the paying in book, for the pram, so I went into the shop knowing that the lady's in there knew me. I told the lady that I wanted to pay the final payment on the pram, but that I couldn't find the payment book. The lady said I'm very sorry my dear, but your partner called in a few days ago and cancelled the order with the paying in book, so we gave him all the money back, he had told them that I had lost my baby. When I asked Mick about it, he said that he didn't want My Mother paying for anything for his baby. As it was his job to provide everything his baby needed, and that he was going to get a job and buy his baby everything. He had used the money to purchase a heap of a car, saying he needed a car first to get a job.

When I came out of the hospital with Michael, I had made up my mind that I wasn't going to put Mick's name on the birth certificate, so it read father unknown. I had no Mother or Family to help me. I had nowhere to go as now My Mother's house was going to be taken back; I had no choice than to move in with him to his friend's house, His friend's wife had left him, so he lived in the house on his own.

Such A Lucky Lady

As soon as I had come out of the hospital, he tried every trick in the book to force me to keep asking My Mother to let him Marry me. But I still said no to him, I just didn't see any future for me with him. I just said I can't, My Mother won't sign yet.

I started Breast-feeding Michael straight away but after a couple of weeks I was told to stop, as I had caught a cold and the midwife said that she didn't want me to pass it on to Michael. So I was told to put him on to a bottle, that meant I had to buy a bottle warmer and a bottle sterilizer along with the bottles and the powdered milk. He would feed very well, not long After I had Michael (most probably my hormones were all over the place) I decided to have my hair styled so I had my very long hair cut big mistake). I had it cut to shoulder length into a bob, I left the hairdressers and cried all the way home, and for days afterwards. The result of that experience means that I hate having my hair cut even today.

I was at home with Michael one day when there was a knock on the door. Mick was out and so, was his mate, when I opened the door one of his mates said that while I was in the hospital having my baby Mick was sleeping with a lady called Sandra, (my family knew her she lived opposite us in Morley Crescent). He said that he thought Mick was out of order not being with me at the hospital. (I just said that I already knew). (I didn't care, but I was mad that I was looking like a fool). Then another one of his friends came and told me the same thing. (this just made me feel such an idiot) I needed to show that I was no easy pushover. Well, there was this young lad that would go around and knock on our doors, to see if he could chop wood for you. Well as luck would have it he knocked on my door just at the right time. He asked if I wanted any wood chopping. (this gave me an idea) I asked if I could borrow his axe for the afternoon for a charge, we both agreed on a price. I was ready to show I was no fool, so first I fed Michael and placed him in his carrycot then put the carrycot on the sofa. I gathered Mick's pride collection of Elvis records and put them on the record player in a tall pile. Then when Mick came in with another of his mates I confronted him about Sandra he just said don't be so stupid, I stated that he had better tell me the truth, or I will teach him a lesson, he just laughed and started showing off in front of his mate.

Well, I went into the living room picked up the axe and crashed it down on his records, smashing some of them to bits, after the second crash. He came in and grab me and picking me up, he then threw me at the wall by the sofa. I hit the wall and fell to the floor, the small Knick knacks on the shelf fell into Michael's carrycot, and the kitchen utensils hanging on the other side of the wall all fell off. He went crazy just kicking and hitting me, I got up a managed to run upstairs, he came after me, and at the top he knocked me down the stairs, I fell to the bottom. But I couldn't move, I could hear him go into the living room, his mate came over to me, on picking my arm up he said you've killed her.
(Mick just said you know what to say she just fell). I could hear everything, but I just couldn't speak or move, Mick gave his mate a fag, and they went out, I could hear Michael was crying, eventually I came to and got up

pulled myself together. I got Michael and walked round to see Sandra. When I got there her dad opened the door, and I walked in, Sandra was in the kitchen, her husband Peter was sitting on the floor with his head in his hands crying. And Sandra's Mum was upstairs with their three little children. I pretended that I didn't know what was wrong, I said: "what's the matter, Pete", He said, "it's your Mick and her", so I said what? Then Sandra came in and said, I'm sorry, I said "what are you sorry for", She said me and your Mick have been having an affair; I've told Peter all about it. I still pretended to know nothing; I told her that I didn't know what she was talking about, and then it dawned on her that Mick had made it all up, she then believed that Mick had just said it so as to finish the affair with her. After that, Mick had heard that Peter had got some mates together, and they were after him with Gurkha knives, his friend that we were staying with, told us that we had to get out, as he didn't want any trouble knocking at his door. So Mick's next brilliant ideas were for us to fly to Jersey and live there. So off we went with two of his mates, we were there for only three days when he decided we had to go back by boat, we had to stay at another one of his so-called mates.

Lady Donna Louise Wilder

Jo-Ann's Family

Left to right;
(1) Kerry Humes, née Shepherd, Rigg, O'Bryan, Ai Humes (2) Terry Rigg, (3) Steve White, Melissa White, née Rigg, (4) Gemma Rigg, (5) Bradley Rigg, Emily Booth, (6) Middle Photo; Paul Davies, Jo-Ann Davies, née Rigg, O'Bryan, Pearce, (7) Craig Rigg, Daisy Parsons, (8) Connor Rigg, Mitchell Rigg, (9) Hannah Davies, Charlotte Davies, (10) Tony Rigg, Ex Husband (11) Robert Shepherd, Kerry's ex Husband

Chapter 16

Haemorrhaging

On the 11th October, we were in the Leigh Park shopping precinct when someone came up to us and said to Mick, sorry to hear about your dad. His father had died that very morning. So we went straight round to see his mum (his dad had disowned him as he would steal from their house). But his mum would always meet him in town and give him some money, he persuaded his mother to let us stay at her house until he could find us somewhere.

A couple of days later he took me to the chapel of rest to see his dad. When we got there, I said I didn't want to go in and see his father. But he made me, saying that I had to. I had never seen anyone dead before, his face and hands were all shiny they looked like candle wax. Mick made me touch his dad and say goodbye to him. I had only met him a couple of times. He never got on with Mick, as he was always in trouble with the police. He had two daughters who were ok with me, the elder one Elaine was a bit posh, she was, married to a very nice well to do young man, who had an excellent job and a new car, they were buying their house. They had a baby daughter Five days after I had Michael we were in hospital together and his young sister Debbie who was very spoilt rotten by her parents.

Lady Donna Louise Wilder

On Thursday 18th October (My 17th birthday) it was their Dads Funeral, it was raining and very windy, that was the first funeral I had ever been to. We only stayed with his mother and sister for a little over two weeks, before, his mother said that she wanted us to move on. (I later found out why,) He had taken something's of his dad's and sold them in a porn shop. Then with some of the money, he got me a ring, as he said it looked bad if I had a child without one.

A few days, later on, the 5th November I went up the hospital again to see My Mother, as soon as My Mother clapped eyes on me, she said that I wasn't looking very well, but told her I was all right. When a nurse came over to attend to My Mother by taking her blood pressure, My Mother asked her if she could take mine so she took my temperature, and blood pressure. She then said that I needed to be seen by a Doctor, and then a little while later I was taken to see a doctor who stated that I needed an operation at once, as I was haemorrhaging. Michael was put with the baby's in the nursery while I had to go to the operation theatre, I had to stay in the hospital for a week the nurses were lovely they put me in a side room with Michael, so I was able to look after him myself.

I never actually found out why this happened (but it does fit with the beating I got I will never know).

My Mother said that we could stay in her house until the council come to take it as everything was still in it, My Mothers told me to get anything that was any good together, as Auntie Jo was coming down to pick all her things up. So Mick and I moved into her house, we got two large egg boxes and filled them with anything that was good enough to keep. (there wasn't much) Just some new saucepans My Mother had recently bought from Blundells; they were Black Diamond non-stick so still looked like new. Parts of a dinner set, some odd cutlery, a few ornaments, two new blankets that were still in their packages. Some clothes, and an anniversary clock with people dancing around in a glass dome. (not much to show for 35 years) The rest was just shovelled up and thrown out the back bedroom window. Then put into a skip to be taken to the dump. My Auntie Jo came down to collect it, and she just went crazy with me, saying that there must be more and that I must have stolen it all, she said how can this be all that your mother has, I promised her that was all there was.

I would take Michael every week to get him weighed, at the baby clinic where I would get his milk first he was on SMA but after a rash; I was advised to change to cow and gate, that one suited him he thrived on it. All the mums would leave their prams and pushchairs outside. Well, this one day, a young mum came in very upset as someone had taken her pushchair, so she asked to use the phone to call the police. I left the clinic and carried Michael home When I got in Mick was excited and told me to go into the kitchen as he had a gift for Michael. I nearly died there in the middle of the room was a lovely pushchair I didn't have to ask him where it came from it was obvious. I told him that I didn't want it and if he didn't take it back. I would tell the police he went mad at me shouting but, in the end, he took it and left it up the road not far from the clinic, I did find out later that the lady got it back.

While I was at My Mothers house with Michael, I tried just to concentrate on being a good mother to Michael. I didn't care what Mick got up to; he could, and did just come and go wherever he liked. As long as Michael had all he needed I was alright. Michael never had second-hand clothes, but I gave in to some toys someone gave to me one time as I could never have afforded to buy them. I just washed them in Milton Sterilizer; I was so obsessed with keeping Michael safe, clean and well fed. He was just so very precious, and he was my whole life. I so wanted to live on my own with just him and me, if only I could find a home of our own I knew we would be ok?

Mick went one day to get a provident loan; he said that while he was in their office the man left the room, so Mick pinched some cheque books, which were laying on one of the desks in the office. Mick and his mate tried to fill them in. Between them two they managed to spell one hundred wrong, so they crossed it out and done it again. We went into Portsmouth town to spend them, first we went and bought Michael a lovely new pushchair in turquoise, and a foot muff. Then we went into a jean shop to buy some jeans, but when Mick handed over the cheque with the mistake on it, the shop owner said, sorry I can't take this you need to return it to Provident and get a new one. We walked out of the shop and down the road when suddenly a police van and car pulled up and put Michael and me in the back of the van. While Mick and his mate ran off, but it wasn't long before the police caught up with Mick, and put him in the back of the police car. We were both arrested and put into the cells. The police were ok with me and even helped me with some hot water for me to make Michael his milk. I had to give a statement where I told the truth that I didn't steal them. I then was charged with being an accessory after the fact. I was taken back home by the police who made a search of the house and found nothing.

I couldn't get any help from the social workers as all they wanted to do, was to take my baby and have him Adopted So I felt I had no way out but to stay with him. After all, I couldn't get any money from the government as Mick was clamming for us both. So had to rely on him to feed and cloth us, Mick used to hit me and humiliate me in front of his friends and so called girls he would bring home with him, (I was supposed to see how wonderful he was and fall at his feet).

When Michael was six months old, I had enough of Mick and the way he was treating me and walked out. He got straight in touch with the social services knowing they would come running, when they found me walking down the road with Michael in his push-chair, a Mr Gardner stopped me and said If I went back to his office where he would be able to help me. So we got in his car, and he took us to his office. Then I was told that if I signed to have Michael placed in a foster home voluntary, then as soon as I found a suitable home. Then I could have him back, but if I didn't he would go to court and I wouldn't get him back, He wouldn't let me leave the building until I did. So I very hesitantly had to sign after being assured that I would get him back as soon as I found somewhere for us both to live. (in my head I thought I would go and ask some old school friends if I could stay in their spare room) I spent the next three days knocking on any of my friends' doors. Only to be told that they couldn't take my baby as well. On the 4th day, I was allowed to go and see Michael at the foster careers house, my poor baby was in a coach built pram in the hallway next to a glass panelled front door, and that I was, told was where he slept at night. His clothes were all on the front room floor, plus one of the many kids had my baby's clothes on. (I'm sorry to say, but that was the last straw).

I just gave up and knew I would never get my baby back. So that afternoon while I was round an old friend's house. I stole a bottle of pills that were on the mantelpiece; they were DF118. I then went over to a supermarket and stole a can of pop. Then I went to a scrap yard and got into a white van, then one by one I took them all. I was crying and convinced myself that I had nothing to live for now. As I started to feel strange, I kept saying to myself. If you don't get some help, you're going to die over and over. Then the next thing I knew I was in the hospital, and they were saying, how many did you take, have you taken then all, how many have you taken, how long ago. I was so determined to die that I added to it 12 hours so they couldn't pump my stomach out.

(God was on my side that day as here I am today to tell all).
I next remember waking up with a doctor asking me in a very pathetic voice, to stand up and touch my nose. (I now understand why). It was to see if I had done any permanent damage. A Social worker came to take me in to care as I wasn't allowed to leave on my own as being so young. I was allowed to leave the (mental hospital) St James's in other words I was, released from St James's so proving I am not mad or even insane (have you?)

That day with a social worker taking me I was then placed with a foster family in Leigh Park. The poor, family was expecting a 17-month old toddler, not a 17-year-old very angry young girl. They were, really nice to me, but I did say that I was going to kill myself when they all went to bed. So they had better hide everything, the lady said what makes you feel like this, you have your whole life ahead of you. Eventually, I told her about Mr Gardner taking Michael away. She said to me wait a minute, and then she went into, the hall to make a phone call. When she came back, she told me that someone high up in social services that she knew was coming over straight away to see me it was a Mr Jones, he had been our social worker after our dad had left. So knew my family and me very well, when Mr Jones arrived he told me that he was going to pick me up in the morning to go and get Michael, he was placing us in a mother and baby home in Southsea I could hardly sleep with excitement. And so it was I got my baby back the very next day. I heard later that horrible Mr Garden got demoted and then

left, his job was supposed to be placing me, with my baby together, in a safe place, and not split us up.
I wasn't in this place long, before Mick found out where I was and started coming around seeing some of the young/mums. When the owner of the home found out, I was told that Mick wasn't allowed to come in, I had no control as the other girls would just let him in. I told My Mother, who still hadn't gotten her own place. She said that she would have a word with her sister My Auntie Pat. So My Auntie Pat said I could go and stay for a week or two, we were hoping he would move on if I wasn't around. While I was staying with My Auntie Pat, I took it upon myself to look for a gold ring, with a topaz stone in it. That My Mother had always said was meant to be hers from her Mother, When I found it I thought it would be my ticket to moving back in with My Mother, and then I could look after her once see got her own place again.

My Mother was still staying with her Sister Jo, But My Auntie Pat found out it was missing as soon as she got home. So that backfired on me, I gave the ring back to My Auntie Pat. I have had to live with the reputation of being a thief ever since; I was taken back to Southsea where he was still hanging around I was asked to leave because of him.

Once again I had nowhere to go, so had to rely on Mick, to find me somewhere, we stayed in some of his so called friends' homes until eventually, My Mother got a house at Bracken Bridge Drive Ruislip. As soon as I found out My Mother said I could move in with her, so I

Such A Lucky Lady

went to the social services and asked to speak to Mr Jones. I asked if he could help me move to My Mothers in Ruislip. I told him I couldn't go back to Mick, so he arranged for me to stay at another foster home. But this time, it was the both of us together, he was going to pick us up the next day and take us to the railway station so we could catch the train to London. Then I was to meet a lady at the other end who would get me to My Mothers. Well, the foster lady was very nice, she lived at the back of a small grocery shop in Bedhampton. After talking to her it turned out that her daughter went out with Mick, and she had his son, who was nearly 4years old. She had got away from Mike just after her son was born. (she told me that I was doing the right thing as he will never make a good husband yet alone a good father).

Mr Jones came the next morning to pick Michael and me up when we left the nice lady gave me a bag of goodies to eat on our journey, and she wished us good luck for the future. So on Friday 29th November 1974. I moved into My Mother's house with the intention of being My Mother's career and a Mother to my son. When the ice cream van pulled up, I went out to buy Michael an ice cream only to find it was a guy I had met back in Portsmouth a few years back. When my mate and I used to see him with his girlfriend, I didn't say anything to him at that time. By Moving into My Mother's house, I knew I would have to take charge of the cleaning, etc. My Mother had already got dogs and cats, who were doing their business, here there and anywhere. My priority was to clean everywhere so as Michael, could walk around without, picking up any poo or germs. After spending all day cleaning and putting things in places, I thought that would help My Mother. She came into the kitchen and had a fit, about me putting her saucepans in the top cupboard. Telling me to get out of her house, I didn't take any notice at that point I just put it down to the after effects of the operation

Chapter 17

Where Needs Must

The next day I stayed clear and went to meet up with my sisters and cousin, we had a great time with Michael at the local park. Later on, that day as Jo-Ann had stayed longer and she needed to go back home to Auntie Jo's house. I asked our brother Richard to walk her home. (I think it was My Motherly instinct trying to protect her). He said very jokingly; I can't as he may get attacked, so at that point I picked up My Mother's phone to call a taxi without asking her if I could, she just flipped and pulled my head down by my hair and punched me in the face. My reaction was to hit her back, only the once (I might add). I don't believe it was with much force. But all hell was let loose when Auntie Jo came round ranting at me.

My Mother once again said to get out, to which I replied that's not very nice to chuck your grandchild out on the streets. She then said he can stay, and she will look after him. (As I was not Married My Mother was my sons next of kin). I was frantic There was no way Michael was going to be living with her without me, so I went out to the Ice Cream van and spoke to Clive, after talking to him about my life so far, I asked him if he knew, or could help me find somewhere I could go! He said he would pick us up Monday morning, and we could stay in his friend's bed & breakfast place in Harrow.

Lady Donna Louise Wilder

So on Monday 2nd December Clive picked Michael and me up. My Mother got straight on the phone and reported me to the Social Services. So they were looking for Michael and me. Clive took us to stay at his friend's place; we got a room with two beds, one at each end of the room. We talked for most of the night, Michael and I, in one bed, Clive on the other. He then said if I were Married, I would get a council house straight away. I told him, I don't have any intention of ever getting Married. But if we got married, it would only be on a piece of paper, and then once we got a house, we could go our own separate ways. His proposal did make sense; life would be so much easier if I had my own home. So on Tuesday 3rd Dec we got our Birth Certificates, and went and booked our Wedding for Thursday 5th Dec 1974 at 2 pm.

Clive's friend's wife had a dress I could wear (it was horrible, cotton with pink and white flowers on it, very 70s). But it was better than anything I had at the time. We picked Jo-Ann & Rebecca up from school so they could come, I have no clue who our witnesses were. After the wedding in Harrow registry office, we went to the Wimpy bar and had a Wimpy meal followed by a Knickerbocker Glory. Our only wedding gifts were from Clive's mates from the ice cream company he worked for, it was a Pyrex dinner set and a set of casserole dishes with a gravy boat, in white with a blue & grey pattern.

We then went to meet Clive's Mum, Stepdad and his sister. We decided that as we had known each other in the past, we would tell them that Michael was his child.

Such A Lucky Lady

They were shocked at first, but they soon took to Michael and me and were happy that Clive had settled down as he had been giving them trouble, by selling illegal and hot cars, etc.

We went to the council where we were put up in a hotel for a few weeks. As we couldn't stay in the hotel all day, Michael and I sometimes went to work on the ice cream van with Clive. We weren't supposed to go, so he would drop us off down the road, go and pick up the ice cream van from the yard, then pick us up and take us on the rounds. As ice cream has always been my weakness, I was in my element. Clive's idea was just to let me eat what I liked as he believed I would soon get fed up with eating it, wrong. No not me, I never got fed up of eating it. I even cut up an ice cream Christmas Gateau that he had for sale and placed a large slice in between wafers.

His parents invited us round for Christmas it was lovely they had gone out and got loads of presents for us all, things like new bed sheets, towels, matching saucepans, & cutlery, etc. But Michael being the first and the only grandchild had loads even a beautiful teddy with a chain around his neck.

We got a flat in Sheepcote Road, Harrow. A week before Christmas. It was bliss all clean well it was when I got my hands on it. We received a hardship voucher that entitled you to go to a big second-hand store. where we could get anything we needed to set up home. I became a real proud housewife. I would be up around 6 am and give Michael his breakfast, and a bath, I would dress him, and then he would play in his bedroom while I started my chores. First any hand washing was done, hung out to dry on the line; that was plastic, so I was able to wipe it over first. The washing would all be hung in size and colour coordinated, with colour coordinated pegs. Or if it was raining, the laundry was placed on a wooden clothes horse. (I had wrapped all the bars with sticky back plastic so that I could wipe than before I hung the clothes on). The rooms were all swept, as I didn't have a vacuum cleaner, the sides all polished, the beds aired and made, (I would strip and aired the beds Tuesdays and Fridays). Windows and net curtains plus lampshades were washed once a month, with the lampshades hung out on the line to dry.

The bathroom scrubbed and bleached, all had to be done by midday. As I would have to do the ironing. All the washing, everything was ironed, even Michael's rubbers & bibs (so as to not have them stick to the bottom of the iron, I would place a terry nappy on top of them. and if things hadn't dried I would iron them dry). Then I would lay the table for our lunch. Michael and I would both sit up at the table with all the sandwich fillings that I had in the house. I would place them all in the middle of the table, and let Michael choose what he wanted, it was always what I wanted him to have. After lunch, he would have another bath and clean his teeth, with another clean set off clothes on, and then we would spend 3 hours playing with anything that would help him with his education. (I had decided he wasn't going to miss out on his education like I did).

Such A Lucky Lady

I got friendly with a lady in WH Smiths book shop on the children's book department. I would go in and get books for Michael every week. I collected all the Noddy books, Peter Rabbit books with a limited edition wooden bookcase, to put them on, plus, loads of the Ladybird books, (Michael has grown up loving books and still does to this day).

On my way home from the local shops, in a shop window, I noticed a card someone was looking for a babysitter, so I phoned the number. We discussed and agreed that I would take care of her baby girl Jennifer (Jenny). She was 14 months old, at 8:30 am on Monday morning the mother & father arrived with Jenny. Her cot, high chair,
playpen and a walker, plus a case full of (clothes, Nappies, toys, food, etc.) and a note with instructions and left, she was a pretty little girl her parents came from Nigeria, the note said that I needed to rub oil into her hair before I brushed or combed it.

Well, Jenny and Michael played nicely, and after her first day, I thought it went well until by 7 pm. Her parents hadn't arrived to collect her, so I put her to sleep in her cot that I had placed in Michael's bedroom. I phoned the house number that I had, but no one answered. As she was asleep I waited until the morning; I walked round to their house but no one was in, so I took care of her. She didn't seem to be distress that she hadn't seen her parents, on looking at her belongings in the case they had packed enough food and milk for quite a few days. At this time, I didn't want to contact the social services, as I didn't what them involved in my life anymore. Then by the Thursday afternoon, when I went back to their house, and I knocked on the door, a lady came and opened the door saying that she was there cleaner and that they were not due back for another ten days. They had gone away on business; I decided that I must talk to social services about Jenny. I went to their offices and told them what had happened, but as Jenny was not in any harm and was safe in my care, they agreed that I could keep looking after Jenny until they had spoken to Jenny's parents on their return. When they got back, the social services advised them to consider employing a full-time nanny/Au pair.

One day there was a knock on the door, it was a man with a letter that had to be, handed to me in person. I opened it and read that I had to go to Harrow courthouse for adding and abetting. I hadn't heard anything for such a long time, and I was all settled, that I had forgotten all about it so didn't tell anyone, I just got Jo-Ann to look after Michael, then went to court on my own. I then was informed, that it was a serious offence and that I would be punished, by imprisonment. I nearly fainted, I didn't hear the time, I just heard prison. I was led downstairs by two lady officers, who just kept saying it's all right, don't worry you'll be home soon. They took me to a cell and stood at the open door, saying do you want a cup of tea or coffee while you are waiting to go. All I could think of was my poor Michael without me. Then one of the officers said not long now, and you're be going home. To me, that meant the Black Maria was coming to take me to prison. But then she said you only have 10 minutes left then you can go home and give you baby a big cuddle from his mommy. I then asked what do you mean is he going to come with me to prison. It was then that she told me that my sentence was to serve one day in jail, and that finishes at 12 Midday.

Well, 12 Midday came, and then I was released from one of the worse days of my life. (I was a free woman).

I never found out what happened to Mick and to be honest, I, really don't care.

When it was Michael's second birthday, his nanny & granddad bought him a blackboard and easel, he was soon writing most of his name (Mich). One day I was just getting lunch ready when I heard Michael calling me to open the front door for him, he had a little bag and inside it was a small money box will a few pennies in plus his hand puppets sooty and sweep, he said that he was going to London.

We lived in that flat for just over a year, and then we were offered a two-bedroomed house in Moorhouse Road Kenton. This house had a front and back garden, again I decorated it and turned it into a comfy home. The lounge I painted each wall in autumn colours, we had glass shelves in one alcove, with lights at the bottom on top of the sliding cupboard that Clive had made, and the other alcove had wooden shelves. We had a carpet fitted that had autumn leaves pattern, dark brown coloured curtains, all tied in with the orange corner sofa we had been, given.

Michael had the largest bedroom, I painted it in a Wedgwood blue, and Clive fitted shelves for all his toys. He had a lovely nursery wardrobe that had been, given to us; it was just right for his clothes. Along with a big book, shelf to house all his books that I would keep buying him. (I still till this day have his full set of Noddy and Peter Rabbit books, plus lots of his Ladybird Books).

The bathroom I painted light yellow with blue towels and silver fittings. Then our bedroom was done in purple mauve and white, the kitchen was more of a challenge as it had painted bricks, so I lined the walls with rolls of polystyrene, and then a thick washable wallpaper in autumn colours. I was still so house proud; I now know that I had a touch of the Obsessive Compulsive Disorder (O.C.D). I would get up and run my bath with just hot water, then when I had finished in the bathtub; I would put Michael in and bath him. I then Would get us both dressed, if I decided that I didn't like what I had put on, I would take it off and put it in the wash, as in, my mind it was dirty. I would take all my trousers dresses and skirts to the dry cleaners as I believed they would be cleaner.

My OCD did at one point take over my life; I would refuse to reheat food in the oven, as I felt it wasn't healthy to leave food laying around. So, after telling Clive that I needed a microwave, and if he didn't get me one his dinner would go in the bin, if he wasn't in when I serve it up. He got me one, then as my hands were getting dry because they were always, submerged in boiling water, they began to get sore and bleed. I told Clive that I needed a dishwasher, and then I wouldn't

Such A Lucky Lady

have to wash all the dishes in hot water, so he got me that as well. But I would still properly wash up all the dishes, etc. before I placed them in the dishwasher,

I sent Michael into the garden to play while I was washing some things by hand one morning while looking out the window checking on him I noticed he was standing next to a flower pot, which still had some soil in and rain water, but no plant. He had a cane in his hand and was poking it from a distance, it then dawned on me what I had done to Michael, he wasn't playing like other boys he was too scared to get dirty. So without thinking what I was doing, I picked up a jug and went out to the pot. I then filled the jug with the dirty, muddy water. I then pulled his trousers and poured the muddy water down his pants. he began to cry, so I then got his hands and put them in the pot with mine, and we had a little mud fight, he then could see it was fun. It was a good feeling; I had taken my cleanliness way too far.

One time while Michael was in the bath, I was cleaning the tiles down with a bathroom cleaner that had bleach in it, when Michael told me that I was spilling it on his head. He had a lovely blond streak for a while. Monday after lunch Michael and I would bake all afternoon, a batch of sausage rolls, butterfly cakes, a treacle tart, fruit cake and a jam sponge, a steak and kidney pie, plus jam tarts. Michael would make his own in his little baking tins; one evening we had invited my in-laws round for dinner, so I stayed up all night cleaning everything in sight, the table was all laid, the food was in the oven, the homemade treacle tart and white wine was in the fridge.

But when the doorbell went, I went and opened it and said: "Oh I'm so sorry I forgot you were coming, so please do excuse the mess."

I decided I would try and have some pets as thought it would be nice for Michael to have a pet or two, as he didn't have any brothers and sisters. We got a puppy, an Alsatian; we called him Sheba, and then Clive came home with a lovely, young all white Alsatian, called Jason. I wasn't happy to have two dogs as they were both going to be huge when they finished growing, but Clive said it would be okay, plus we got a little kitten that Michael named Kitty. They were only allowed in the living room kitchen and the garden, because Jason was a long haired white Alsatian, wherever he laid down he left a dog size hair print, so I was forever hovering. Jason would go to work with Clive, then not long after a friend of Clive at work offered him some money for Jason, so Clive sold him. Clive always went out to work, I never knew what he was doing, but he upset a lot of people with his (Jack of all trades master of none attitude) He would always bring things home, but I would never ask where they came from.

When it was Michael's third Birthday he was having a party, So I ordered him a cake, in the shape of the number three, he had his first bicycle with stabilising wheels. I arrange for him to stay at his friend Tom's house while I got everything ready. When I went to pick him up from his friend's house, Tom was playing in the living room with his toys, and Michael had been told to stay in the kitchen. Tom's mum said that they both were upstairs playing, and when she went up to check on them, she found that they had gone into her bedroom (that her husband was decorating). And found a tin of gloss white paint, they had both painted all the windows and frames. So she separated them until I came round, (I wasn't at all happy, as the punishment it didn't seem to be fair to me). I didn't say anything to Michael as I felt he had been, punished enough, so he had his party and lots of presents.

By the time Michael, was 3-years-old he was doing 50-piece jigsaw puzzles, and he was becoming a real bookworm, he loved his books and still does, I believed that it was my job to teach him the best I could so I didn't want him to go to a playschool/nursery.

We were on our way home one day and in the middle of the road outside our house was poor Kitty, she had been hit by a car. We called the vet but after examining Kitty, it was decided that she needed to be put to sleep. (our Alsatian Sheba was pining for kitty). I then had to explain to Michael. So thinking that children don't like injections or tablets. I thought the best thing was to say that Kitty had a special sleeping medicine so that she could go to sleep and then go to heaven where she can play with all the other little cats and play with all the balloons. So every time Michael had finished playing with a balloon, he would let it go for kitty to play with, Rebecca and Jo-Ann would come over lots of times, at one point Rebecca was miserable staying at mothers, as the house was in its usual state of animal mess everywhere and rubbish and everything everywhere.

So early in 1976. Clive, and I took Rebecca, and went to see a solicitor. Who told us to get in touch with the Health and Safety officers. We all got together and arranged that My Mother would go to see Jaws at the cinema. I think it was Richard that took her. While we showed the Health and safety officer around My Mother's house. He said that it wasn't very nice, but in this day and age people do live like this, so nothing was done. Rebecca stayed for a bit but then she decided to go back home to My Mother's as she had lots more freedom, plus she was missing her friends.

Chapter 18

Baby's Black Eye

One day around April time in 1977 the council were working on all the houses in the street. I had gone to the front door to discuss what they were doing; Michael was upstairs playing (so I thought). He came down the stairs, but when he was on the second step from the bottom he jumped, something he had done many times before. But somehow Michael tripped and fell out the front door, right onto the corner of the doorstep. I picked him up and as I turned him to face me, all around his eye was dark purple, I was panicking, and then one of the workman said, that as it had bruised straight away, it was a good sign. I took him to the doctors straight away; The doctor had a look at Michael's eyes with his torch thing. He said Michael's eye looks fine, but as his eye was still very swollen, I was to bring him back in a couple of days. When I did the doctor said that it would be better for an optician to take a closer look, as he thought Michael had a lazy eye.

When the appointment came through, the bruising had all gone. After all of Michael's eye tests, I was told that Michael was, and had only been using one of his eyes. And that they wanted to operate to straighten his eye. But before they could do that he was to wear an eye patch over his good eye to force him to use his weaker eye. So for a few days, he was bumping into everything.

He didn't like it so he just sat on the sofa cuddling his soft toys, as he couldn't see anything. After a while, his sight was restored in his lazy eye, where it began to get stronger. The day came around for Michael to have his operation, I tried to turn it into a big adventure, telling him all the lovely toys he was going to wake up to after he had had a little sleep, he was in his surgery gowned when a nurse came into the room saying.

"Hello, Michael here is a special sleeping medicine to make you go to sleep."

Well with that Michael went completely out of control, kicking and screaming. No, no, and closing his lips tight. I told him to stop being silly and do as he was, told, but he wasn't having any of it. In the end, I held him tight while the nurse opened his mouth and poured in the medicine. But Michael spat it out, so she gave him some more and held his nose until he swallowed it. He kept up the fight, refusing to go to sleep; I cuddled him until he finally had to give in and he fell asleep. They told me that Michael would be in the theatre for around 45 minutes. So I popped to the toy shop to get the airplane, and a doctor's bag and an outfit that Michael had said he liked. I was back in 30 minutes, so I waited right outside the recovery room for a little bit, and then a buzzer started going off, two nurses came one went into the room while the other one told me to go and wait in the waiting room when I said what was wrong?
They stated that there was nothing to worry about, (what no one had told me or even warned me off, is sometimes people go into shock). Michael was, placed in his room,

Such A Lucky Lady

and the nurse came and got me. Michael was very sleepy, I just held his hand and told him mummy is here it's all over now, have a lovely sleep, we will play with your new toys when you wake up. When he began to stir I said Morning Michael mummy's here; he said "go away "so I said what's the matter? He said, "I didn't want to go to, heaven to see kitty", I felt so awful and wicked I had forgotten all about, kitty. (poor child had thought his mother was putting him to sleep, and he was going to join kitty in heaven). In June we went to Cornwall on holiday in our caravan, Jo-Ann came with us. On our journey, Clive would just pull over and get out of the car to admire the beautiful views. Jo-Ann and I weren't a bit interested, so we didn't make any comment, on one of his stops he said just look how lovely this view is. As we were looking, Jo-Ann said look, look over there, at the top of that hill, we all looked over, but couldn't see anything different. She then told us to keep looking, if you look long enough, you may see a worm pop his head up, well she and I just fell about laughing, but Clive got the right hump.

On the 6th June, we were staying at a campsite in the caravan doing a jigsaw puzzle as it was raining, when we noticed lots of people walking past the caravan, but we couldn't understand where they were all going, it went on for a long time. In the end, our curiosity got the better of us and not wanting to miss out on something that everyone knew about but us. We decided to follow everyone, Well, after all our walking and walking we then got to see what all the fuss was about; it was a beacon for the Queens Silver Jubilee. When I asked

Michael what he wanted from Father Christmas that year. He said he wanted A piano, A Guitar and some Lego. So Nanny and Granddad got him the Piano, a good friend of theirs who had no grandchildren got him the Lego, and I got him his Guitar, we told him that Father Christmas wanted to give him lots of other gifts. So Father Christmas had asked us, to buy him his presents, so they, were put under the Christmas tree, and he had a sack at the bottom of his bed with all the thing Father Christmas had brought him.

My Mother was moved again to a house just off the Bath Road right by Heathrow airport. I would travel with Michael on the bus to see her when Clive was at work. As he didn't approve of my family and done everything he could to keep us apart. (But at the end of the day you can pick your Friends, but you can't choose your family?).

While we were there, I would hold Michael on my lap as things hadn't improved at all in My Mother's House. He wasn't allowed to touch anything in there. I even had certain clothes we would only wear when we went round. Once I was sitting at the end of My Mother's bed with Michael sitting on my lap, when he piped up and said, "Nanny look at all the mess on your floor" she said how naughty Rebecca and Richard were, for making all the mess.

When it was time for Michael to start school, I decided that it wouldn't be a good idea to send Michael to the local school. As it was only two houses away, I didn't like the thought of looking out of my window all the time to see him playing on the playground. I know I would have been up the school all the time complaining if I was to witness anything happening to him that I didn't like. So in the summer holidays, I found a good school that was on a private estate, so I was thinking he would get a better education as he would be mixing with educated children. I arranged to meet the headmistress to view the school; she impressed me, and I liked the school, so thought this is the one. The road to my son's future education, and then college, followed by University, where he would be getting a Scholarship, as a doctor, solicitor or even a scientist. I went out and tried to buy him his school uniform, but as he was so small, I had to get his blazer and overcoat from a specialist shop, that sold to the private schools. I stitched cash's personalised name tags that I had ordered on all his clothes; he even had a school cap and scarf along with a leather satchel the works.

Well, the day was here, my baby was now ready for school. He was only going in the mornings for a couple of weeks, then the following few weeks he would stay for lunch, and then it would be full time. I felt sick to my stomach, the thought of Michael not having me with him all day was now upon us both. We walked hand in hand to the school gates. He was very excited; he didn't seem at all fazed that I wasn't going to be with him or see him until lunchtime. When we arrived at the school gates, all the parents and their children were waiting for the school gates to open. On looking around I found Michael & I were among the very few white faces in the school apart from the teachers, his teacher called him and the rest of her class to follow her and off they went. Michael was more than happy to run off to his classroom with her. I walked slowly back home and sat down and cried as I realised he wasn't a baby anymore, then pulling myself together I hurried up to the school to hear all my son's adventures; he came running up to me with his new friend Christopher. Saying can my friend come round to play? Christopher's Mum came over and introduced herself, saying that we could go round hers tomorrow for lunch if we liked. She lived in a beautiful house not far from the school, I was very surprised to find that Michael hadn't missed me as he said he knew I would be at the gate to meet him. Whenever Michael fell over like most children do he would just lay there crying until I picked him up, I told him that unless there was blood, then he wasn't, allowed to cry for no reason. It seemed, to work as when he fell over he would have a look before he burst into tears.

Then one day at school he fell and hit his ear on the side of his chair, his teacher didn't hear or see him fall. Michael placed his hand on his ear while he queued up at his teacher's desk, to tell her that he was bleeding. She said if it wasn't for a tear drop falling on her desk, she wouldn't off have known as he didn't make a sound, he was crying quietly. As she looked at him, she could see, he needed to be, seen at the hospital. So I was phoned and told that he had fallen and cut his earlobe. I thought it was where you had your ears pierced, a teacher from the school came and picked me up and took us both to the hospital. It looked like someone had cut a V shape

Such A Lucky Lady

out of his ear. Michael had to have some stitches 5 in total. Plus, I got him a gift for being so brave. For my 21st Birthday, My Father gave me £25 which I bought a brown three-piece trouser suit and a cream blouse. Clive took me to Baileys nightclub in Watford. It was a bit boring as we just sat all evening he wasn't one to get up and have fun.

I had been having lots of trouble with my periods since Michael had been born. I was under a top gynaecologist in Edgware hospital, who after giving me a D and C (Dilation and Curettage) and a laparoscopy. Told me that my Fallopian tubes were, twisted and blocked and that he would like to have a go at a new procedure, that had a 10% chance of working. (not very high but I thought it was worth ago). He was going to remove my Fallopian tubes from my womb, and replace them in a different part of my womb, with artificial tubes inside. They had to stay inside for two weeks, and then I would have them removed. I would have to remain in the hospital for two weeks after the operation. I agreed as I had intended to have at least another baby, so in September 1978 the operation went ahead, and it was now just a waiting game.

When I was in the hospital, Clive would do Michael his breakfast, as Clive had a cooked breakfast he done Michael the same. Michael wasn't, used to having so much every morning, especially the baked beans. So in the end, he was put off baked beans, one day soon after I came home from the hospital he asked not to have them. One day he came home from school, and Clive had put pictures up in his bedroom off baked beans, and he had even remove the labels from the tins and put them on the walls, then come the following Christmas in the shops there were lots of stationary things, etc. About with Heinz baked beans on, so Clive as a joke got lots and put them in Michael's Christmas stocking plus a large catering size tin of baked beans.

On Christmas morning, Michael would have his stocking at the bottom of his bed, and everything in there came from Father Christmas. And presents under the tree came from us, his family and friends. so on this Christmas, he came downstairs to show us what Father Christmas had brought him. But without the bake bean things, he put them in his cupboard, so we didn't see them.

As Jo-Ann was coming around a lot, and she was expecting her first baby. One day we discussed the possibility of adopting her baby if she wanted. Or even her carrying a baby for me. We offered to pay her £300 that was a lot of money for us then. At this time, Louise Brown had just been born using a test tube. So all kinds of things were running through my head, I just knew I wanted another baby so desperately, (today it would be seen as quite an acceptable request to make of your sister and probably very typical).

Jo-Ann went ahead and had he baby Kerry. In the December, she found it very hard living at home with My Mother as the house was so untidy. Jo-Ann even got someone to come and have a look to see the state of My

Such A Lucky Lady

Mother's house. The lady had to step over dogs mess the lot. After she had been shown around, she said that this is not that bad, she had seen much worse. Eventually, Jo-Ann was helped with somewhere to live with her baby. Again the time came when My Mother was moved, this time, it was because the houses were going to be knocked down. They moved her to 88, Great Fields Drive Hillingdon Middlesex. I didn't get to go to my Brother Richard wedding, his first one back in 1979 I can only assume that Clive threw the invitation away like he did with Jo-Ann's and Martin's.

Lady Donna Louise Wilder

Jo-Ann's Grandchildren

1st Column
Brenden White, Lucy Shepherd, Holy-Ross Jacqui Rigg,
2nd Column
Lewis White, Hayley-Mae Parsons, Jaiden Joseph Alexander Gow, Jayden Rigg
3rd Column
Katie White, Lily-Grace Humes, Zac Rigg

Chapter 19

Bent Solicitor

Clive's parents who were homeowners had talked to Clive about getting on the property ladder, lots of times, like his sister, had just done. So he decided it was the time for us to move on. We found a house in Horndean that had been a repossession; the owner had built an extension without planning permission. They agreed that we could move in as long as the first thing we removed was the extension. I started buying things for our new house. New light fittings in mahogany and gold with glass shades, a lovely set of three coffee tables in mahogany with the world maps on with brass corners. New bedding, towels pots pan's the lot. Clive's parents gave us their gold corner sofa and armchair, and there teak dining room table and six chairs. We had new carpets fitted throughout, the lounge carpet was a shag pile in brown with a gold fleck in it, and the bathroom was white it looked and felt like Cotton wool. (When my stepmother Jenny came over she was upstairs in the bathroom for ages just stroking the carpet).

How he did it, I just don't know? We were able to move in, remove the extension and all without pay a single penny deposit when I asked him about it; he said that the solicitor had paid it for us, Clive even managed to get the solicitor to add his name onto Michaels Birth Certificate as the father. I found Michael, his next school when I went to meet the head it turned out that her father was my old headmaster, Mr Franklin from Warblington, my secondary school. Michael started in this school September 1999. Clive got a boat, and Michael loved it down Langston Harbour, we told him that the tender was his very own boat. I made a lot of friends, and we would have Tupperware, and jewellery parties at each other's houses, I was brave enough to have my ears pierced for the first time.

One day Michael had an appointment for a check-up about his eyes. At the Queen Alexandra's Hospital, while we were in the waiting room Mick showed up, he came over to me. As luck would have it, Michael was playing with some toys in the play area. So he didn't see or notice Mick. When I asked what he was doing there, he said that my sister Rebecca had told him that I was going to be there at that time. I told him to keep away from us and that Michael and I were happy and didn't need him in our life. Michael's name was called to go in and see the doctor, I got up and just told Mick once again just to leave us alone and keep out of our life. That I'm glad to say was the last I heard or saw of him. I didn't see the need to tell Clive that I had seen Mick.

A little while later when we went to pick My Mother up from GreatFields Drive in Hillingdon. As she was going to come, and stay for a few days with us. I had a quiet word with Rebecca; she was going out with a lad called John, his parents lived in Gosport, so they were always travelling down south on John's motorbike. She must have seen and told Mick where I was going to be when she was down that way. I asked her why would you do that? All she said was that she felt sorry for him not seeing Michael, she thought he should be allowed to see his son. I told her to keep her nose out of my life. My Mother came down to stay for a few days; all was well until the morning that we were taking her back home. She had been staying in Michael's bedroom, that morning she was late getting up after Clive had gone out to work, I went up to see if she was alright. She was sitting on the side of the bed; she said I'm sorry I've had an accident. All I could do was to say never mind; it's alright. (Thinking she had broken or spilt something, not for one second did I think that she had wet Michaels Bed). But deep down I was cringing, luckily it was her last night staying in Michael's bed, I threw the bed sheets away and I wouldn't let Michael sleep in his bed until it had dried out, after I had washed the mattresses and brought a new mattress cover.

We had Christmas at home than a few days later we went to Clive's sisters in Norfolk, we had to stay the night. Her house was a mess, and I felt very uncomfortable about staying, we were going to be sleeping in the front room, but Michael fell asleep early. So his sister suggested that he sleep in her son's bed, and her son would sleep in his travel cot. Well, I carried Michael upstairs and placed him on the bed with the lights off, and went downstairs where we played some games and drank. In the morning I went upstairs to get Michael, only to find that he may as well have been sleeping in the dog's bed. As I think there were more dog hairs on the bed covers that Michael had been sleeping with, than was on the dog. It was a long-haired Alsatian; I'm glad to say that was the last time I saw her.

Clive would go fishing with Tony, a friend we had met back in Kenton. Sometimes Michael and I would go as well, but only if the sun was shining. Michael loved using his tender to go out to Clive's Boat. He was so chuffed with himself just holding on to the oars and helping Clive row. He wasn't at all afraid to go into the sea, even once fully dressed and with his life jacket on in October, it would have been far too cold for me, I always had Clive take a bag with extra clothes in for Michael.

We were down the beach one day, and Michael needed to go to the toilet, so I took him first, and then Clive took him a little while later. Then Michael said he still felt like he needed to go. So as the toilets were a bit far away, Clive said just go in the sea thinking he was just going to do a wee, well he did a bit more than a wee, we said you should have told us you needed to do a number two. The next day a tanker was washed up on the beach, Clive told Michael that his torpedo hit the boat.

I was, so determined that Michael wasn't going to grow up like us, by stealing anything, he was, told that if it wasn't yours, then you don't touch it or take it. Well, one time when Michael was six years old. I found a tiny ball off plasticine in the back of the car, when I asked Michael where it had come from, he said that he had taken it from school. So I took him back to school, and I made him tell his teacher that he had stolen it. (I was trying to get him to understand that it was wrong to take anything that wasn't his). I had just about given up having another baby when 18 months after my big operation, I found out I was expecting a baby. I phoned my Gynaecologist he was just as excited as I was.

Then in June 1980 just as I hit three months, I started to bleed. The hospital told me to go to bed and rest which I did. Jo-Ann came down with Kerry, to help with Michael, and so did Richard & Tina his wife, with their baby son Shane. I stayed in bed the whole time just watching TV. Well, in the end, it just wasn't to be. I then was taken to the hospital, where I had to let nature take over and deliver my dead baby. Then I was given another D&C, before being placed in a ward with new mothers and their baby. I had been, told that I needed to wait for, my body to get over the loss before I tried again for a baby. In the school holidays in the July Michael and I went and stayed with Jo-Ann for a few days, we took Michael & Kerry to London Zoo and the history museum, as Michael was crazy about dinosaurs.

When I got back, I was hit with a bombshell from Clive. He told me that we had to pay some rent for the time we had been living in the house, it was a total of 10 months rent which we didn't have, as usual, Clive had done a crooked deal. So we had to pack up and move out. We had nowhere to go, so we landed up moving to Milton Keynes in August 1980. We went to stay with one of Clive's friends and his wife (I didn't know them). We went to Milton Keynes development corporation, where we applied for a house, they told me, we would be able to go onto the waiting list as we were homeless. We didn't have to wait that long; I arrange for, Michael to go to Conniburrow school in September. I then volunteered to help in the school. Clive's friend's wife wasn't happy with us staying in her house, as she was out working, and her husband and Clive were going out a lot which left me in her home. So it was agreed with Clive's friends that they would ask us to leave by the end of the month. (September) So that way we could get a house a lot sooner. I went around and found all the empty houses that were on Conniburrow, and then went back to the development corporation with all the addresses. Telling them that we were going to be out on the streets very soon. We left all our belongings in Clive's mates house and moved out, we went and stayed with his Mum & Dads in Leighton Buzzard. For the weekends, then Monday mornings a teacher from Michael's school.

Mrs. Margaret Meir would take Michael and me back to Milton Keynes, so Michael would still be able to attend school. And a friend I had made at the school called Janet, whose daughter Nina was in Michaels class, let us stay at her house. Michael and I stayed in Nina's bedroom; she had a snake in a fish tank. One night I was awakened by a splashing sound only to witness the snake eating a goldfish that had been swimming in a tinfoil dish in the middle of the tank, on Friday after school Margaret would take us both back to Clive's Mum & Dads. Then on Friday 31st October we were offered a house, so I didn't go back with Margaret, I went and picked up the keys just as the offices were about to close. The address was 45, Ransoms Avenue Conniburrow Milton Keynes MK14 7BB. It was a three bedroomed

Such A Lucky Lady

townhouse; it was enormous. Michael and I moved in straight away; I didn't care that we had no electricity gas or water, I just wanted to get in immediately. Officially our moving date was Monday; I made it into a great big adventure for Michael. I got some candles, and we had a lovely evening, we had crisp, coke and snacks to munch on while I read Michael ghost stories by candlelight. Clive was off arranging for all our belongings to be, moved into the house. as soon as the water gas and electricity were turned on, I went on a cleaning spree. Clive was still up to his old tricks bringing home things he had got from the back of Lorries. I carried on volunteering at Michael's school.

One lunchtime I was on playground duty, when two girls came up to me with a toy gun that they had found on the playing field. I put it in my pocket, but not before another child had seen me with it. So not long after I, was approached by a group of, 7 to 9-year-olds, who were, convinced that I was an undercover cop. (a policewoman) As there had been things going missing from the school, and it had been, mentioned in assembly. I didn't say I was, but also didn't say I wasn't. They were convinced. Even more, when they started discussing that I had black leather gloves on, one little girl stated that she had seen me writing in my notebook. (I think that would off have been when I was writing in the accident book).
I felt settled and content with my life, as I had a husband that was providing for us. Not always on the straight and narrow, but, at least, we had a roof over our heads and food on the table. We weren't wealthy but comfortable.

Lady Donna Louise Wilder

There was a market every Tuesday and Saturday in town. The first time we went it was very busy, we stopped at this one stall, where the man was standing high up on the stall. He was shouting out about what he was selling. It was a digital watch, man's, or lady he started the price at £50 then dropped it down, and down, people were raising their hands to buy one, and then the price dropped to £5, Clive asked if I wanted one, I said yes, well that was it. I was hooked right line and sinker; I would always go to that stall after that. I just loved the atmosphere and the buzz. I would go to town and religiously go Straight to that stall.

I brought Michael some toys for his birthday from that stall, then as Christmas was just around the corner, I started looking for bargains. I got a digital clock radio and a tape recorder for Michael for £10 each. But the tape recorder didn't work after Clive had a look at it on Boxing day and he said the head had gone. So I went back in the New Year to return it, only to be, confronted by the stool own, who after asking his helper to go and get a screwdriver from the back of the lorry proceeding to remove the plug. He then started to ask me if I was married, to which I replied I'm very happily married thank you. He then told me to return the next market day. Well, I did return every Tuesday & Saturday, until Tuesday 10th February when as I arrived at the stall, a different man appeared, when I asked about my tape recorder he went to the back and came back with a box with a new tape recorder in it. Saying this has been in the lorry for weeks. (This was because Wally had gone to have a vasectomy). Well on Saturday I had finished my

Such A Lucky Lady

shopping, and I was walking through the market when I felt an arm around me. I turned and said what do you think you are doing, don't touch me. It was the man from the stall he said sorry he wasn't around to give me my tape recorder back and just laughed. He then started walking with Michael and me towards my home; he offered to carry my bags when we reached the other side of the bridge to Conniburrow, he tried to kiss me but I just turned my face away and shook his hand and said thank you for carrying my bags, he said by and off he went back to the market. A job came up for a welfare assistant as I was getting along with the teachers and even the headmistress Mrs, Iillings, who had even invited me to her house for her Christmas party. I was encouraged to apply for the job, but I told them that with having no qualifications I didn't stand a chance, but they said that I should go and give it a go, so I did. well as I was sitting in the waiting room with all the candidates I just thought I've got no chance. Then that evening I got a phone call congratulating me on getting the job, all I had to do was go on a first aid course and that they were going to foot the bill.

Clive got a caravan, it needed doing up a bit, but just needed a woman's touch I wasn't put off, I went up the market, looking for lots of great bargains I found them all from the stall, where the man who had walked me home worked. I got a pump pot, saucepans, frying pan, etc. sun loungers all from his stall. I said we were going away on holiday; he then said don't forget to send me a postcard, to which I just laughed. But he told me I'm serious, you can send it to my warehouse. We went away in April but came home early as it was cold and started snowing. After the holidays, I went back to work at the school.

Clive went about doing whatever he was doing; then he got a Jaguar car, so he then was in the carport most of the time working on it. Then he said he was going to get another video machine (using my name to buy it as he was blacklisted). So he could copy from tape to tape. So Clive told me to ask anyone that I knew at work or any of my friends if they had tapes we could borrow. Well I asked at the school, but no one had any, and then when I went to the market, I asked the man on the stall. I said "I don't suppose you have or know anyone with any video tapes we could borrow", he stated that he had some. So it was arranged that I would phone him, and he would tell me the titles that he had. He would then bring the tape the next time he was in the market.

He wrote his number on a piece of paper which he gave to me; I put it straight in my pocket, without even looking at it. When I got home, I told Clive that the man in the market had given me his number as he had some videos' we could borrow, Clive said for me to phone him, but when I looked at the name on the paper, Wally. I started to laugh, thinking no one would have a name like that. When I phoned, a woman answered saying Yer (yes). I said "sorry to trouble you, but is your husband the man who works in Milton Keynes market" I then heard her say "it's for you" her husband, Wally, then proceeded to real of the titles of the videos he had we decided on one which Wally said he would bring it to the market where I was going to collect it on his next visit. I went up the market, as usual, done a bit of shopping, and picked up the videotape. I bought a couple of Britannica Encyclopaedia books, which Wally was selling for 50p each. You had just to take pot luck, with the volumes that were on offer. There were 32 in the set, but Wally said he didn't have time to sort them out. After showing then to the school, they were interested in buying some for the school. So I went up after School and asked Wally if I could try to sort out a set for the school, and myself. He let me sort through them all in the back of his lorry. Well not being able to carry them home, I went and bought an old lady's shopping trolley, to put them all in. I never did find a full set, but not too far from it, the school was happy with what they got.

Clive went ahead and started copying the video tapes, I then had the job of returning the tape with a free copy to Wally at the market. Well, I went up to his stall and openly offered him the tapes. When he said put them away, not here, you'll get done for pirating. I was scared; he told me to go to BHS British Home Stores. I'll meet you upstairs in the restaurant. I went upstairs and ordered a coffee and orange juice for Michael. I was just about to pay when Wally said. I'll pay for that to the cashier to which I said "no you won't" I went and found a table right in the corner away from everyone,
Wally came over, and I handed him the videotapes under the table. He then gave me another one for Clive to copy, on leaving down the escalators, my heel broke on my shoe; Wally said let me buy you a new pair "again I said

no you won't" I went to the nearest shoe shop and got a new pair. Then a few days later I was looking at a light weight coat for Michael on one of the stall's in the market when Wally saw me he came over and Told the lady on the stall to change me less, (I must admit it was nice to get a bargain).

Before I had met up with Clive again, he had a fight and had one front tooth knocked out and another one had a big chip in it, plus he had a stammer both he could off got help with but never bothered. As Clive had a good education and he knew I hadn't, he would always make me feel like I was thick. He would try to make himself the big man; he would always talk down to me especially in public he was a bully not physical but emotionally.

One day Clive had gone to work, but he had opened the post. He shouted up I've put the bins out for the dustbin men. I continued to get ready for work when I left to go outside I saw that some of our rubbish had been, spilled onto the drive. On picking it up, I noticed an invitation that had been torn up, it was inviting us to my sister's wedding. (Clive had torn it up and put it in the bin so I Wouldn't see it so we couldn't go) When he got home, we had one almighty row. I told him I was going with or without him to the weddings. My Sister & Brother were going to have a double wedding. Jo-Ann was going to marry Tony, and Martin was going to marry Caroline in the same church at the same time. But they were going to have separate receptions, Martin's was in a hall just down the road from Jo-Ann's one that was in her flat.

Such A Lucky Lady

Chapter 20

Stolen Heart

Wally would walk me home from the market to my house many times, Clive would be in the carport doing something to his car, so Wally would stop a have a chat with him while I just went indoors. Then one day after they had finished talking, Clive came in and said that he had arranged with Wally, to bring the next tape round to the house on Tuesday, at lunchtime, as Wally needed the tape back the same day. So on the 16th June 1981, I left school at lunchtime and arrived home to find Wally waiting on the doorstep, with a bag from the Wimpy bar. He said he had bought me some lunch as he thought I wouldn't have time to do any.

Well, I let him into the kitchen while I took the videotape and went upstairs to the lounge to set the video machine on to copy his tape. I then went downstairs to eat the Burger and chips that Wally had bought for me, when we had finished eating, I began to tidy and wash up. Wally by now was standing with his back to my washing machine that was next to the sink, as I walked from the sink around him to wipe the side down, on my return to the sink he pulled me to him a proceeded to kiss me. Well, I didn't resist, and to be honest, I enjoyed it.

But, after I felt so very guilty. I said to myself this shouldn't off happened. I went upstairs to see if the tape had finished, but it hadn't, then when I got back downstairs, Wally said he would like to meet me and take me out for a nice lunch. As I couldn't remember Clive ever taking me out for dinner, I thought that it couldn't hurt. I wasn't going to let Wally kiss me again; it would just be lunch. And that's all. So I agreed to meet Wally at the market on Thursday lunchtime, so he could take me out for lunch, I gave Wally his tape and he went back to the market, and I went back to my work at the school.

When Clive came home, I had decided not to say anything about what had happened in the kitchen, as no one needed to know, I wasn't going to let it happen again. Clive asked if Wally had brought the tape round, I told him that the copied videotape was upstairs. When he came down from upstairs, he said, where is the original tape, I said that Wally had taken it back with him when I had finished copying it. Clive then said, so you let him in the house on your own, because I was feeling guilty.

I began trying to justify myself, so we started arguing. When out of the blue there was a knock at the door, when Clive opened the door, My Father was there, he came in so we pretended nothing was wrong (as you do). I went upstairs to see Michael, and then Clive came up and said you may as well go back to with your father now, instead of me taking you this weekend. (Michael and I were already going, at the weekend to stay with My Father, his wife Jenny and my step-sister's Karen & Kelly, then I was going to visit My Mother; Clive was going to take me down then pick me up on Sunday afternoon). I wasn't looking forward to My Father going, as I knew we would continue arguing where we had left off. So, I jumped at the opportunity to leave with My Father, I couldn't wait, I gathered some clothes for Michael and I and packed them in a case, and off we went. Clive said I'll see you Sunday afternoon about 4 pm; when I got to My Father's place the girls were already in bed, I put Michael to bed I stayed up a bit then we all went to bed. We'll all through the journey to My Father's; I was wondering how to contact Wally, to tell him not to bother coming down on Thursday, to take me out for lunch, as I wouldn't be there. In the morning after My Father had left to drop the girls off at school before going to work, I asked Jenny if, I could phone an old friend, well the old friend was Wally. I called his number, but it just rang and rang, then Jenny came into the room. I cut the call off but pretend I was still talking to my friend, saying it would be lovely to see you and the kids, I can pop over this morning, ok I'll catch the train and be over soon by then, I put the phone down,

I gathered Michael, and off we went, I just had to get out and think. I went to the phone box down the road and tried to call Wally again, this time, he answered, I just said don't come down to Milton Keynes as I'm at My Father's, Wally said where's that? When I said its North Ealing, he told me to get on a train, and meet him at Hayes Station at 1 pm, and then he put the phone down on me. (I later found out that it was because his wife was just coming in from the car, as they had been shopping after dropping their kids off at school).

Well, I didn't know where Hayes station was but, I managed to find it, Michael was having a great time travelling on the trains, and being off school. We arrived at Hayes Station, around lunchtime, so we went into the Wimpy bar to have some lunch. We were sitting by the window, and I was looking at the cars going around the roundabout; I remembered that Wally had said that he had a Mercedes car. All I knew about those cars was that they had an emblem that had 3 points on it. So every Mercedes that went around the roundabout, I took a look at, and then at the driver. All but one, as I happened to turn away after seeing the car, but missed seeing the driver. Well, after finishing our lunch, we took a slow walk back up the town to the railway station.

Only to see, that one car parked up by the station, and not far away from it was Wally. Will tell you the truth, it didn't look like Wally. As this was the first time, I had seen him dressed in smart clothes. He was wearing tailored black trousers, a white shirt with a silver fleck pattern, with a gold Belcher chain around his neck, tan shoes with a padded light brown leather jacket.
My first thought was, Wow; I like what I see.

We all got into Wally's car, and he took us to Heathrow Airport to show Michael the airplanes Michael was in his element, and then he dropped us at My Mothers. Wally and I arranged to go out for dinner that evening; I asked My Mother to look after Michael, telling her that I was going to meet up with an old friend. After settling Michael down for the night, I got myself ready as best I could with what I had with me. I met Wally on the other side of the field next to My Mother's House. We went to the pub and had a meal and drink, then later on in the evening, we went for a drive, and we landed up in a car park at a big hotel called the Crest hotel, by Heathrow. Where Wally said, I hope you don't mind, but to save you any embarrassment I have booked us into this hotel for the night. I just didn't know what to say, I was just stunned, all I remember is walking in a bit of a daze down the corridor where the carpet went up the sides of the wall saying in my mind, you know what is going to happen if you go in that room? You know what he is going to be expecting? Over and over until before I knew it, I was in the hotel room well, I will let you use your imagination as to how we spent our time together. (I will just say we didn't sleep very much if at all).

Early in the morning, we left way before breakfast, Wally dropped me back at My Mother's House, we arrange to meet later at 6 pm. I spent the day with Michael and My Mother just talking, and I went up the local shops to get some lunch for us all, as because My Mother still had animals in the house and was still unwell so not very house proud. (Or maybe my standards were way too high). I just wasn't happy with preparing food in her house. So a takeaway was the best option. I met Wally and after another lovely evening, we ended up back at the same hotel. This time, we both went up to the reception, where when asked for our name Wally said Mr. & Mrs. Slip. When we got into the room I questioned why Slip, he said that was the first name that came into his head; it just so happened that is was the registration of the car that he was driving. Well, again we left early just before breakfast, the next day being Friday 19th June I met Wally at 2:30 pm, this time, we just parked up and sat and talked about our life with our partners, then out of the blue, Wally said if we weren't both already married. Would you marry me? I said, but we are, but if we weren't I suppose. Wally said as you're everything I have been looking for all my life. Then early that evening I had, I guess a panic attack. As it dawned on me that I was going to be stuck here with My Mother, not able to see Wally, as he was going to be back in Milton Keynes. So I asked him to stop off at a telephone box.

Where I phoned Clive and said, please can you come and pick me up right now. He said no, as I'm picking you up Sunday. So I told Clive, if you don't pick me up now, you won't see me again, he said he will come later that evening. Wally took me back to My Mothers, I then waited, for Clive to turn up he came around 8 pm, as he pulled up, I just couldn't look him in the face. I just got Michael into the back seat and our bags in the boot, and I got in the front passenger seat. I just told Clive that I was so tired, and pretended to fall asleep.

I think Clive knew something was very wrong, as he even stopped off and bought Michael a chocolate milkshake, something he had never done before. He even let him have it in the back seat of his car, (that was a first). When we got home, I went and put Michael straight to bed, as it was late and by the time I had unpacked my bags. Clive was already in bed when I entered the bedroom I just froze. There was no way I was going to get into bed with him after what I had done. I had no plans I just knew that staying with Clive my life was never going to get any better. I wouldn't be any worse off bringing Michael up and living on my own. I knew I could manage to pay the bills with or without a man in my life. I had been getting fed up with the threats of the bailiffs knocking on the door all through our married life, as Clive would not pay the bills on time. Even when he had a court fine, he messed them about in paying them.

I said to Clive, you know when we got married; we said that if it didn't work out for us. We would go our separate ways. Well, that time is here. He jumped up out of bed, grabbed his clothes, and went down stairs; I stayed in the bedroom, and then I heard the front door slam and him shouting, and jumping on the car. He got in and screeched off down the road at a high speed. I just got undressed and climbed into bed and went straight to sleep; I then was awoken early in the morning by Clive leaning over me crying please please I'll do anything, please don't do this.

Lady Donna Louise Wilder

Richard's Family

Left to right
(1) Tina Staunton, née O'Bryan, Bagwell, (2) Huy Tran, (3) Jack O'Bryan, due April 2016, (4) Richard O'Bryan, née Pearce, Thi Bich Van O'Bryan, née Tran, (5) Charlotte Ford, née O'Bryan, Neil Ford, (6) Shane O'Bryan, Nicola O'Bryan, née Marks, (7) Sharon Nottley, Haley O'Bryan,

Chapter 21

On My Own

Well, I just knew that I was doing the right thing, for me and hopefully Michael. As if I had any genuine feeling for Clive I wouldn't have been able to go to sleep. I should have been pacing up and down worrying; it just proved to me that I didn't love him and that he was not what I wanted or needed in my life to survive. We talked and talked I told him that ever since we had been in this house, he hadn't lifted a finger to decorate the place, or even tidy the jungle/garden that was in a dreadful state, very overgrown. All he was interested in was spending any money we had on dodgy deals before paying our bills, and, more importantly, he knew how much I hated the, two tattoos on my arms. (I was still covering them up with tennis sweat bands). I said that had he even taken the time to care for me he should off paid to have them removed.

After Michael had got up, I got dressed and was just going out the front door to go shopping, when Clive said where are you going, we need to talk don't we? I just told him that I've said all I needed to say, then I carried on going out the door with Michael. As it was Father's Day on Sunday I took Michael to buy Clive a gift; he got him some records and a card. I, of course, went up to Wally's stall. I told Wally that I had told Clive that I didn't want to be with him anymore. I also told Wally that it wasn't because of him, it was that I had realised that I could quite happily live better on my own if I had to. Wally gave us a lift back in his lorry with all our shopping bags, when Michael and I got home Michael ran upstairs to hide his Father's Day gifts while I went into the kitchen with all the shopping bags. On the kitchen table was the biggest bouquet of flowers I had ever seen. Clive said they came for you. I don't know who would have sent you them? Then also on the table was a large box of chocolates. Clive went over to them, sat down on the chair and lifted the lid saying in a very pathetic voice. Oh, look someone has been eating your favourite ones. But what is this in its place, wow look, it's a pair of earrings (he had bought a pair of gold heart earrings). I just said, please stop. He told me that he had booked to have the tattoos removed tomorrow in a tattoo shop in Dunstable. Clive had also got some paint & wallpaper books, as now he was going to do the house up and he said he was going to change,

Well, I wasn't going to miss the chance of getting my tattoos removed, so I agreed to go the next day. First, we went to Dunstable Downs with Michael to see the gliders and let Michael fly his kite, which he had since Christmas still in its packaging. Then we went to the tattooist who said that he could tattoo over them with some form of acid. I would still be left with scar's, and I would have to keep them moist and not let them get dry by smothering them with an antiseptic cream, and banged them up for at least three months. I went ahead and had them done it hurt a lot, but I had to do it. I took some painkillers and went to bed early. Clive slept in the spare room. In the morning I phoned the school and told them Michael was not well, so he and I wouldn't be at the school that day. I spent time playing with Michael while Clive kept trying to make amends but by that evening he knew we were over, he said right that's it, you're not going to have anything. I told him that the fairest thing was to sell everything we owned, apart from any of Michael's things. And that we should both have half the money each. (Money talked to Clive) He said yes that's right that's what we're-do. But when I reminded him that it also included his car, van, and tools, he was none too pleased. So he comes up with, he would have the car and van, his tools the portable TV plus the new video player. I could have the house, which was a corporation house, and all the furniture in it. I agreed with everything apart from the video player, as it was in my name and I didn't think he would keep the payments up, he promised he would keep up the payments and even change the name from mine to his.

So he loaded his car with his belongings, I got Michael and myself ready and decided to go up the shops. Clive said I'll drop you off, so he took me to the market and walked with Michael and me to Wally's stall. He then shook Wally's hand, and said to him to take care of me, Wally's first thought was that I had slit my wrists, as they were both bandaged up, Wally wasn't aware that I had any tattoos. Wally finished setting up his stall, and then he took Michael and me for lunch in British Home Stores BHS. Wally said if I needed any help just let him know, I told him that we were going to be ok and that I was fine. I went home and sat down that evening, and I felt so relieved and finally in control of mine and Michael's own life's, Wednesday morning I was up early and ready for my new life to begin. I went through all the bills that Clive had left me and done my best to sort them out. The only bill that was up to date was the rent. Michael and I went to school that day, as usual, and then when we got home, I cooked our favourite meal which was BBQ spare ribs. I did a big dish of them, just as I took them out of the oven and placed the oven dish on the table the phone rang. It was Wally, his wife had gone out for the evening, so he was in looking after his two children. He asked if I needed anything, and did I need him to help me with anything, and we must off have been talking for a long time as when we had finished Michael had eaten nearly all of them.

On Thursday 25th June that evening, I remember sitting on the sofa looking out of the window and listening to the top of the pops, just daydreaming and for the first time, I was listening to the words of the number one song. "One Day in Your Life" sung by Michael Jackson As I was listening, to all the words!!!! I thought yes. I will always remember, Wally. As he had made me wake up to the fact, that I needed to change my life. So I will always remember him, and he would stay in my heart, but I didn't need him now I just wanted him to be forever there.

On Friday when I got home with Michael from work, Clive was waiting outside the house. He had come round as he still wanted to see Michael, and ask if he could take Michael around his mums on Saturday. Michael said he

Such A Lucky Lady

wanted to see his nanny and granddad, so I said he could go, Clive asked if I was ok. I told him that I was doing just fine. He asked me if I had finished with him because I had someone else. I said no, I'm on my own. (well I was. as I never thought Wally would ever leave as he had far too much to lose apart from his wife and kids). He said that he had moved in with his parents, for now, we said that we would stay friends. So on Saturday Clive picked Michael up for the day he said he was going to bring him back around 6 pm, so I had the day to myself. It was very strange as I felt a bit lost without Michael being around. I walked over the market where Wally gave me a box full of savlon antiseptic cream for my arms. (they looked revolting just like Tapioca pudding). They were still very sore. I told Wally about my sister and brother's wedding; I told him that I, really wanted to go. He said that he would take me down anytime, just let him know, and he will take Michael and me. I told him the date so he said he would be able to take us down on Thursday 16th July.

So I went to find an outfit, I got a pale blue skirt suit and a burgundy pair of ankle strapped shoes, and matching bag. When I got back home, Clive turned up with Michael, and I told him I was going to go to Jo-Ann and Martin's weddings. He then said that he would take us, to which I said no way, you never wanted to have anything to do with my family, so don't bother now, it's far too late. I was getting along okay with living on my own, I was paying the bills as much as I could, Clive was giving me a little bit of money towards the bills. Unfortunately, he didn't tell me that he owed so much.

Clive hadn't paid some of the utility bills, so we were behind with then. I contacted them all, and they said that they would allow me to give them a bit extra per month until I was up to date. Wally said that he would like to pay them for me just to help me out until I got straight, I was so grateful as it was a big weight off my mind.

Such A Lucky Lady

Chapter 22

Double Wedding

Our summer holidays started early, as we finished school on Wednesday 15th July. Wally picked us up the next day as planned, and took us to My Mother's as I was going to be staying throughout the holidays between, My Mother & Jo-Ann's. Wally asked if we could meet up the next day, so on Friday 17th July Wally and I met, we were sitting in his car next to a stream in Uxbridge. Wally was very fidgety I said what is the matter? He told me I need to tell you something before we go any further, but I didn't know how to. He went on to say. I hope that I don't lose you because of this? He started off by saying you know I have two children with my wife, well before I got married, I had a son and a daughter by another woman. He told me that he wasn't seeing them, as that was the mother's wishes. But he was still paying maintenance for them both and had done throughout their life's. I told him that it didn't have anything to do with me, as that was in his past, the look of relief on his face was a picture he was so relieved. We had a big cuddle followed by a little kiss (or was it the other way round).

Soon after Wally gave me his Gold chain to wear just to let me know he was serious about us, all I had to give to him was a gold ring with a Garnet in, he wore it on his little finger.

Lady Donna Louise Wilder

On Saturday the weather was lovely, both brides looked beautiful, Wally finished work in Milton Keynes, then went home and changed and came down to see me. I introduced Wally to my Family at both the receptions, telling them he was a good friend. After he had gone home, my family and some friends said that they thought he was very nice.

A few days, later on, Tuesday, Wally asked me if I wanted to go back to Milton Keynes, to check on the house. So every Tuesday and Saturday I would get up at the crack of dawn, and wait outside, either My Mothers or Jo-Ann's house, for him to pick me up. Leaving Michael with My Mother or Jo-Ann for the day, as it was far too early to take him with us.

On the 1st August 1981, Wally's sister Sheila was getting married, and he was giving her away as he was the eldest brother. Wally was in desperate need to have his hair cut, but every time he left to do so he got waylaid and came to see me instead. So on the day of his sister's wedding, while his wife and children were getting ready, he told his wife he was going to get his hair cut. But again Wally came to see me instead, so never got it done. He said he told his wife that every time he went to the barbers they were always busy.

I started going to work with Wally; he took me on Monday's to Kingston market; Tuesday was Milton Keynes, Wednesday was a day off, and Thursday was off to Dartford in Kent, Friday's was buying so we would go

Such A Lucky Lady

to the East End of London Saturday back to Milton Keynes, Sunday was Black Bush.

When I went back to Milton Keynes at the end of August, to check up on the house. I gathered up the mail that had piled up in the hallway, and most were just junk mail. But one letter had important written on the envelope in red when I opened it. It said that the bailiffs were going to be calling to remove belonging to cover an outstanding debt in Clive's name. I went into a big panic; Wally said to pack all the valuables, and he will bring the van over to the house when he had finished at the market. He and his helper will load all of my things into the truck and take it back to My Mother's, as she had a garage that was just full of junk, I would have to put it in there for safe keeping. So that is what I did, anything that I didn't what to lose was packed TV, furniture, ornaments, etc. anything that didn't fit in My Mother's garage was put in the bedroom that I was using with Michael. It was all around the room, even under the bed.

I phoned the company up and told them that there was nothing in the house that was worth taking, and that Clive no longer lived with me. They said that they would be in touch to let me know what they were going to do about the bill. As I didn't want to go back until I knew what was going to happen, I started thinking about Michaels schooling. Knowing that I had better sort somewhere for him to start near My Mothers, so I arranged for him to go to the local school just through the park by My Mother's house, he started the next week.

Lady Donna Louise Wilder

When I went back home the next time, I had received a letter from them saying that they were not going to take the case any further.

When it was my 25th birthday, Wally brought me a hair dryer set, plus a ski suit with a pair of ski boots, to keep me warm at the market. As I was wearing high heels, and I didn't have suitable warm clothes to work outside in the market. I think he got the idea for the hair dryer because I would roll my hair every night, then sleep sitting up. So my hair always looked its best in the morning, and the ski suit as when we were at work in Kingston I was standing in front of the stool collecting the money, when it started raining then pouring, I was like a drowned rat by the time the rain had finished with me.

Wally's wife had a tip off that he was seeing someone, so one day she went for a look in his briefcase, she found a poem I had written and a couple of photos of me. Like any woman, when he came in from work she confronted him. He didn't deny it; he told her that he had intended telling her after Christmas. As he didn't want to upset the children, and ruin their Christmas. She said that if he loved his kids, then he wouldn't leave them; Wally told her that of course; he loved his children. He was going to be leaving the marriage. But he was going to go right after Christmas. It upset him to think that she could use the children. After he had told me, I said that she was wrong in using them like that. I said if he liked, I will come round and tell her that she shouldn't use or bring the children into the marriage break up. He said if you

Such A Lucky Lady

like you can. So the next day when I went round to see her. I made sure I was dressed up to the nines, in my Sunday best, so to speak. Then I made my way to their house.

Wally had told me that he was going to be in, as he had a man calling round to take a look at his car. I knocked on the door where Wally opened it; I said please could I speak to your wife. He turned and said to his wife, it's someone who wants to talk to you. With that, he told me to come in.

Well when his wife saw me, she must have recognised me from my photos, as she just shouted, get out of my F... ing house. I said I will go as soon as I have said my piece; she said F...ING get out. Just then the man turned up to see Wally's car, so he went out to see him, and just left us both together with their son who was coughing, as he had, whooping cough. His mother stopped to see to him, still shouting get the F... K out of my house. I said do you think it would be a good idea to send your little boy upstairs, so he doesn't have to listen to our conversation.

She then quiets down a bit, and I said it's not nice to use your children as a weapon it's got nothing to do with them the break up of your marriage. It's between you and you husband, just because your husband is having an affair doesn't mean he doesn't love his children. I said I'm not the first affair he has had throughout your marriage. She then said he can have as many affairs as he likes as long as it's not with you. I told her as long as I'm happy, and he wants me. I will be the other woman. That is until I, or he, decides to finish.

Wally came in just then and said do you want a coffee? She then began shouting again, and that's great you think you can take My husband and now my coffee, I didn't want a coffee. I have said all I wanted to say, just please don't bring your children into it. I was just going to leave, when Wally said to his wife, I'm just going to drop her off ok. She didn't say a thing; he just followed me out the house. I got into his car, and he took me to Jo-Ann's. (She had recently moved to West Drayton). As no one was in he stayed for a while. I think we had a coffee or something?

A few days later one evening at My Mothers, there was a knock on the door, I went to the hall landing window to look out, there were a man and an old lady at the front door. I opened the window and said hello can I help; the man said are you, Donna? Yes. I said what do you want, he said can you come down we need to talk to you. Thinking it was something about one off Clive's jobs that had gone wrong as usual. I said I'll be straight down. I had every intention of explaining that we were no longer together, so it had nothing to do with me, I was going to give them his parent's address and phone number, so took my bag down with me.

When I opened the door, the old lady was the first person I saw, or should I say heard. She was shouting you F...ING B...H; I'm going to F...ING kill you, you F...ING B...H you have ruined my son's life. His brother

Such A Lucky Lady

said look; I'm Wally's brother Ken, we know what has been going on with you two, Wally has told me to tell you to leave him alone. I said don't you tell me to leave him, if he wants to finish, then he needs to say it himself, as that's not the message I'm getting from him. He is the one coming after me, so it's no one's business but ours. Ken then said you're not the only one he is seeing; I just said Oh!!! Really. As they drove away, his Mother shouted, just keep away from my son. When I told Wally the next day what had happened, he said that his wife had told the family, and they were trying to talk him, into attempting to save his marriage he told them that it was up to him.

Wally's car wasn't working, and his wife needed her car, so Wally's said he was going to be relying on his brother, to come and pick me up in the mornings. But his brother refused to get involved, then one Sunday I was up ready waiting by the front door of My Mother's house. After waiting for over an hour, I thought I must have been late and missed them. As I had been helping on the stall and it was getting busy, I decided to make my way to the market myself. Well with no sense of directions, I just followed my nose (as they say), and hitchhiked all the way to Black Bush Market, from Hillingdon.

When I got there, Wally told me that he had no way of letting me know, that his brother wouldn't pick me up. (we didn't have mobile phones like we all do today). Not wanting his brother to get one up on me/us, I told Wally, that I would walk to his house, and be there in the mornings then. So I would get up earlier, and walk to his street, so his brother didn't have to go out his way to pick me up. Then one evening it started to snow, I decided to phone Wally and tell him that I was going to arrive earlier and that I would then sleep in his car, outside his house for the night. It would only be for a few hours as we left very early in the mornings.

Plus, I had my nice warm snowsuit and boots. Frist, he said no, you can't, but he soon gave up trying to persuade me otherwise, as I usually do what I want. I said he could put a flask off coffee in the car for me and leave the car door unlocked. Well, I walked around and sat in Wally's Car, all the lights were out in the house, apart from the landing light for the kids. Wally would sleep downstairs most night so as to not wake the family with his early starts.

Then all of a sudden Wally appeared at the car door, whispering its far too cold everyone's asleep come indoors. We walked round to the back and through the patio doors, as quite as a mouse. We both just cuddled up on the sofa I had no intention of falling asleep in case his wife came down, well I could hear the little boy coughing throughout the night, and then I heard someone walking around, and then the creaking of a door opening. In a panic, I hid behind the sofa and the dining room table and chairs, Wally just stood with the cover stretch out in both hands, pretending to be yawning and stretching, as his wife came downstairs to get their son a glass of water. They didn't speak a word to each other; she just took the water upstairs. Wally got dressed and made himself a cup of tea. When he saw his brother had turned up outside, he let me out the patio doors. It had snowed in the night. So I left a trail off big footprints, that lead from the back, all the way down the side of the house, to the pavement right into his brother's car, Wally's brother still wouldn't talk to me. So the next day, when we were going to Milton Keynes market, and his brother was still refusing to pick me up. Wally told me that he would pick me up in the lorry on the way to the market, after his brother had picked him up, and taken him to pick the truck up from there warehouse. Then when we got back to the warehouse at the end of the day, his brother would drop Wally and me off at the top off Wally's road, as I could easily catch the bus from there to My Mother's House.

Then next day being Wednesday I met Wally at the top of his road, we spent the whole day together, just talking about our plans, then later he left me at the bus stop. Wally went off home while I waited for my bus, he came back just before my bus came, and he was all flustered and in a state, his wife had left a note saying, I can't do this anymore I'm going. Well, he didn't know where his children were, I told him that she wouldn't hurt the children.

We walked back to his house, and he phoned all her friends and family, but no one was saying anything there were no clues as to where she had gone. He then got a phone call from her saying she just needed to get away and that she had booked herself and the children into a hotel and didn't know if or when she would be back.

Wally didn't want me to go, so I stayed that night. Then the next day I went back to My Mother's not knowing what Wally was going to do. All he would say was I hope she doesn't do anything stupid, and he was in a right old state. I didn't see him the next day, but I was up and ready the following morning just in case Wally came to pick me up from work, and sure enough, Wally did come. He told me that he had spoken to his wife, and she was going to be coming home that afternoon. We worked the market, and he couldn't wait to get back home to see if she had returned. I told him just to drop me off at the top of his road; I would catch the bus home because I needed to get some bits at the shops. He had to drop his brother off, so when he drove off I walked down to the corner of his street to see if I could see if she had come back. As I approached the corner, I noticed she was putting the catch up on the porch door, wearing a low-cut black dress, and was made up.

Well, that just did it for me I imagined the scene, a table laid for dinner, with candles and a bottle to celebrate them working on getting their marriage back together. There was I, it was nearly Christmas, I had no prospects of a happy, healthy life, I was stuck, in between My Mothers and Jo-Ann's, a man who had his bread buttered on both sides, and with jam on it. He had his wife, children, a nice cosy house, and me whenever he wanted. I had a lovely large house back in Milton Keynes, where Michael had his own, bedroom, I needed to snap out of being so selfish, and stop living in cloud cuckoo land, I had to put my life back on track.

I decided to phone Clive, and tell him about Michael, being in the hospital. Because he had been, bitten by a dog. I just forgot to say it happened three months back. I said he was fine and that I just thought he should know, he was very concerned, but I told him he was ok. He asked if I was alright, I broke down and just said "I want to come home", Clive took that as I wanted to come back to him. He said he would come right down to get me. I told him that I had moved lots of things out of the house, so he said he would borrow a van from his friend and come straight down. He was going to meet me in Harrow outside Debenhams. I then phoned Wally and told him that I was going back home and that Clive was on his way to pick me up, as I was fed up with living like this, he said. Where are you, I told him I was at the call box on the corner. I heard him say to his wife, she's going back to her husband, so I'll take her and drop her off then she'll be gone ok.

With that, Wally came up in his car, and I got in he drove me to Harrow, all the way he was saying don't go, I don't want you to go, please don't go. I told him I have to go; telling him that I've got to leave I, really do. I told you I'm going home I, have to get back home, I, really need to go. He dropped me at Harrow; he was very upset, but I had to think about myself but, more importantly, Michael, I needed to get Michael back to some normality. I got into the van with Clive and we drove off, I could see Wally's car in the wing mirror he was following us for quite a bit, and then we turn off the road.

Lady Donna Louise Wilder

Richard's Grandchildren

Left to right;
(1) Ethan Ford, (2) Adam Dubz, Shane's son) (3) Kacey Ford, Ryan Ford.
Center; (4) Keeley Ruby Louise Ford.
Bottom left to right;
(5) Logan O'Bryan, (6) Libby O'Bryan, (7) Lainey O'Bryan.

Chapter 23

Homeward Bound

Clive said that as it was a bit late, that we should book into a hotel for the night, then go and pick Michael up and load the van in the morning. He found a hotel for that evening; I started talking about how I had to move out of the house, as the bailiffs were calling for money. And how Wally had helped me by paying some of his bills that he had left me. I said if it hadn't been for Wally helping, we would have lost everything. I even told him that I had been around Wally and his wife's house (it wasn't a lie was it). I said it had been very hard for me living with My Mother and Jo-Ann's, without all my home comforts. Plus, as Christmas was nearly here, I wanted to get back home.

I was dreading getting into bed as I hadn't worked out how I was going to reject him. I went to use the bathroom, and for the first time in my adult life, I had never been so happy and delighted to find I had started my Period. I wasn't due for another week or so, but I was so pleased it decided to come early, that made my job easy to turn Clive down. We talked a bit, but at no time did he or I, talk about what he had been up to while I had left. In the morning, we went down for breakfast, as we were sitting at the table, I suddenly burst out crying. As in the background, there was music playing, and this one song came on that just said it all.

Lady Donna Louise Wilder

Song: I can't say goodbye to you, sung by Helen Reddy.

Clive said what's the matter; I just told him that it's been so hard these last few months. We finished our breakfast and left to go and pack the van and pick Michael up, and drive back to Milton Keynes. When we arrived back home, I got on with putting the things back in their places around the house, while Clive refitted the carpets and put the furniture all back. Michael was playing in his bedroom that was all neat and tidy, and then after most of the place was looking more like home again.

Clive said I need to tell you something; I have been seeing someone. And I'm supposed to meet her tonight, and I don't know what you want me to do? I said well it wouldn't be very nice not to turn up; I wouldn't like it if someone didn't turn up when I was waiting for them. He told me that what he will do, is go and tell her that your back and I won't be seeing her anymore. Well, he got ready and left around 7 pm. I didn't mind as I had no intention of us getting back together. My plan was to get everything moved back in the house, as I couldn't do it on my own, and I didn't have the money to pay someone to do it for me.

Well, Clive played right into my hands, as he didn't get back home until gone 2 am. When he got in, I said in a very sarcastic way. Well, that was a quick goodbye I must say? He told me she was very upset, and then I asked, have you slept with her, or anyone while you have been on your own, he said, I'm a man what do you think? He then said how long is it going to take for you to get over it, my reply was, I don't know, it could be a month, a year, I don't know. He then said it's not going to work, is it. I just told him that I don't think so. In the morning, that happen to be our 7th Wedding anniversary, Clive packed his bits in the van to leave, yet again. Michael and I said goodbye to him, as he drove away we started to walk over to the market, then just as we turned the corner, Wally was there. He had seen Clive's van in the carport and was hoping that I would come out.

Wally grabbed hold of me, lifted me up, and kissed me, he then took my hand and held it tight as we walked back to the market stall. So his brother and everyone could see we were together. He said he was never going to let me go again; Wally stated that he was still going to leave right after the Christmas holidays were over. Wally had made up his mind that he wanted to spend his life with me and as I was back in my house, and that's where I was going to stay. I agreed that he shouldn't upset his children's Christmas, so I was going to have Christmas with Michael on our own in my house.

I didn't go to work with Wally for the next few weeks. I spent my time getting Michael back into his old school, Putting up the Christmas tree and decorations. Clive would come round and take Michael out on the weekends; he would take him to his parents as they wanted to see Michael. Clive began to let Michael do things he knew I didn't, or wouldn't want him to do. Like to drawing on his hands with felt tip pens let him have sweets before meals. He then brought Michael a bike for Christmas, without checking on what size he needed. He brought it to Wally's stool, and left it with us, as soon as I saw it I knew it was too small. So Wally and I took it back to the shop and exchanged it for a larger one, we had to pay a bit more so Wally said he would pay for it.

Wally would phone me every day, until on Saturday 19th December 1981. Wally and I had said our goodbye's after he had finished at the market. So I wasn't expecting to see him until Tuesday when he would have been down for work. Wally left and went back to his warehouse, to load up the lorry for the Sunday market in Black Bush when Wally got home his wife decided that she wasn't going to let him stay until after Christmas. She wanted him out now, so when she told him to go, he went and packed a bag and drove down to me. It was late in the evening when Wally knocked on the door, saying she has told me to go.

(I couldn't see this poor man out on the streets now could I)

So I let him stay in my house, after all, it was nearly Christmas as they say "Goodwill to all men and all that."

Wally went to work the next day; I stayed at home. He went round to see what his wife was going to do about Christmas; she said that he was to come back to their house, and Spend Christmas Day and Boxing Day with his children. But he told her that he will only be spending Christmas Day, as he will be with Michael and me on Boxing Day. She wasn't happy about that; she didn't want the children to know that their dad didn't live with them anymore. So it was decided that Wally would go home every day and put the children to bed and read them a story. As Wally never got home until it was the children's bedtime nothing was different for them, this went on for a long time; he continued to give his wife the same amount of housekeeping (money). So, all in all, nothing changed apart from she didn't have her husband living at home, he was never there even when he lived there.

On Thursday 24th December, Christmas Eve, Wally went round, as usual, his wife said that he has to come on both days, as she didn't want to tell her parents yet that they had split up. He told her no he wouldn't, as he was still going to spend Boxing Day with Michael and me. But she said if the only way you can be here on both days is to have her here then she will have to come. With that, he phoned me and told me her crazy idea. I said don't be stupid the last time I saw her she was going to kill me; he told me she said, that she knew they were over, and had excepted that they were over for good. I said if that's what she wants then you had better come and get me so that I can go round, and she can say anything, which she needed to say to me, and get it all out in the open before the morning. He told her, and she agreed. So that's what was done.

Wally drove to Milton Keynes, to get us Michael was in his night clothes PJs, as we were going to be back later we drove to Hayes, and when we arrived, she opened the door and said come in, sit down, what do you won't, tea or coffee. The children were already in bed. I sat down with Michael next to me at one end of the corner sofa; she sat at the other end, and Wally was in the middle. She started just chatting about whether Michael had ever had, whooping cough. And then it got around to us coming round on Boxing Day. So Wally said that we will come down Christmas morning, drop Michael and me at my sisters, and then he will spend the day with his children. Later he would pick Michael and me up from my sisters, and we will have to book into a hotel for the night, so we can come round on Boxing Day. Then his wife said you're never going to get a hotel this time of the year, so why don't you all stay here Christmas night, (it was very hard for me not to show my disbelief in this crazy idea).

Wally had a smug look on his face when she saw it; she said don't think you're be sleeping with either one of us, you can sleep on the sofa, and Donna can sleep in with me. Best if you come round first thing in the morning, with Michael's presents from Father Christmas, then the children can all open their presents together. Then you can take them to her sisters, spend the rest of the day with the children, then pick them up at 8 pm. then you will be here for Boxing Day. I was in complete shock; I just couldn't believe what I was hearing. (maybe she had expected her marriage was over and was making the best of a bad situation). We drove back to Milton Keynes; we decided that we would open our presents the day after Boxing Day. So gathered a small amount of Michael presents to take with us, and all the food that we had got in for our Christmas dinner, that we were going to have on Boxing Day, we took and gave it to my sister.

Such A Lucky Lady

So early Christmas morning we drove to Hayes, we arrived at her house and knocked on the door. I had My outfit on a hanger when she opened the door, the expression on her face just said it all. I said can I hang this somewhere to which she said abruptly, not in my room, so Wally took the hanger and took it upstairs with my overnight bag. Michael and I went and sat on the sofa. Wally came down the stairs, and the children were very excited and wanted to open their presents. Michael began opening his next to me while Wally was at the other end of the lounge playing with his children. She just sat on the sofa, not saying a word, as soon as all the children had finished opening their presents, she then said, to Wally you better drop them off now than.

Well off we went to my sisters, I said. I think your wife is having second thoughts don't you? But he said that's what she is usually like, well I had a nice time at My Sisters, Michael was having fun playing with so many toys that his cousins had. And he was free to play and eat whatever he wanted as long as he left room for his dinner. My sister was going to her in-laws that evening at 7 pm. so all the food we took she took it with them to give it to her in-laws. She left me in the house and said just close the door behind you when you leave. Well, 8 pm came and went then 8:30 pm then just before 9 pm. Wally turned up; he had a face on him like thunder. He said the B...H has changed her mind; I must admit. I was very pleased that she did, as I wasn't looking forward to spending the night in bed with her, (I had visions of waking up with a knife in my back, or not leaving that house alive). We then had to drive back to Milton

Keynes; Wally was not in the best of moods. So I just kept quite while he was letting off steam, he was mad as we had no food in for Boxing Day. The shops were closed, back in those days. As it was, I laid the table with a Christmas tablecloth and mats and cooked us Omelette beans and chips. Our Christmas wasn't the best that year. I think we have made up for it over the years.

Chapter 24

Together

Well, the outcome from here on being, that Wally carried on going to see his children and putting them to bed after work. So it was quite a while before they knew he had left. Wally was still giving his wife the same amount of housekeeping as before. But one day, when he went round when she opened the door, he picked her up and turned around with her, and placed her outside, saying now you go and get a job, and I'll stay at home all day looking after the children. Wally did this because after paying for everything, she wouldn't even give or offer him a cup of tea; after all, Wally hadn't taken anything from the house except his belongings.

He agreed that she would have the house, and all its contents. While he would continue to pay her maintenance until the children finished school. But that wasn't enough for her, she approached Wally's business partner (he was a sleeping partner). Asking him and his wife to make things difficult for him at work. They tried their best to convince Wally that he was making an enormous mistake, as he would lose everything, so he would be better off going back to his wife. They told Wally that they didn't want me working or helping out on their stall. They had a big row, and Wally told them that if I didn't go, then he won't be going. Well, they had to go to the market all by their self's that day. (They had no Idea at all, how much the goods should be sold for, so some things they even sold at a loss).

Wally borrowed a lorry from a good mate of his, who said that he could buy it from him and pay a bit off each week. We went to a loan shark, where we took a loan out for £500. We then went to the East end of London where we bought some stock from the wholesalers and started up on our own. He told his wife that she will have to get a job, as now he will only be able to pay for the children. Her response was to say she would see him in the gutter first. As there was no reasoning with her, he said ok. If you want to play dirty then were sort it out with a solicitor, that way we will both get half the house and everything.

He left it at that for a bit. She then decided that she didn't want to speak to him about anything, not even the children. She got her solicitor to send a letter saying that Wally had to go through him to talk to her. We'll both Wally, and I applied for our divorces, mine went through straight away. I got my divorced on the grounds of Clive's adultery. Wally's was on his adultery. But his divorce took a lot longer, as his ex-wife was still arguing about any little thing, Wally still said that he didn't want anything from the house, just that when the children left school, that the house would be, sold and he would be entitled to have his half.

Michael was playing in the back garden with his friend one afternoon, when his friend told him to ask his mum and dad if they can go to the park, well Michael came to the back door and started saying, Mum, Dad, Wally, poor thing started stammering. He didn't want his friend to know Wally wasn't his Dad; Wally said he could go as long as he didn't go anywhere else. Michael was allowed to have his friends round to play, which was something Michael couldn't do before as Clive always had something stolen hidden in the house. I think Wally earned Michaels approval when he said that he could have a Birthday party, and was allowed to invite his whole class. Michael was so excited, Michael, had his friends in the back garden that year. Then another year as it was raining, they all went to our carport.

Michael decided that he wanted to call Wally Dad. As he said to me one night, you and Wally will get married one day, won't you? I said yes, I suppose we will; Michael said then I may as well call him Dad, from now then. I told Michael if that is what he wanted to do that was fine, then I received a phone call from the school saying that Michael want's to be called Wilder; I said if that's what he want's then it was all right with me.

Michael and Wally got on well together so much so that when I asked Michael, what he wanted to do when he grows up and leaves School. Michael said he wanted to be a market trader like Wally, or a DJ like my brother Richard. So quick thinking, I said well, why don't you join the Army, Navy or Air force. Because you would only have to do three years, then you can save all your money and buy yourself a brand new van, and market stall plus all brand new DJ things, with all that money, you would have the best.

Lady Donna Louise Wilder

Wally had gone to work, and I was home alone (well apart from Michael). One Saturday, I had just finished in the kitchen and gone upstairs to wait for Wally, to come back from work. Michael was already sitting on the sofa watching the TV. As I went to sit down I heard a noise, I stopped in mid-air, listened, and then continued to sit on the sofa, thinking the noise must have been the fridge making noise. Not long after, I would say 20 minutes, or so, my next door neighbour popped round to ask to borrow a tin of beans. When she noticed my patio door was open, but from the opposite side, of the handle. Puzzled, I went over and closed it. I looked around; everything seemed to be in its right place, I didn't notice anything missing. So of she went with her tin of beans, saying I'll return them tomorrow, to which I said that's ok don't worry.

We'll, I went back upstairs and continued waited for Wally, to come home from work. When he came in before I even had a chance to tell him about the patio door being open, he said where's your bag gone. You see I hardly ever used and still don't very often a handbag. My one at that time was sitting on a little trolley that was next to the fridge; I would keep the usual lady's things in there, like My house keys, purse, pens tissue, family allowance book a bit of make-up, etc. There was nothing very important in there, just the everyday things, you may need to grab, like my lipstick. It was a scary feeling, knowing that someone had been in my house while I had been upstairs. We think what had happened, was as I usual went to work with Wally. We believe Someone had noticed that the house was usually empty. So they thought no one was home that day until they got in and heard the TV. So lucky for me they were a kind robber. My bag was found a few weeks later in one of the outside cupboards belonging to the flats on the corner of our street, they had taken the two watch pens, and two watches, I had intended to get new batteries for them.

One day I was cooking dinner as usual when Wally came into the kitchen. I asked him if he could stir the gravy while I dished up the dinner, and then the next time, I was making the gravy, Wally told me, you don't do it like that, let me show you.

I would go into the kitchen, to make Wally a cup of tea, but because I had picked up the cloth to wipe up after, I then would end up cleaning the windows, or the cooker, so Wally said it was easier for him to make his own, tea in future. Little by little he began to take over the cooking in the kitchen, as he would sometimes be waiting for ages for his dinner. That way we are both fed quicker. How our housekeeping its done in our home is that I am responsible for all washing and ironing including washing up, Wally responsibility is to do the cooking, so we are fed and watered. We both tidy up behind ourselves, we are both quite organised neat and tidy people. So as Wally, knows better than me, I have let him take over the kitchen, and it's funny as after moving in my man suddenly become a master chef. Even though he never had even boiled an egg before.

As Wally is deaf in his right ear, he finds it difficult to hear where voices and noises are coming from, I just can't help playing and messing about, I have confused him many a time. I would be walking upstairs to our lounge, with him not far behind, and then as I reached the room, I would run and hide behind the closed curtains. He knew I had gone into the room, but couldn't see me; then I would call him quietly, only to watch him look for me in the opposite direction. One time I was hiding under Michael's bed, but he looked out the window thinking my voice was coming from that direction. (it was three floors up.

Then there was the time I put a hair brush under the covers on his side of the bed, and hid in the ottoman at the bottom of our bed, peeping out so I could see him in the reflection of the mirror. He came into the bedroom, got into bed, then said a few choice words. Then said, I know where you are, I know you're in the wardrobe, he was lying in bed looking in every direction, I was in stitches. It went wrong one time, when he was in the bathroom having a shave, I went in to talk to him, then when I had finished, I turned the light off, taking the light cord with me, and closing the door with the light cord outside. I then turned the landing light off, and stood in the spare bedroom, behind the wall, just where the landing switch was, I knew he would turn it on. As I heard him coming along the hall landing ready to turn the light on, I at the same time, put my hand around to turn it off, but I touched his hand at the same time, well he flew down the six steps and hit his leg. (ouch). On a side cupboard that had been placed there temporary, as we were decorating the spare room. He wasn't too happy with me but the pain didn't end there for him, as I had placed the hairbrush, inside the bed again, ouch.

On the 19th June 1983, Wally and I got engaged. I had a sapphire and diamond ring; he paid £75 for it, we had a meal together at home just the two of us, when Michael had gone to bed. We got a couple more market days, so by now we were working Weston international market on Sunday, Colnbrook on Saturday, we tried Hemel Hampstead and Bletchley, but they weren't any good. We were able to make ends meet. We very soon paid the loan sharks back, and the lorry from Wally's mate. Then Wally heard that his friend was selling a catering trailer, so we brought it, and went into selling fast food in the markets. That was a great move for us. We went a bit overboard by providing real crockery, cutlery, and we even gave our customers a china mug instead off paper cups. Everything matched it wasn't long before we built up a really good name for ourself's. We were very busy all day long,

At one time I found that one of my boobs seemed to be shrinking, but didn't worry too much, but after wearing a dress that had stripes on, it seemed to show up even more, than on the second time of wearing the same dress, it showed even more. Plus, I had been tightening my straps on my bra but only on one side. I didn't say anything to Wally, and he didn't say anything to me. I bucked up the courage and went to the doctors on my own, well after undressing and being examined I was told that it was all in my mind. I came home all upset and told Wally, he straight away phoned up to speak to my doctor who told Wally that he would not discuss his patience with him. So Wally and I went back, this time, Wally said that apparently you don't know what is wrong so he should send me to someone that can diagnose the problem. My doctor still insisted that it was all in my mind. If we insisted, he could send me to a Psychiatrist or a Gynaecologist. Both we thought were not any good for what I had already worked out, that it was a hormone unbalance. Well, we went for the Gynaecologist, we were, sent to St Bartholomew's Hospital in London a few weeks later by which time my hormones had righted them self after being, examined they came to the same conclusion.

Chapter 25

OUR BIG DAY

On Saturday 16th June 1984 we got married, at Hayes Methodist Church Hayes End. I found my dream dress, in a department store named Debenhams. It cost £125.00 I had Michael as my page boy in a three-piece suit, four bridesmaids, that were my nieces, two were in white and pink and two in pink and white, plus my younger sister Rebecca, as chief bridesmaid, in dark pink. (I had to buy it in white and buy a packet of pink dye, I placed it in the washing machine with fingers crossed, and just hoped for the best). I then sewed hundreds of pearls on that took me over 7 hours to do. (It was worth it though as it looked lovely at the time). My brother, Martin, gave me away as we weren't in touch with My Father at the time.

We had a fantastic day with My Mother, all my brothers, sisters, nieces and nephews. We had invited Wally's children to be in the wedding party, but his ex-wife kept them from coming. Wally had his next-door neighbour, Dave, from Hayes as his best man. Most of his family came, plus lots of our friends. He even had his friend Graham and Val. Graham was Wally's best man the first time Wally Got Married back in Oct 1970.

We held our reception in the Maurice child memorial hall Carfax Road in Hayes. We had a sit-down buffet for

100 family and friends, then later we had a disco, with a running buffet for 150 guests. My Brother Richard offered his time and disco for our wedding gift. Our first dance was to for your eyes only, sang by Sheena Easton.

We prepared all the food ourselves and even provided a free bar. I baked a three-tier, heart shaped wedding cake with fruit, (and laden with plenty of brandy). I declined to attempt to bake a sponge cake, as I'm no good at baking sponge cakes, they never rise high enough. I got it professionally iced, in white with pink hearts all around the sides. But the pink kept fading, so I used a paintbrush and with pink icing repainted them over and over again, right up to the last minute, just before the cake had to be, taken to the hall. I made pink and white crackers, with a wade whimsies ornament inside for the women, and a key-ring for the men, I even wrote out jokes for everyone. (I didn't think it appropriate to put silly hats inside).

As far as I was concerned, getting married in a church was a must for me. It felt like a real marriage, compared to my first wedding in the registry office. At the time our wedding was beautiful, I couldn't have wished for more. (That was until we renewed our vows 25 years later when it felt like we were doing it all over again). Our wedding night had to be, spent at The Crest Hotel where it all began back on the 17th June 1981.

On Monday, we went on our honeymoon, to Lloret de Mar in Spain on the Costa Brava for two weeks. Michael stayed with Jo-Ann while we were away, I knew he would have a lot of fun staying with her, as she is a lot more lenient than I was or am. He would have been allowed to stay up very late, and eat in-between meals, even have water fights inside the house. I have always said all her children have had a great childhood. They would do all the thing they liked to do. We popped into Jo-Ann's one day to see them all, only to find, my sister at one end of the kitchen worktop, with two of her children, they were playing with some play dough. While her husband Tony, was at the other end, with the other two kids, they were playing with some paints. Then from nowhere, Jo-Ann throws a little bit of play-dough down Tony's end, and then one of the children at Tony's end threw a little bit of paint down Jo-Ann's end, that was it. (War had now been, declared). Play dough and paint went everywhere.

Wally and I just got out of the way very quickly. We just left the kitchen in complete shock. Jo-Ann then would say right that's enough, now all tidy up and they always did. While Tony would make us a cup of tea/coffee. I was far to house proud, and I wouldn't have been able to cope with all the mess.

When Michael was due to go to secondary school, the local one in our catchment area was Stantonbury Campus. It was a very modern school, where it was acceptable to address your tutors by their, christen name. Plus, they were allowed to wear anything to school, as they didn't have a standard uniform. It didn't sound right to me, I believed that it was important, and I didn't understand how addressing you elders with their, christen name instead off Sir or Miss showed any respect. I thought that the idea of the uniform told where you belonged. Whereas at the Radcliffe school in Wolverton, not too far away they did, plus they provide all that I thought a Strict good school should, they even had a boarding, part at the school. I had made my mind up that Michael was going to attend Radcliffe; it was my duty as a parent to make sure Michael had every opportunity to do well in his education. Michael wasn't too happy about it, so I explained my concerns. Well a couple of days later, we received a letter sent to us both it said,

Please Mum & Dad

Can I please go to Stantonbury, as all my friends will be going there, I promise that I. will always have respect for my elders, and I will wear whatever school uniform you say.

Please love from Michael.

He had written it and posted it in the post box himself Well after that when he came in from school I said I will go and have a look at Stantonbury but don't hold your breath, as I don't think I am going to like it. I was wrong, everything I saw made me change my mind. When we got back home, I said right you can only go if, you wear only black or Grey trousers, a white shirt, with any colour school jumper, plus black shoes. I also told Michael that if ever, I found out that he showed any disrespect to his elders in any way. He would not only be

Such A Lucky Lady

going to Radcliffe, but he would be going to Radcliffe boarding school. So Michael started attending Stantonbury Campus wearing my kind of school uniform, every day for over Two years. I found out later that he would take his own clothes to school and was changing, so I didn't know.

Just after Michael's 11th Birthday Wally, and I had been having a few words about something and nothing, as that is what we usual have words, about. I was doing my usual I'm not talking to you, you've upset me, so now you can have the silent treatment. I sat on the sofa arms folded gritting my teeth. While Wally just ignored me and started helping Michael with one of his air fix kits, that he got for his birthday. Wally being a man, got out a fishing knife, which lived in its sheath. So it shaped every time it went in, or out of the sheath. That meant it was extremely sharp; Wally started trimming the little bits of the model with it.

When all of a sudden, I heard the drip, drip, drip, on the newspaper, they were working on so they didn't make a mess. He had slipped and sliced his ring finger, right across his top knuckle. I could see he needed it seen to by a doctor, so I went and got a flannel for him to wrap around it. (I didn't what him bleeding on my carpet). I drove him to the hospital, when we arrived, he said look, it's ok. As he had done as he was, told for once, and held his hand up and squeezed the flannel, it looked like it had stopped bleeding. But I said let's just get it looked at, we went in, and a doctor took a look, as he touched the top of his finger, it just flopped over, it was just hanging on by a small bit of skin. They told Wally that he needed to have microsurgery, to repair the tendon, which he had sliced, though. If not he would not be able to use his finger, he would be left with a floppy finger. He was put in a wheelchair and wheel away. I just said by I will see you tomorrow, and went home. I phoned later that night, and they told me that Wally could come home, after lunch the next day. So I went to pick him up, Wally was still waiting to be seen by the doctor when I arrived, with his arm raise up. When the doctor left, the nurse said right. You can go home right after I give you another injection, a tetanus one. All the way home he was like a big kid saying you left me all on my own.

We told Michael that we would all be going to Spain next year, and so we did, this time, we went to Salou, on the Costa Daurada, for two weeks. We all had great fun, apart from the time, Michael and I were floating around on two separate inflatable Lilo's. Wally was floating, with one arm and leg, on each of our inflatable Lilo's. We started drifting towards the rocks, as Wally went to put his feet down to start treading the water, he felt the current was very strong. He pushed Michael's inflatable Lillo, into the shore and told him we are going back now, and then he pushed me all the time he was struggling, trying to get us back without letting us know, we were in any danger. There was a tremendous storm in the night. Everywhere was flooded, when we ordered a taxi in the morning, to go into town when it arrived and we opened the door to get in, loads of water came pouring out.

Such A Lucky Lady

I nearly always see the funny side to thinks, so it's not long before I'm turning something into a joke by playing pranks, especially on my long-suffering husband. I was having a bath one day, as I went to shave my legs but realising that I had run out of blades thought I would use Wally's razor. His one at that time was the one that has a blade on both sides. I lathered up my leg, and began shaving, when I cut my leg, thinking it was like any other nick, I had done many a time on my legs, I just carried on shaving the bath water begun to turn a bit red. It wouldn't stop bleeding like all the other times, on looking. I had cut my leg quite deeply. When Wally saw, he called me all the names under the sun and told me never to use his razor again, telling me that is why they make lady's razors. I had to have it bandaged up for some time before it healed up. (I seem to take a long time to heal).

Sometime after I used my razor and nicked my leg, hardly at all but with my sense of humour, I just couldn't resist bandaging my leg up from ankle to knee, then going downstairs to the lounge saying I had cut my leg again. Wally said "you better not of used my razor", I told him it was the new one that he had bought me. He very carefully removed the bandage to have a look at the damage, only to find a tiny weenie little nick, that wasn't even worth a plaster yet alone a bandage.

By now Michael was allowed to make his breakfast in the mornings, but it was only a bowl of cereal. Well, he was doing fine, until one morning he decided he needed the under counter lights on. As the switch to turn it on was located under the cupboard over the sink. Michael couldn't reach it, even with his roller boots on. He decided to climb on the work top, then reached under the cupboard, trying to locate the switch, as the outer casing had gotten broken. Michael accidently touched the inside of the switch. There was a loud bang; that woke us up. I went tearing down the stairs, to find Michael, just getting up from the floor. He had received an electric shock. He was a bit shaken, and he had lost his colour, but other than that he was fine. Not wanting to make a fuss, I said I bet you just did that so I could fix you some Ready Brek, which was his favourite breakfast at that time. I added a lot more sugar and gave him a cup of tea with plenty of sugar in it as well. I felt he was all right so sent him to school, but I did phone the School to inform them of his shocking morning and asked them to keep an eye on him throughout the day.

Then just after our marriage, we both went to see our doctor, as decided that we wanted to have a baby. Knowing that Wally would need to have his vasectomy reversed, and I would need to be checked out, well our doctor suggested that we should first go to marriage guidance to make sure that is what we both wanted. With that Wally told him that we were not happy with his decision and that we wished to change our doctor, first he wouldn't sign us off his list, but after Wally had finished, we got another doctor. The new doctor referral was for Wally to see a private surgeon and me an appointment to see a gynecologist.

Such A Lucky Lady

Chapter 26

Test Tube

As Wally had his vasectomy before we had got together, (back in February 1981). We decided that we would like a child together, Wally had to go private and have his vasectomy reversed, and the outcome was a success. I had to have my Fallopian tubes cut and replaced into my womb once again. Weeks after my operation, I had a dye injected into my uterus, to see if my tubes were open. Unfortunately, the nurse forgot to get the air out of the syringe before she started to inject the dye into my womb, it was only after I had nearly bitten through my hand and stuck my nails, into the poor nurse's hand. That, it was discovered what she had done. It was very painful at the time, the results, they were still, blocked.

So we were put in touch with a private hospital to try IVF. (Test tube). Well, I was able to produce plenty of eggs, which were then, fertilized. Then three were placed in my womb. When we found out that I was expecting, we were over the moon. Wally's preference was for us to have a little girl, just like me. We had both decided on Cassandra, as we liked Cassy, for short. And Matthew, after Matthew Wilder, as we both thought it had a nice ring to it. But I was only able to carry for three months, we didn't give up, we tried five times in all. But just as I reached three months, things just went wrong, it wasn't to be, we contemplated adopting, but, they told us, that

Lady Donna Louise Wilder

we were not able to adopt, as we had both, been, married before. I think that was why I turned to child care as I loved being with Children. I thought it would be the perfect job for me.

When Rebecca had her first baby in 1987, she named him Matthew, knowing that was the name we had plans to use had we been successful, in our attempt with IVF.

Michael had a pair of ski boots (moon boots/snow boots). That he loved to wear, to and from school, so much so that when they got a hole in them, he would put plastic bags inside to keep his feet dry. Well, one day, when Michael came in from school, Wally noticed the state of Michael's boots, so he told Michael, to take them, and throw them in the dustbin, out the front as the dustbins were going to be emptied in the morning. Michael began to protest, but Wally just said just throw them in the bin. Very reluctantly, Michael did, but on his way back he went to go upstairs, just as Wally, turned, and said from the kitchen, while he was peeling potatoes, we will buy you some more when we go to the market tomorrow. Michael's reply was, they won't have any to fit me, at the same time, sticking his two fingers up.

Wally happened to see this in the reflection, through the glass kitchen door. But thinking his eyes were playing tricks on him until the fingers went up a second time. Well, he flew into the hall, grabbed hold of Michael's cardigan from behind, as by now Michael was legging it up the stairs. Wally said, what the bloody hell are you

Such A Lucky Lady

doing, to which Michael said, I was just waving my arms like this. Most of Michael's buttons had fallen off by now, he had to sew them all back on himself, and as it happened Michael was right, as they didn't have any boots to fit him come market day, so he had to wait until the next week.

One day the police came knocking on our door, it was the time when a baby, had been stolen, from The John Radcliffe Hospital in Oxford. As I had been a patient at the hospital, trying for a baby, and I fitted the description, they had to check me out. Luckily, I had all the papers for The baby's that I was looking after at the time.

As Michael got older and could go to the shops on his own, he was told that he must always get a receipt. I told him that if he didn't have a receipt, and someone else stole the same item that he had just bought, the police may think it was him. So anytime he brought anything he always got a receipt.

When Michael started having his pocket money, he was told that he was to save one-third, that was to be, saved up. One-Third to spend on, special things, like gifts for the family, friends, etc. and the rest on comics or extra sweets. (As for sweets, ice creams, crisps, etc. came in with the shopping). We had told him; he wasn't allowed to have bubble gum or chewing gum. Well, one day as I was doing a spring clean, in his bedroom. I came across a secret hide, under his bookcase, the front plinth had come loose, so he had been hiding small things under it.

Lady Donna Louise Wilder

I found empty chewing gum wrappers, a full packet of Wrigley's Juicy Fruit, and a couple of tricks, like the soap, that makes your face black, the sugar cubes that foamed. Well, I gather he had done the jokes on himself as we hadn't seen them. I placed all the things on his bed, apart from the whole packet of Juicy Fruit. I waited for him to come home, from school. As he came in the door, I started eating the gum smacking my mouth, and I said: "Wow, it's so nice when you find something nice like this when you are doing the housework." He didn't say anything he just went up to his room and went straight to his secret hiding place.

When Michael was around ten years old. Wally, and I were upstairs decorating his bedroom when I heard him come in from school. I shouted down, "Michael there is a pound note on the kitchen side, run down to the shops, and get some large potatoes. So of he went, but after he had got the potatoes, he had a lot of loose change, so he decided to go to the sweet shop and spend two pence. When we had nearly finished the decorating for that day, I went down to make dinner, only to find we had run out of bread. So I called Michael to go quickly to the shop, I told him that I've just remembered that we needed some bread so move fast before they close. But he went to the sweet shop again first, so when he went to get the bread from the corner shop, he didn't have enough money. So Michael came home without the bread. When I said "how come", as looking at the receipt and knowing how much bread was, you would have had enough. He then owned up to buying the sweets. I just saw red, and I said "get upstairs and get your pyjamas on now", I went mental. I picked up one of his flip flops and began hitting him, on the bum. (shouting don't you ever steal again). But I didn't get any response, he didn't flinch, he just said I'm sorry, I won't ever do it again. Wally came in as I was still hitting Michael with his flip flop, like a mad woman. Wally told me to stop; that's enough, I went downstairs, shaking with anger, Wally checked to see that Michael was ok. Michael told Wally that it didn't hurt one bit, he said it was like being, hit with a feather. Thank goodness. They don't make them like the one's My Mother used to use on us. What with him taking money, from his savings to buy his tricks, and now some of my money. (I know it doesn't add up too much). I just felt I needed to nip it in the bud so to speak. Unfortunately, for Michael both his birth parents, were a bit light fingered. So the mold needed to be broken.

We had started employing staff to help in our business; so our business would still be running while we were away on our holidays. When we got back, I started child-minding, and Wally began working at Chelsea, & West Ham football ground, with his trailer. And then some pop concerts, in 1986 at Wembley for The Wham Farewell, and Simple Minds Milton Keynes Bowl, Wally's mate's then got a market and asked us to run the market for them. It was on the Poyle industrial estate near Heathrow. We had the late Ross Davidson, best known for his role as Andy O'Brien in EastEnders, to officially open the market. We even employed some off duty Grenada Guards, from Windsor Castle to master the car park.

Lady Donna Louise Wilder

As someone had stolen our trailer, Wally's mate came up with another challenge for us. He offered him work as the manager, in his fish and chip shop in Wraysbury. That he had acquired, plus work his burger wagons/burrow on a Sunday in the market. After a bit when the insurance paid up, Wally had a burger wagon built. As luck would have it, the owner of the market had thrown his mate of the market, so Wally was able to take over the pitches. We had to get another wagon ordered, so now we had two burger wagons in Milton Keynes. I could only work Saturdays as I was still child-minding throughout the week. So we had a helper for my one, on the Tuesdays, but Wally worked both Tuesday and the Saturday.

I had gotten a friend to make a Father Christmas outfit, so Wally could play Father Christmas to my childminded children. He did a fantastic job, I have to confess, I have had the pleasure of sleeping with the said Father Christmas.

Michael stated that he would like a spectrum games console for Christmas. We told him that they were very expensive and that we don't know if we would be able to afford to buy him one. Well, of course, we did get him one, wanting to see what all the fuss was about, I plugged the lead into the socket, on the wall, and then I plugged the other end into the machine. It went bang, and nothing was working, as I had blown it by plugging it in wrong. We quickly took it back to the shop and exchanged it for another one. I never touched it again. Then I came up with a cruel idea, I knitted a black jumper, with a picture of a spectrum on the front. On Christmas morning, after opening most of our gifts including the large present that every time Michael opened it there was another box inside, until the last one, then it was just a book. I then gave him the jumper, saying sorry son, but this is the best we could afford, and then we gave him the real thing. I did the same thing with the BMX bike he wanted. But that jumper I knitted in light blue, I even knitted Michael a cardigan like the one Starsky wore in Starsky and Hutch.

One time I asked Michael to strip his bed and bring down his bedding to be washed, but like most kids he obviously had better things to do as he went on out, as usual, forgetting to bring it down with him. I went into his bedroom, to make his bed and to get his washing. I found he had it ready by the doorway to bring down. Thinking to myself well, at least, he had done half the job. I took his bedding down and put it into the washing machine, and continued my chores. A little while later I could hear a strange noise coming from the washing machine, thinking that most probably one of Michaels Star Wars figures had got caught up in the wash. Well, when the washing was over I emptied it, only to find whatever was in there was no more. As little bits of it were dropping onto the floor, then on close inspection it turned out to be legs, yes real legs, and then a shell, I started jumping around feeling sick, when I realised what it was, poor thing, it was one of Michaels tropical crabs. It must have got out of his tank and must have crawled amongst Michael's washing.

Lady Donna Louise Wilder

We were all settled down for the evening when there was a knock on the front door; two policemen had come to ask Wally, questions about a commando knife, that they knew he had. As one had been, found in a man's body, in his back, then dumped in a car at Heathrow airport. So they knew the kind of knife they were looking for, and Wally had one. (I had bought it from a catalogue for Wally as he was into collecting them a few years back). They had checked who had brought them, and our address had come up, all Wally's knives, had been, packed away some time ago, and buried somewhere in the attic. It took a while, but luckily Wally found it, so it proves he wasn't the killer.

When we had been, married for ten years, Wally brought me a full set of rings, engagement wedding & eternity, for our anniversary as we were in a better financial position by then,

(I think that was why I turned to child-care, I loved my job so much).

We had some great holidays, some were just for long weekends to Spain, we would go out to join my mother-in-law, who was going on holidays a lot with her friend Alf. She liked Majorca and Benidorm, the first time we discovered Benidorm we had gone for only four days. As we had a lovely time, we decided that we would all go for our two-week summer holiday. Before we got round to booking it for us, Michaels school were doing a skiing trip to France, and Michael said he wanted to go, so we all agreed he would be going skiing with the school, and we would go to Benidorm. So we booked our holiday, but then a few weeks before we were all going Michael, said that he didn't want to go, as he would rather come with us. So we tried to get him a room in our hotel, but it was fully booked. The agent suggested a hotel just down the road, for Michael.

We all talked about it Michael thought it was a great idea, I wasn't too sure at first, but after a while I agreed it would be okay. So we agreed that as he was nearly 16 years old, we would take Michael to his hotel room, making sure Michael was settled Then after breakfast. Michael would walk down to our hotel, and spend the day and evening with us, and his Nan & Alf (Wally's Mum and her friend). On the first morning, Michael came and stayed and played in the swimming pool for a bit, and then Michael went back to his hotel for lunch. But when Michael came back he came with a new friend and his parents. And said, could he have some of his spending money, as he had made a friend at his hotel with this boy, and the boy's family said that they would keep an eye on Michael at the hotel; they asked to take Michael with them to a water park. So all in all, we hardly saw Michael, throughout the two-week holiday only to come to collect his daily allowance. Then on the last evening we insisted he spent it with us, you should have seen the face on him not very happy at all.

Lady Donna Louise Wilder

Rebecca's Family

Left to right
(1) Rebecca Webster, née O'Bryan, Pearce, (2) Matthew Webster, (3) John Webster, (4) Rachael Webster. (5) Daniel Webster, (6) James Webster, (7) Adam Webster, (8) David Webster, (9) Hannah Webster, (10) Emily Webster,

Chapter 27

FRIDAY 13TH

On Friday 13th January 1989, I was at home child-minding, Wally had gone to work in the fish and chip shop. After the lunch time rush, he closed up as usual and went to the bank. On the way back to work, as Wally was driving he suddenly came over a bit strange. He was approaching a roundabout and knew he needed to break. But Wally had lost all his coordination, Wally got around the roundabout, and managed to pull over, just opposite a police station. Just as he stopped, and got out by holding onto the side of the car, and staggering to the bonnet. Two policemen saw him, and came over, thinking they had a drunk. They asked if he was ok? He told them something's wrong; I need an ambulance. With that, he vomited and fell to the ground. One of the policemen, said, have you just eaten a curry?

Well by the time the ambulance arrived, Wally was unable to move, they took him straight to Hillingdon Hospital. Where they did tests, they thought he had a heart attack. I was phoned and told to get to the hospital as soon as possible. As I had the children with me, I told Michael to take care of them, while my friend Judy's husband Paul, took me on the 50 miles, Journey to the hospital. When we arrived, a nurse was waiting for me, and led me into a side room, she sat me down, and said, We're very sorry, but we're doing everything we can, I thought oh my God he's gone. Just then a trolley was being wheeled out to a waiting ambulance; I saw it was Wally. As I got up to go and see him, the nurse said, they need to take him to the Charring Cross Hospital.

As they had eliminated a heart attack, they were now looking at the possibility, that he had a brain tumour. I said I want to go with him in the ambulance, but the nurse said I couldn't, as there was not enough room for me as well, as they needed the doctor and nurses to be with him. The ambulance pulled off with the sirens and lights going. Paul then drove me to the Charring Cross Hospital, but after a while, a nurse said that I wouldn't be able to see Wally, until the next morning, as they will be doing lots of tests on him for a long time.

So Paul dropped me off at Wally's Mum's house. I was going to stay the night; Paul said that he and Judy will sort Michael out back home, and not to worry, just to call as soon as I heard anything. Later that night, Wally was well enough to phone home. (As we didn't have a mobile phone back then). Michael told him I was at his Mum's, so he called me there, Wally said that they had given him a CT scan, and first they found a shadow, on the right side of his head. So they did another one, and it was still there. They were relieved to see that it was because Wally has no eardrum on that side. So no tumour was found, he was put in a ward for the night while they waited for his results from all the other tests they had done. I told him I would be down first thing in the morning, but first, I had to go and get him some pyjamas, and toiletries. Two of my sister-in-laws took me to the shops then my Mother-in-law and Alf took me to the hospital. I couldn't believe the change in him; he looked like he had just come home from a long holiday. Wally looked all tanned, they kept him in the hospital until the Sunday morning, as they were still unsure as to what it was, and that had caused this to happen. When he left the hospital, it was decided that it was probably a virus, from the flu that he had before Christmas, they think the virus had been travelling around his body but exploded when it reached his brain, they told him that it was vertigo. He was fine after that.

As a teenager, when Michael was nearly 15 years old, he would come in from school, and go straight up to his room, where he would put his headphones on to listen to his music, on his Walkman. While playing games, on his spectrum, reading a book, or fill the whole floor with all his Star Wars figures and ships. But this one day when he came in, I was in the upstairs lounge doing some ironing, I said Michael come in here a minute, as I want to talk to you, he came in and sat down very reluctantly. (Just like the character Kevin from Harry Enfield). Well, I began trying to have a conversation. First, I asked how is school? OK. What are you doing at the moment? Nothing much What's your mates doing? Not Much. Well not getting much out of this conversation from Michael. I just said off the cuff, well my friend said that she saw you down the red way, and what did she tell me she saw you doing. (thinking he was going to say, she saw me, throwing stones, climbing trees). Well just picture my face, when he said yes, I know, she saw me smoking. Lucky I wasn't eating at the time, as I would have choked. Still Pretending I already knew, I said in a very calm manner, "go downstairs and get me two pint glasses, then bring them up here", I was so shocked when he came back up he said is Dad coming home soon? I told him no dad wasn't due home till later. I said now go into the cupboard in the hallway, and get that big bottle of whisky. I want you to fill those two glasses right to the top. Because as soon as I have finished ironing this last shirt. We're going to celebrate, you becoming a real man. Then were going to go down to the off-licence, and get you some cigars, as we don't want you smoking cigarettes, you have to smoke cigars, like a real man. Michael was facing the window so I could see his reflection; he was trying to open the bottle. (which I might add I didn't want him to as it was a gift). I said come on son, pour us both a man's drink. At which Point. Michael turned around, and said, I don't want to be a man, I want to be a boy, I think he got grounded. (I don't know of him ever smoking after that).

Michael had joined the Milton Keynes sea cadets and seemed to like it. He had said that he wanted to join the Royal Navy when he left school.

On Friday 13th October 1989, I got a phone call from Michael's school, asking if he had come home at lunch time. I told them that he hadn't why? They said that Michael and a couple of other boys had been seen getting into a police car, near the park. I straight away phoned Milton Keynes police station and told them that the school had called me; they said that they didn't know anything about it and that they had no boys at the station.

Such A Lucky Lady

I went straight into panic mode, thinking Michael had been, taken. The policeman said to phone the police station in the next town Bletchley; they told me the same I was in a right panic when the police from Milton Keynes called to say that they had found him; he had been placed in the women's cells, as the men's cells were all full. I was so relieved; then I asked what had he done. The officer told me that he, along with the other boys had vandalised a fence. Well as I had a very good and well-behaved son, who knew right from wrong, all it can be, was he had climbed over a wired fence, and his weight, had bent it a bit, nothing much to worry about, boys will be boys. Well, I went straight to the police station, at the reception desk, I asked if I could see my son.

As I was going through the partitioning door, I turned and said to the officer. Had thy asked Michael about what had happened, he said yes, but none of them would say who had done it. (they had asked them while in the police car, so I understood that they wouldn't grass on each other while in their presence). I told the officer to give me a minute with Michael, and he will tell them everything, they needed to know. Then I said Do you have medical facilities here? As you're going to be needing them? The police officer led me towards the Women's cells, where Michael had been held. When they opened his cell door, and Michael came out, he was petrified. He knew he was going to be in lots more trouble with me. They had him remove his shoelaces and his belt, the first thing Michael said when he saw me, was I didn't do anything Mum I promise, I just said right

Lady Donna Louise Wilder

you tell the policeman everything from when you left school right up until you were put in the police car, right. Not even waiting for a reply, I turned to the office and said, he will tell you everything now. We all went into a side room, where I started saying to Michael. Well, this is going to put an end to you joining the Navy, now isn't it, as they don't take criminals. Well after Michael had told his version of what had happened, I think the officer could see he was in for it when he got home, with me. After the officer told us that we could leave and go home. But they would need to speak to Michael after they had finished speaking with the other boys.

What had happened, was that all the boys were playing a game of Sky hitting, as they had come across some small pieces of broken fence laying on the ground, that was from an empty house. So they used a bigger piece of wood, to hit a smaller piece, which they threw up into the air. But one of the boys wanted a larger piece, so he broke a bit off the fence. Unfortunately, a lady in the next house had witnessed him doing it and rung the police. When Wally got home, we told Michael that he could be done for criminal damage, as if he and his mates hadn't touched the broken fence, the owner may have been able to fix it. A few days later the police phoned to say that Michael was to go in for a caution.

Wally took him to the police station, but when they went into the room there was a very stern-faced chief inspector who said to Michael, well Michael in your, own words, what did you do? So Michael said "I didn't do anything" well with that the sergeant banged his hands down, on the desk, and stood up saying very loudly, well were see you in court then. Wally said what do you mean? Well, I can't caution him for doing nothing, so that was it. As soon as they came home the phone rang it was the police officer who had arranged for the caution, who said, what went wrong.

Wally told him I don't know; Michael just told him that he didn't do anything, and the chief inspector said, where see you in court then. The officer, on the phone, told us to leave it with him; I will call you back in 5 minutes. Well, I think that was the longest 5 minutes of Michaels life. He was sitting at the table, having to listen to me going on about, how he had ruined his life, and would never be able to get a decent job, with a criminal record hanging around his neck. He did look a bit white, and then the phone rang, and the officer said to Wally. Take it that Michael has had his caution and that nothing was going on record. Wally told Michael, who then seemed to get a bit of a colour back on his face. Then the officer said to Wally, could he have a word with Michael. The police office told Michael that he had been in the Navy himself, and if Michael still intended to join up and needed any help with filling in any forms he would be happy to help him.

When it was Wally's 40th Birthday, I was struggling to come up with a suitable gift. He said he didn't need or want anything (Just me). So in the end, I decided on a Ferguson Video Camera, you know the ones that take the full VHF tape. Well back in those days it cost over £1,000 plus, and a large tripod. While, waiting for it, to be delivered. I asked Wally again if there was anything that he had thought off that he would like. He said he wouldn't mind a gold bracelet, I then thought maybe I should have got him that. A few days later I just happened to be walking through Boots the Chemist, when I noticed a big, chunky, gold colour bracelet, on the sale rail at a bargain price only £7.33. It was a bargain not to be, missed. I came home giggling all the way (with a smile on my face). Straight to my jewellery boxes, hunting for a suitable box, to dress it up a bit. I even found a 9ct sticker that I very accurately placed emphasising it was 9ct gold.

I wrapped all his gifts up and hid them away. The night before his Birthday. I said, I, really hope you like your presents. But if you don't, Please, Please, don't tell me, until after all your friends have gone. He just said, I know whatever you get will be lovely. Well early in the morning, I took him his cup of tea, and handed him the gift with the bracelet in it, saying I hope you like it, love. On opening it he could see at a glance, it was a pile of rubbish/ junk, (as Wally would say it's a pile of S—T). Well as we had a joint bank account he knew I had spent a lot on his gift. I quickly said do you like it, my love? He just said "have you got the receipt", as it needs to be, put in a very safe place. (he had thought I had been ripped off). I tried to help him, take it out of the box. But he said no darling, don't take it out yet, I need to have a shower, and get dressed first. I then went to remove the 9ct sticker off, but he said no don't love just leave it a bit. I then gave him the tripod; he was a bit baffled as we only had a small 35mm camera, I did say I hope that it wasn't too big for our camera. Wally did say it was a bit big, so I said, never mind; we can change it as I still have the receipt. Wally went to have his shower while I said I will go and cook him his breakfast. When he came down I said have you got your bracelet on, then he noticed another large present when Wally opened it, he then realised the money was, spent on that and not the bracelet.

We had to sort out Michael's birth certificate, as he landed up having two. The first one with his name as O'Bryan, as that was the name I was, known as at the time Michael was born. The second one with Farrant, that Clive had somehow managed to get. So we went to a solicitor, who worked out that the second one was not legal, so then we decided to have his name changed by deed poll to Wilder (with his approval), so he became Michael Antony Wilder from then on.

Lady Donna Louise Wilder

Rebecca's Grandchildren

Left to right
(1) Harry John Webster, (2) Alfie Joe Webster,

Chapter 28

From A Boy to A Man

Wally took Michael to the Navy Careers Office in Bletchley, for some information. Michael was able to take the Navy qualification test instead of waiting for his school qualification results to come through. They told him the dates that were available, and he chose one, he told them that he wanted to join up on 25th June 1990. They said that he would be signed up for 22 years. (Wally and I thought it was three years, so it was a bit of a shock). My friends said, to me, that you don't want Michael to go into the Navy, as most of them are gay or alcoholics. I dismissed the gay bit, but we thought we would introduce Michael to alcohol before he went. So we started on larger, beers, even Shandy, but Michael didn't like any of them. We just gave up;

Wally then told and showed Michael how far one and a half miles was, as he needed to be able to run it at a particular time. But when he came back, he was knackered I then had a good look at our son and decided that no way was Michael man enough to fight for our country. My son, Michael, was a skinny little boy, not a big tough guy that would be sufficient enough to fight. I was afraid he would lose his confidence when he failed, but I didn't have the heart to tell him that I thought he would fail. My impression of the armed forces was of big tough men, who were very sporty, and who were men like Sylvester Stallone, Arnold Schwarzenegger, or better still Steven Seagal, all could look after them self's and our country. All Michael had ever been interested in was reading, music, films and computers. So an office job would off have suited him, nothing physical. I wasn't at all happy he was going to join up. I felt, I had failed, just like My Mother did with me, as I couldn't wait to move away from home, and now here was my very own child ready to leave me. I hadn't seen that I had in fact, done a great job in bringing him up. I had brought up a very confident young man, who was ready to move on into the big wide world on his own. Michael left to join on his chosen date for his six-and-a-half-week training.

A few weeks into his training he phoned us one evening, as he was talking to us I said there is a lot of noise in the background where are you? Michael said I'm in a pub having a drink with his mates, so I said oh that's good, what are you drinking? He said diesel, to which I said what's that? (You see I thought diesel was a fuel that you put in cars, etc.) Michael told me that it was cider, larger, and black currant, commonly known as a snake bite. Well, so much for Michael not liking Shandy. Very near to the end of Michael's training, we received a letter from HMS Raleigh, saying that, if Michael didn't manage to master folding his overalls to an A4 size, then he would not be accepted into the Royal Navy. I couldn't believe that they may turn him down, as now I wanted him to succeed with his dream. I knew I had to let go of the apron strings. Michael managed to complete it in the end. When Michael had done all his training, we were invited to his passing out parade. Michaels Nan and Alf

Such A Lucky Lady

(My Mother-in-law and her friend) came with us for the, Passing out Parade. We all were so very proud of him as he passed out, it had to be the proudest day of our life.

Our little boy was now a man ready to fight for our country. Michael then moved to Plymouth. Then three weeks later he passed out for his Stores accountancy. When we went down again to visit, Michael took us to the Navy's pub that they all used, well the carpet was so sticky, my shoes just stuck to it, as it was so full of beer. To think that Six weeks earlier Michael wasn't interested in drinking anything, other than coke a cola. When he left home, Michael was just a young lad, and now in such a short time. He had turned into a man; you could see that every one of them was looking out for each other, and they were a team.

One thing I had always wanted to do was scuba diving. So when we were on holiday in Grand Cannery one year, we were staying at Playa del Ingles, they were offering a trip to Puerto Rico, where they would give you a lesson in scuba diving. Wally booked for us to go, as he knew how much I would have like it. We were in the harbour doing the equalizing bit, with the instructors. When I went down, I couldn't equalize, and it hurt my ear. But I told the instructor, that I'm all right, as I so wanted to do it. But when I looked over to see how Wally was doing, He looked very disappointed, and Wally started shaking his head telling me that he was unable to do it, because of him having no ear drum. But knowing how much I wanted to do it, Wally said if you can find another person to go down with you, he didn't mind. Well, as luck would have it, a young lad also couldn't do it, so I paired up with his mate. We all went out on a boat; that was it I just couldn't wait to get into the water and go down to see all the fish. I was off like a shot, we had to hold hands and stay together, I could feel he wasn't as enthusiastic as I was. He was trembling a little; he had no chance of letting go of my hand, as I was going right down to the bottom, and he was going down too. I didn't care about the pain in my left ear; I just needed to go down to the bottom. It was fantastic. When our tanks were running short of air, we had to surface, so I let go of his hand, and I just floated on the surface, as I hadn't finished looking at all the fish, so I was swimming around in the roped off area. When unbeknown to me my tank had got caught on the rope, some people on the shore saw and were shouting that I was in trouble, my hero came to my aid in the form of my husband, he dived from the boat and swam over to free me.

When Rebecca, came to Milton Keynes to visit, it was around her eldest son's fourth birthday, in September 1991, by this time she had three children. We were talking about her eldest son, who had started going to playgroup, I had noticed that he wasn't speaking very clearly, he couldn't pronounce his name, his sisters or baby brothers name very well. I gave Rebecca a card with money in it so that she could buy my nephew a present from us. A few days later Rebecca phoned to say thank you for the card and money. While we got chatting, I said, it's a shame your eldest boy, couldn't go to playgroup, for more days, as by mixing with other children his own age, it would probably help him pronounce his words correctly. She screamed, down the phone, what are you saying, he's thick? I said no of course not, and I told her that as she was talking to her two baby's in baby talk, he was still using it. She went crazy, shouting, just because your sons, in the navy, well any thick O, can join up. What do you know about kids you've only had one, I tried to say "yes, but I have looked after a lot more." she then said, and didn't you think that God can see what a nasty evil bitch you are, that is why you can't have any kids? (I've guessed I wasn't allowed to give any advice)

After Michael had been in the Navy, for a little while, he came home on leave. He had arranged to meet up with a couple of his mates from school/sea cadets. Andrew, and Darren, all three were on their way back from a local pub, they were crossing the bridge, between Bradwell Common and Conniburrow, when a car pulled up, a pile off yobs, got out, and started to attack them, some of them had nunchucks. Poor Darren had his front teeth knocked out, Andrew, was knocked unconscious, and was down the side of the bridge, luckily Michael, just curled up into a ball after the first punch, and didn't even try to fight back. As he said, he knew they were, outnumbered. We had a phone call late that night, from Andrew's, brother Mark, who was at the hospital, with his parents. Telling us that Michael was at the hospital as well, and what had happened. We went straight to the hospital. Where we found the other two boys straight away, Michael was nowhere to be seen, the reason was that he wasn't, injured too severely, Thank God. he had gone back to the scene was with the police. The lads were in the wrong place at the wrong time.

I had started a hobby doing cross stitching with a friend, who had been doing it for years. She told me about a place that sold some beautiful things for doing this hobby. I asked Wally if he would take us their one Wednesday afternoon, well my friend and I were in our element. Wally, who was waiting patiently for us, noticed how busy the shop was, so when we got home, he asked me about my new hobby, as he hadn't seen it in our shops. I told him that only John Lewis had a small amount. That then gave Wally something to think about,

A few days later he said, how about us selling it in the market. Thinking about it sounded like a lovely way to enjoy my hobby, what with my very own business. So we approached the necessary companies, DMC and coats, who came round to see us. They were not happy at first, as their products were not what you would find in a market. But we convinced them that we were willing to prove it was a good idea. Wally proceeded in encouraging the other stall holders, to move up just a little, by the time he had finished he had made enough for a stall, that was 12ft x 20ft.

We also bought white baby things, and decorated them up with ribbon and lace, like pop under vests, that when finished, would look like a little ballerina leotard, plus socks, parasols, shawls, we attached lace and roses on to them. The business was called Buzzy Fingers & Little Miss Lace. We opened to a lovely large crowd, and sold loads; I told the parents of the children that I was looking after, that I was going to have to give them all notice, as I wasn't able to be available all week. But they said, they would be quite happy, to make other arrangements for their child on Tuesdays, if I could still have them the rest of the week. So for the next couple of months, we were getting visitors travelling, especially to come to our stall, I would invite potential, customers, to our house, for free lessons. Then before long, I was running a club called, The Stitch and Bitch Club. Which grow out of control, so I had to do them twice a week. Then Wally took me to show a little shop he had found in a small shopping precinct. It was perfect for our business, but I was hesitant as I didn't want to lose the children, but I knew it was an excellent opportunity for us, so we went ahead and opened a few weeks later.

Then soon after, in Milton Keynes Shopping Centre, a specialist stall came up. So we applied to have it, all was going well until a very well know Department store found out. So the Shopping Centre said that we would not be able to have the stall, as we would conflict with another trader. We then told the management, of the shopping Centre. That we would be contacting the local Newspapers. As we were not happy, that a larger company should have the sole monopoly. We did tell our story to the local paper, which then phoned the Shopping Centre Management to ask for their side of the story before they went to print. We then were contacted by the shopping Centre Managment, to be told, that they had decided, that if we promise, not to undercut the said department store. We would be able to run our business on the stall, inside the shopping Centre. We had been selling our embroidery threads at 1p cheaper then in our shop so our customers would place an order and we would bring them to the Centre, at the shop price.

In the shop, one day, unbeknown to us, was someone from the Cross stitching magazine. They came along to see our business after they phoned up and asked if we would like them to do a write up on our shop. Of course, we said yes, as it could only be good for business and so it was, we began to get groups of dedicated stitches travelling to our shop and the postal side then started to get very busy as well.

At the stitch and bitch club. We wanted to raise some money for Willen Hospice, where I had known some lovely friends, who had been looked after there. So we sponsored a local lady to stitch a lovely design of three Victoria girls flying kits, and then we gave them a large cheque along with the stitched picture that we had framed for them. So they could hang it the reception area,

We were doing so well that we had to employ staff for the two business, as we had now extended into the shop next door. We even had a small coach load off lady's turn up one day After seeing the fantastic write-up in the national cross stitches magazine. Lucky for us they had phoned before they came.

As we were so proud of Michael joining the Royal Navy, we brought him his first car, for £500. He started having

Such A Lucky Lady

his driving lessons in Plymouth then one day he phoned us up to say that he had a date for his driving test. Once Michael passed, we paid the deposit for him on his first new car it was a Seat. Well, it wasn't until Michael phoned and said about his driving test that I remembered that I hadn't taken mine, I had been driving illegally for the last eight years. You see Wally had tried to teach me a few times, but that turned out to be a big mistake, as I couldn't handle, being, told that I was doing anything wrong. I just couldn't get the gears right; I just gave up. Then Wally got a Cortina Ghia that was automatic, so I had a couple of goes in that. I got a little bit better, but I still wasn't, really interested in driving.

Then on the morning after our stag and hen night, just two days before our wedding. We were in Hayes Middlesex, but we had to get back to our House in Milton Keyes, to pick up everything for our wedding that we were having in Hayes, on Saturday 16th June. We had lent our car to my brother Richard, so he could bring his DJ equipment, so that meant we had to borrow Wally's best man's car, it was a Jaguar. Well, Wally started to try and drive home, but when he got to Harrow, he was feeling so ill with his hangover, he then said that we had to go back to Hayes unless I wanted to drive home.

Well, I decided that I would. And I did, it was brilliant as Wally was fast asleep and wasn't watching my every move, I gained so much confidence after driven around 40 miles parking the car in our carport, under our house without knocking it down. I Put my future husband to bed, and then I drove to the shopping center and parked in between to other cars without damaging them in any way, as I needed to pick up items that we had hired. Well on the day of our wedding, I didn't give it a second thought I just got into our car and drove to the hairdressers, to have my hair done. And then after the wedding, I would just get in the car and go where ever not giving it a second thought. It wasn't until Michael mentioned that he had a date for his test that I remembered that I hadn't taken one myself. I arranged to have some lessons to clear-up any bad habits I may have picked up. As luck would have it, I hadn't picked up any bad habits, so I was able to pass 1st time.

I only had a Couple of little mishaps in our cars I don't think they were too bad. I told Wally when I got home, after trying to do a turnaround once right where there just happened to be a lamp post bang in the middle of the pathway that was separating two cars. It only needed a new wing on the passenger side. Wally had to get it resprayed silver and burgundy. Actually, I think I did Wally a favour, as the Cortina looked lovely. Then there was the time I moved Wally's car, as we were having a new American fridge freezer delivered. The man in the lorry asked if I could move Wally's car, so thinking I could run it without wiping the dew from the windows. As believing, I knew the angle to go in, as I was reversing the tail lift was lowered on the lorry, so Wally's car had a look of a Piano accordion. But most importantly I was unhurt

Chapter 29

God's Garden

Early in 1992, I recall my sister-in-law Christine, gathering all her family, together. As she needed to tell us all that she had Cancer. And that she didn't have very long with us, she was the first family member I had known to have this intolerable decrease. We would go and visit her in Torquey. Then one day we got the dreaded call to say that she didn't have much longer. So Wally and I along with lots of her family travelled down to be with her before she passed away. I was in her room, at the Hospice along with her immediate family, and a nurse. She was making a rattling sound, then she took a deep breath, and that was it. I was standing at the end of her bed. Everyone was crying, but I just couldn't understand at the time, why, no one tried to give her mouth to mouth to resuscitate her. (As that was my first thought), I knew it wasn't my place to, but I thought that someone should off. I had never experienced someone dying before, I'm now older and understand that there was nothing that could have been, done.

Christine's Husband, our brother-in-law, passed away through carbon monoxide poisoning soon after.

Then, not very long after, two dear friends passed away from the same diabolical disease, Cancer. Leaving their young families behind. One had four beautiful little girls, the other one, two lovely little boys God Bless.

We have also had to say our farewells to a few of the family, that were far too young to be, taken from us all. God only knows why? God Bless them all.

As I have had the unpleasant, and misfortune to attend many funerals, and cremation so far. I have decided that like everyone it is an experience I wish I could avoid. I have decided that when my number is up. I would like to be, buried. Not for any other reason other than I just can't come to terms with their only being ashes and not a body to mourn.

We had some home improvements done on the house, like all three bedrooms, had bath En-suite's fitted. New UPVC windows and doors. An extension to the kitchen, the Carport was enclosed, making another lounge. And the upstairs room was extended, onto the balcony. And professionally, made to measure curtains.

Well, Michael bought a house in Saltash, just over the Tamar Bridge. With his Girlfriend at the time. Angela, they Married on the 11/06/1994. Both Michael's Nan's were at his wedding, My Mother looked, really lovely in her navy blue and white outfit, so much, as Michael even made a comment. As she had, indeed, made a great effort. His marriage finished about seven years later. He then left the Navy, after serving for 13.5 years. He got a job as a DJ. (As he said many years before that he wanted to). At a Men's only club, he soon was made

Manager. Then he met and Married, Kelly on 11/07/2014. They lived in Plymouth for a time, before moving to Chalfont St Peters, where they run a pub, called the Poachers. Then one evening, some men broke into the Pub. Michael was told to hand over all the takings. He was made to open the safe, and then they set upon Michael; he was beaten up. The robbers were demanding more money. Michael told them there was no more. So they then smashed bottles of spirit, onto the pool tables, then set them alight. One of them kept Michael held down, so he couldn't get out, then when the robber, made a run for the door, Michael managed to get up and get himself out of the Pub. Michael had told Kelly, that in the case of, any emergency she was to get herself and her son Ben, out and not to worry about him, the place was burnt out. So they had to rent a house until the Pub, was refurbished, Unfortunately, the time it took, they lost their regular customers.

Then the insurance company refused to pay up for everything; Michael is now classed, as disabled, as now he has nerve damage. He has to walk with a stick and finds sitting in one position very painful at times. They have recently moved on 10/07/2015 to Gosport to be near us, so after 25 years I have my Son back.

We received a call that My Mother had accidently, set fire to her house. She lost everything apart from what she was wearing at the time. My Mother was then put, into bed and breakfast. In a lovely kind lady's house. Until the council found her another home. This time, it was a small downstairs flat in Hayes. Every so often after work from the Sunday market, we would pop in and see her, as she had started all over again in a new place it was not so bad, she was keeping on top of things. But all of us had moved from the area, by now, so she would travel up to London, to see her grandchildren, from Martin and Richard. She would take the children some sweets, so she was known, as sweetie nanny by them, Jo-Ann and Rebecca lived in Gosport, and I lived in Milton Keynes, so she only saw us three when we visited as it was too far for her to travel.

We were going to be spending Christmas with Michael and his wife at the time, in Plymouth. So after we had finished work, Christmas Eve, we started our long journey, it was dark, and there was a lot of traffic, at one point on the M5 there were no street lights, so it was very dark. At around 8 pm Wally was driving in the middle lane and decided to overtake the two cars in front, so he accelerated and moved into the fast lane, only to be confronted with what looked like up ahead a pile of sand, that was what it looked like from the headlights. With no place to go, as he was along side the other two cars that he was overtaking, he had no choice but to drive straight at it. By this time my fingernails from my right hand had in bedded into his leg. We hit the said pile of sand, only to find, in fact, it was a whale off hay that had very recently fallen from a lorry. As we hit it at a great speed around 80 mph, we broke the netting that was around it, spreading it everywhere, we had taken off about two foot.

Such A Lucky Lady

(that might not seem much but you have to remember it was in a car and not on a plane.
(plus, by the way, Wally is no Evil Knievel). Through the headlights you could see every strand of straw flying by, it was all in slow motion. Eventually (I thought this was it I was off to meet our maker). (Secretly hoping I had earned enough brownie points to go up and not down).
After what seemed like forever, we landed back where we had started from, behind the two cars that we were trying to overtake. We then careered over to the hard shoulder were after we had finished shaking realised we were still alive. But the hay was now all over the road, and cars were swerving trying to avoid it. One car was spinning upside down; we went and checked that everybody was ok. Wally then removed the netting from his car that had wrapped its self all around the bumper. We then went on our way but not for long, as the water temperature gauge started rising, we pulled over, and there was water coming out. So we called the RAC who took us to our final destination so to speak. When we awoke Christmas Morning, we were aching all over. Our insurance paid to transport us back home and repaired the car, but soon after Wally replaced it, as it never ran the same.

We were able to get more staff to help out, as the shop business was thriving so much, so Wally decided to sell one of the burger trailers to a friend. Then not long after he sold the other one as the cross-stitch business was so busy it was taking all off our time.

Lady Donna Louise Wilder

As all the hard work with Our Cross-Stitch Business was paying off, it looked like we were differently on the up and up. We decide to arrange a treat for our staff, for all their hard work, by booking a Christmas meal at a hotel, that we're putting on a meal with entertainment. When we arrived, we were very pleased to find that we were rubbing shoulders with the big boys, Argos, B.T British Telecom, Etc.

I'm very passionate about the nostalgic things as my lovely husband knows only too well; he has brought me some great gift throughout our marriage. Unfortunately, I have had to part with some of them as we have downsized, plus I can't take them with me when my number is up? I've had the beautiful grandfather clock, a full-size rocking horse, the silver cutlery set in the mahogany box. A bone china Royal Doulton dinner set, the porcelain dolls including a Christening baby doll, he even brought me a Masonic ball to replace the one My Mother wouldn't let me have, but this one wasn't, broken. Then when Michael got married, I started buying toys for any Grandchildren, I may one day have. Well, to begin with, I bought a doll's house, I was in my element, buying everything to furnish the play mobile townhouse. I still have at the back of our store cupboard; I haven't been able to part with it yet.

It was strange getting in contact with my Auntie Maureen and Uncle Barry, after all, this time. My Auntie Maureen always looks so very glamorous. I think she is such a sophisticated lady. I have always admired the way she presents herself, I obviously have the same taste in material things, as we both at one time had the same sofas, collectable clock along with matching candlesticks same shaped dinner set, just the opposite pattern, table mats, it's uncanny. Auntie Maureen said one day that we must come out with them for a curry, as they had found an excellent restaurant. Wally told them that he didn't like curry (the truth was, he had never even tried a curry), So Auntie Maureen said she would cook a few different curries' in a mild sauce for him to taste, we all sat down at the table to a beautiful spread. I said that I wouldn't drink, so I was going to be able to drive us both home. So first the beers came out, and then the wine started flowing, followed by Ponche from a silver bottle from Spain, then out came the Sloe Gin. not forgetting my dear cousin Baz, offering Wally some Wacky Backy. By 2 am, we were all still sitting at the table. When Wally got up, to use the bathroom. (which was downstairs as Aunties house at this time was a bungalow). As he was staggered back out from the toilet, I took one look at him and knew it was time for us to leave (he looked like death warmed up) we said our goodbyes, and off we went,

I had just made it out of my Auntie and Uncles gates, when Wally said, stop the car, I'm going to be sick, and so he was. I had to stop many times, on the M25 and the M1 all the way home. I put Wally to bed; he was in a very, bad way. The next day, and the day after that, he spent most of it in bed asleep, or on the sofa. By Monday he was just about able to go to work, but lucky he had staff as he couldn't do anything much, he felt so bad. He reckoned it was my Aunties fault because she had given him food poisoning. As it turned out, he had alcohol poisoning. It took him years to try curry again; now he can't get enough of it.

Our next door neighbour, who was always sending her children round to us, to borrow money, for the electric, gas, or bread, beans, etc. would only speak to me if it were to borrow something from us. Then this one day after many times of her passing me on the street, where she would Completely be ignoring me, once too often, but would always say hello to Wally. I said to Wally that I wasn't going to help her out anymore. So when she sent the children round the next time I was going to say sorry, I have run out, or I had no spare money. So this time, she sent one of her children round, he said mummy said, could you lend her a tin of peas, when I said sorry I haven't got any, he then said or a tin of beans, I thought you're a cheeky mare. She then would go up to Wally on his burger stall pleading poverty with her two children with her, so out of the kindness of his heart, Wally would give them a burger each she was just taking advantage of his kindness.

Then one day she asked Wally to borrow £20, saying she would give it back to him. He decided to help her out by giving her the money, telling her not to let Donna, know. So he didn't say anything about it. Well, she had decided she wasn't going to pay him back with money. Because she could blackmail him instead. She kept on coming around to see him at work when I wasn't there. He started feeling uncomfortable, as he knew I could turn up at any moment. Then this excuse for a woman then began, telling her ex-husband, and people who knew me, that she was having an affair with her neighbour. One Day Wally and I were both in the shop together when Wally popped out to the bank. He had only been gone for 5 minutes, when our next door neighbour's ex-husband, came into the shop, he said can I have a word with you, I told him. Sorry, but I'm busy at the moment, as I had a few customers in the shop. So I said what do you want, he said do you know where your husband is right now, as I can tell you he is in a hotel room with my wife. I just said yes I know they are, (just to humour him). As a customer of mine was waiting to be served. I knew Wally wasn't. A few days later, at my stitch and bitch club in my house. A very, good friend of ours that ran a taxi service said that one of her drivers was talking to my neighbour, as he was giving her a lift to work. And she told him, that she was having an affair with her neighbour, so as my friend knew all my neighbours, she and I were puzzled. Then not long after, another one of my friend's phoned she said, Hi, love, I hope you are ok. If you need someone to talk to just call don't sit indoors on your own, I've just heard that Wally has left you and move in next-door I said I'm not on my own Wally is sitting right next to me.

I knew our neighbour, was and alway had been jealous of us, as we were happy and it showed. When we spoke about it, Wally said you know what she is like, don't take any notice of her she is just sad. Well, I couldn't argue with that. On arriving home, the next day we parked up, and both got out of the car. Our neighbour was on her balcony; she immediately said, Hi Wally, but

Lady Donna Louise Wilder

just ignored me, I was fuming, as Wally responded by saying hello back.

We went indoors, and I told Wally that he was out of order, as he was playing right into her hands, and was just leading her on. Wally said, not to be so silly; saying she is just trying to wind you up. (I can tell you she was doing an excellent job). Wally went and made a cup of tea; we both went to sit, in our garden to drink it, and then when I had finished, I took my cup indoors, only to see her pop her head over the fence to say, Hi Wally. Wally just came in and said just ignore her. I said that was easy for him to say, she then turned her music player up louder she was playing her songs that were lovey Dovey songs. Just happened to be the songs that we liked and that meant something to us both. (I think when you are in love you can make any song mean something to you). Then as I was at the sink she walked by our back gate looking in, by now Wally could see I was getting stressed out by her. So after we had watched a bit of TV. Wally said I've run you a bath love, why don't you go and have a nice soak.
(nothing strange about that, as Wally, often runs my bath for me, he is lovely like that).

Well, I went upstairs, and stepped into the tub, and just as my posterior, (bum) touched the water. I had a funny feeling that something wasn't quite right, I had a very quick bath, whipped on my bathrobe, and went downstairs. Only to find Wally, wasn't anywhere in the house. Then on my way pass the telephone, I noticed the receiver was on the side.

I went to the front door, just in time to see Wally, coming out from next doors carport. I went completely ballistic. Wally tried to explain, but I wasn't having any of it. Wally said I'm sorry, I should have listened to you, it's my fault I lent her £20, weeks ago. She said she was desperate, and needed it for the electric. I knew you would go mad, so I just went round and told her don't bother to give it back, you can keep it. I went upstairs and grabbed some clothes, then I stormed around to her house, and told her to keep away from my husband, and I told her she was a sad bitch. (well words to that effect). Still very confused and trying to put two and two together. I went back indoors and started ranting and raving at Wally. Saying that he had led her on and that our marriage was over. I removed all my wedding rings and threw them at him, and our wedding photos that were on the wall. Saying that was it, I'm leaving. Wally pleaded with me to listen saying nothing was going on he promised. I just was so confused trying to work out when he had the time to have an affair with anyone yet alone her. A so-called friend. I just had to get away and try to work it all out for my own peace of mind. I packed a large suitcase with some clothes including my dressing gown and a pile of towels, (as I knew I wasn't going to be leaving for good, I just needed the case to look like it was full).

I also took the briefcase that had all our week's takings in; Wally grabbed hold off me begging me to stay, and let him explain, but I just wouldn't wait. I just pulled away from him and left in our car. I had no idea where I was going to go. I was crying as I was driving and found myself at our shop, the shutters were down, so I turned off the alarm and opened the shutters, and went inside our shop. Walking back and forth up and down,

(I admit I was talking to myself). Trying to work out what I should do. I decided I needed to show Wally that he had betrayed me by going behind my back and helping her out without consulting me first. So I tried to book a hotel as I was going to disappear for a few days, thinking that will show him. But as it was August bank holiday all the hotels were booked up. So that plan backed fired on me.

I then thought I'll go to my sisters and stay with her. I phoned Wally and asked him to meet me outside our house, saying that I need a quilt and pillow to take with me. When I arrived our friend Geoff came up to the car and said what on earth are you doing; you may as well cut Wally's right arm off. Wally came out with my quilt and pillow and laid them out in the backseat saying please darling please don't go. But, I knew I just had to get away. As I drove off, I knew, I didn't want to drive all the way to my sisters, and involve her. As deep down I knew we would work this out. So after wracking my brains, I decided, that the best place for me to sleep the night would be at the local police station. I parked outside the police station, under a street light, and went inside. At the information desk, I asked if they had a spare cell that I could stay in just for the night. I told him of my domestic situation; The officer said no sorry they are only for criminals, and that I should just go home. I then told him that if I went back, I would land up going next door and then they would be called to arrest me for killing the woman next door. I told him I was just trying to cut out the killing bit so to speak.

He just laughed. I said I was going to stay in my car for the night just to calm myself down a bit. So if they could just keep an eye on me from their security camera. It was very busy that night with police cars pulling up all the time, people in handcuffs, being taken to the police station. So I wasn't able to get any sleep, even if I was able to turn my over active mind off. Around 5:30 am I took a slow drive back to our shop, where I was able to have a wash, and get changed into some clean clothes. I waited, for our staff to turn up, as I was still in business mode. I was giving her the orders, which I needed to be, put together. Telling her what I wanted her to order, from the rep when he arrived later that day. When Wally turned up, so I finished what I was doing, and went out to the car to drive off. Wally told me that I couldn't take the car as it needed to have its service.

So I grabbed the case and proceeded to walk down the road. With that Wally got in the car and started, driving, after me. Wally was driving along. Telling me not to be so silly, and just to get in the car. So we can go home, and talk it over. I just kept saying I'm never going back to that house again as long as she is living next door. In the end, he persuaded me to get in the car so he could drop, me of at the train station where I said I was going to go to my sisters and stay. When we got to the station, I got out of the car while Wally went to find somewhere to park. I asked for a ticket to the next station stop which was Bletchley, as I still had no intention of truly leaving. Wally arrived at the station. Just in time, to see me going through the turnstiles.

Wally got a platform ticket and followed me onto the platform. Where the train had just pulled in, I carried onto the train, and off I went, leaving Wally thinking that that was it (He had lost me forever). When the train reached Bletchley, I got off with my suitcase, and boarded a bus, to Stony Stratford. Where our shop was, as you can see, I was going around in circles not really knowing what or where I was going.

While I was at our shop, Wally turned up once again; he said, please let's go somewhere and talk. I again told him I'm not going home, so we went to Willen Lake, where we sat on a park bench, to talk about our future. Wally got himself a cup of tea from the tea bar, and he brought me an ice cream, as he knows it is my weakness. It was quite warm, so Wally took off his gold chain and placed it in his shorts pocket, we talked, and it was, decided that we had no choice but to move if we had any chance of getting over this together, we had to get away from her next door. I very reluctantly went back home.
When we arrived home, Wally wasn't thinking straight as he placed his gold chain on the stairs and not where he would usually put it, which was on his bedside table. So come the next morning when he went to put it on he couldn't find it. He thought that he must have lost it in the park (I knew differently but kept quiet as I wasn't talking to him still) he said I'm just going to the park as think I must have dropped it there. Hopefully, no one has

found it. Well, I know my husband so well, as he would think that I thought he had given it to her next door as he had done with me when we got together. So I let him think that by saying REALLY? When he got back, empty handed his first words were I know what your thinking and the answer is no I haven given it to her. Again I said REALLY? As he was going up the stair, I heard a great big sigh of relief as Wally found it right where he had put it. I didn't tell him for years that I had known it was there all the time.

Wally arranged for an estate agent to come round the next day and price up our house. Even though I loved my house, and we had done so much to it, I just knew I couldn't bear to live next door to her anymore.

The estate agent came round and priced our home at £55,000, but before it even went on the market a friend of mine, heard we were selling, so phoned and asked if she could come round to make us an offer. As she had been in our house many times, she knew what they were getting. When she and her husband came round, and before they made an offer, I said if they were interested they could buy it for £52.500. Without even hesitating it was agreed. When Wally came home, I told him I had sold the house, and for what price, he said he wasn't surprised, they wanted it at that price, and that it was her place not mine to make a lower offer. We went to look for a new home,

Lady Donna Louise Wilder

My Half Brothers And Sister's

Left to right;
(1) Karen Pearce, (2) Kelly Pearce, (3) Jane Beverly Pearce, née Lifford, (My Stepmother)
(4) Robert Pearce, (5) Nicola Pearce, (6) Jordan Pearce,

Chapter 30

Time To Move On

We decided to sell our house and move to a new estate; we found a lovely four bedroom detached house, with a detached double garage; we had a huge mortgage but with our predictions we were going to be okay.

We decided to sell the burger business, as the cross stitch business was taking over, we had just about settled in, and we were enjoying our lovely big house, with the new conservatory fitted. My Mother was having more health troubles again. So, it was decided that My Mother needed to have a triple heart bypass. She was in Harefield Hospital, awaiting her bypass, we travelled to the hospital to see her before her operation. We were talking to her when she said, would you believe it, I haven't seen any donor cards in here. I asked her if she needed anything, she told me she could do with a flannel and some tissues, so Wally, who hates hospitals went off to the shops to buy My Mother her bits.

On his way he found a donor card, He took one and gave her it, along with her other bits he had just got for her. I also was checking, that she wasn't worried about anything. (Other than her operation). She said that she hadn't paid her insurance policy. As she had it with her in her bag, I said to give it to us, as we will pay it for her. She said she didn't have the money to give to us. We told her we would pay it for her, and that she wasn't to worry about it. It was only a small amount. After her operation, she was going to need to take it very easy and needed somewhere to convalesce. So Wally said to me, that he thought the best place would be to ours. As we were on our own without young children or pets running around, plus we had the conservatory, which she could sit in and rest. Wally also said it's not that I want your Mother staying with us, it's just that it would be a better place for her to get some rest. I too wasn't that keen on the idea, but it made a lot of sense, we put it to My Mother while Rebecca was at My Mother's bedside, Rebecca said oh no, she isn't. It's all been arranged My Mothers, is coming to mine, with that we just kept out of it.

When Rebecca left to go home, My Mother said she had no money with her, and needed a clean nightdress. We told him that we would give her some money and that we would go and buy her a nightdress from the shops. But she said that she wanted her other bag, that was at Rebecca's house, as it had something inside, that she wanted with her. So Wally drove us to Gosport to get My Mothers things that were at Rebecca's house. When we arrived there, I knocked on the door, but no one came to answer it. So Wally went around the back, to see if anyone was in the backyard. He pulled himself up to look over the high fence, but couldn't see anyone, we phoned but still no one answered, as Wally went to go round the back again, he saw Rebeccas husband John ride off on his push-bike going off to work. Wally called after him, but he didn't respond. We put a note through

Such A Lucky Lady

Rebeccas door, telling her that My Mother wanted her bag, nightdress, and some money and could she take them on her next visit. On our next visit to the hospital, My Mother told us, that Rebecca didn't answer the door. As she wasn't happy with us, as she believed, that the only reason we paid My Mothers insurance, was because we were hoping that My Mother wouldn't pull through the operation? And we would have a claim to it. Plus, Wally giving My Mother The donor card as well, as we didn't want her to survive she also said told My Mother that Wally had been trying to break into her house.

Well, My Mother did go and stay with Rebecca's, and while she was there, she wrote a letter, to both, Jo-Ann, and myself, word for word the same. Except my one mentioned that she was returning a cheque, that we had sent to her for her birthday. Along with a cheque for the money's that we had paid for her insurance. Finished off with from your ex-mother.

Lady Donna Louise Wilder

My Cousins On The O'Bryan Side

1st column;
(1) Paul Kingsley Hone, (2) Colin Stewart, (3) Elaine Davis, née Mountford, Stewart,
2nd Column;
(1) Stephen Kingsley Hone, (2) Mandy Church, née Hone,
(3rd Column;
(1) Mikala Ackerman, née Baker, Hone, (2) Debra Stockley, née Stewart, (3) Mechelle Gooder, née Stewart

Such A Lucky Lady

The Letter,

Donna
Here is the £24-00 you paid to C.I.S. For me. After all, that has been said and done, and all the lies told I have decided that enough is enough and that I have forgiven you too often in the past, and all I got from you is disrespect and disloyalty so now I am going to make a clean break, from you and Jo-Ann. I do not want to see or hear from you again Now I hear you both think I am going senile, well if I'm senile you must be brain dead. From your ex, Mother.

Apparently My Mother wrote them and then asked Rebecca to post them as she couldn't get out, (I know that if My Mother had asked me to post something as hurtful as that. 1st, I wouldn't have posted them, and the 2nd I would have, at least, had contacted my sisters, to say mothers asked me to post these nasty letters to you both. So just ignore them, till she's feeling better. When I received my letter, I was shocked but thought it best to give My Mother some space. And hopefully, once she moves into her place. We can visit when Rebecca wasn't around. Which we did, and we got on fine, just as before.

After Six months of living in our beautiful home, I had a dispute at work with one of the reps from DMC. It was about some stock. I had ordered and just received from them. I wasn't happy with, as the delivery parcel was full of stock from another large store, and still had their price tickets on, which I was supposed to remove before adding my own. I ask him to arrange for another delivery, but fresh stock. He then told me that I had to accept it. I told him that in that case, I would be closing down My business, he just laughed at me and said you won't do that. I told him you just watch me.

I went home and told Wally, that's it, I'm not doing it anymore, I'm not being told how to run my business. Wally said what are we going to do. As we had the mortgage to think off, I just said we will have to find a job down the job centre. So we went to the job centre, to look for a job. A job that paid the most. We found one working in a cooked meat factory. We took it to the lady at the counter and said that we were both interested in the job when she found out that we hadn't been unemployed for longer than six weeks, she said that we couldn't apply for it. So we took down all the details, went home and phoned up the company. We were told to call in and pick up an application form plus we needed our CVs. (CV was something new to us, we had never had one before).

We went straight down to the factory asked for the application forms and filled them in. We were then, told that they would be in touch for an interview soon. I then asked if we could have an interview now, the reception made a call, and a lady came out, I just said that we needed a job and that their company needs us. She smiled and said that she would interview us both now. So Wally went in first after a short while he came out with the lady and as I got up, she said I don't need to interview you as you know you have the job. The woman

Such A Lucky Lady

said when can we start, we both said whenever, she then said well, you can both start tomorrow night if you like; we would be doing then night shift 6 pm to 2 am. So we removed everything from the shop over the next two weeks and put it into our garages. We then sold a lot of it at the Stitch and Bitch club. We started doing the night shift, at first, and then we both went on to do the 12-hour shifts, that was four days on with four days off, followed by four nights on then four nights off. We had to wear Hygiene white coats, white Wellington boot a hair net with a hard hat and no makeup, nail varnish or Jewellery. Very soon they offend Wally a Team Leader job and me QC. (At long last I had letters after my name QC). No, Not Queens Council, it stands for Quality control.

As we needed to keep afloat so to speak, we were desperate for any overtime that was going, so we would both put our self's forward for any that was available. When there wasn't any overtime, we both signed up to an agency. Where we did some fascinating jobs. (NOT).

One of the job was, we had to put food baskets, (the ones that the supermarkets have their fruit and vegetables in). Through a sanitising machine, another one was removing an electrical cable from an item in its box and replacing it with a UK Cable, and then there was the one where I had to pack medication at a laboratory.

Then we both went to another job, that made plastic milk bottles, shampoo/conditioner bottles for L'Oréal. And many other kinds of bottles, there seemed to be a lot more work there plus plenty of overtime. We both left

Beni foods, we had been there for nearly two years and went to work at Alpla again; Wally was picked out to go and work in the warehouse, as a forklift driver. I carried on working on the factory floor, and then the manager of the Quality Control department told me to go to the office and ask for an application form and apply for QC. As there was a vacancy coming up. I went into the personal's office, when I requested the application form, I was told that there weren't any jobs going. I later found out that the woman thought I was after her job. It was just the push I needed as I was starting to feel I needed to look for something else. As luck would have it, I was approached to do childminding for two little girls, so that was it I went back to child-care.

Wally stayed, working in the warehouse. But he was soon made the manager, but after a few days told them that he didn't, what to have the responsibility, and he offered to train a younger man for the manager's job if they made him assistant manager, which they agreed to do and so they did. Along with his other requests that were a pay rise and only to work 6 am to 3 pm and not work weekends or bank holidays. Wally didn't think that they would. He was just trying his luck. Well, he was lucky as they agreed to all his requests.

Chapter 31

Our Wilderness Land

As the area, on both sides of our house had become landlocked, and no one was taking care of it. We approached the builders and inquired about buying it as it would make our garden bigger. Well, we were very surprised to find that we could buy it for a nominal fee of £1. Yes, you read it right. Just one pound. Well, after checking our finances, and cutting back on our alcohol consumption, to make sure we didn't go into debt. We sent them a cheque by recorded delivery. When the new plans came through for the land it was gigantic, so we squared off our garden by taking it to the back ends of one neighbour's garages, and the back end of our garage. Then we gave the rest of the land to each of our two friends on either side of our garden making their gardens a bit bigger, behind our garage we placed a large shed, then down the bottom of our garden behind our neighbours we put a large summer house.

(I wish I still had the summer house now, as it would have made a great den for me to write this book).

We used to have a company come round to feed and care for our grass, and then one day they told us that there was a slight problem; they said that we had leather jackets that had invaded our grass, and that it needed to be, treated. Well as I had never heard of them before, I

Lady Donna Louise Wilder

just had a picture in my head, of a load of biker's Hells Angles with their leather jackets on riding around on their Harley Davison's on our grass. It turned out to be Crane fly's, commonly known as daddy long legs eggs laid in our grass and needed to be, treated as the grass was dying in places.

As we were living in a new estate word soon got around that there was a child-minder right on the doorstep, so it wasn't long before I was fully booked up with children. I was allowed to look after six children under the age of 8 years old but any child over eight years old didn't count. They told me that I shouldn't take on the older children if they were going to take my time away from the younger ones. At one time I was lucky enough to have three sets of twins. As with everything I do, I went too far. We decided to convert our double garage, into a den for the children. So we partitioned the front so we could still store our things safely. We then decorated it with wallpaper, top and bottom with a dado rail. A suspended ceiling that My Father put up for us. We laid a new carpet, and as we had just renewed our living room furniture, we put our old furniture in there for them. When it was finished. The children were over the moon. They had our old TV and video player, that was in made from yew TV cabinet, with closing doors. Two dark green leather three setters, high-back Chesterfield sofas with a pouffe. A computer, two play stations and two Nintendo's, piles of stacking boxes full of toys and playthings. I even got them a large round Lego table, that had five seats. (The kind you would see in a car showroom to keep the children happy).

Such A Lucky Lady

Only the older children were allowed to play in the den after school. Soon word got about down the school, about the den. So I would have Mums at the school, asking if their child could come round and play. So very soon I was having up to 12 children playing in the den, after every school day. The rules were very simple, if you touch or play with it, you are responsible for making sure it is left as you found it. To encourage them to drink water, (so to be healthy) they were offered a glass of water and one sweet, or if they wanted pop or juice, there were no sweets, as children like sweets they all chose the water.

I started looking on eBay for equipment and toys, to use for my job. I got a bit hooked on the site, so would look for things that I didn't even want or for that matter need, but when I found something, that was a bit different, unusual or unique. I would put a bid on it, only like £1 or so. But it wasn't long before all the £1s added up, as Wally received one day our monthly bank statement, it was pages and pages long, adding up to around £300. Whoops, poor Wally just didn't understand a bargain.

One time we had some of our neighbours around for drinks where it was discussed that it would be nice to have dinner parties, like back in the 80s. When it was the in thing to do. I said I would do the first one. So Wally and I went to Marks and Spencer's, and we got a three-course meal for eight people. It all came in foil trays, so it all went straight into the oven. The deserts came in glasses. As I always looked after everything I owned, I still had a full eight-piece dinner set still in one piece.

Lady Donna Louise Wilder

After everyone had finished they said it was lovely, and then one lady said, you must tell me who your chef is, so I said now what was his name now let me think. I know Mark, and his mate was Spencer. As she was leaving, she said, please don't forget to give me Marks phone number.

Then at the next dinner party, the lady got out her Christmas dinner set and spent all day preparing everything it was lovely, but I couldn't cope with all that work. The next one was the lady who was asking about my private chef. Well, she decided she didn't want to be outdone by us all. So she had a new table and chairs, plus a new derby dinner set, the works. When Wally leant back in his chair, it cracked (opus). Then the last couple who were Scottish said I think I will do chicken in a basket on paper plates, but she didn't, they done haggis, we had never eaten it before, but it was very nice. While we were talking with our neighbours, one of them enquired as to what university, (don't laugh). We had attended. As they were all university graduates, now with professions as a bank manager, accountants, and even a headmaster. They were pretty shocked when Wally said that he had been expelled from school when he was 14 years old, and with no qualifications. Wally was then, asked. Were we fortunate enough to inherit our wealth? Wally told him that we had worked for everything that we have they were a bit surprised.

On the eaves of our house, two pigeons decided to nest, so Wally phoned a pest control man who came round and shot them, Wally asked him what to do if we ever got

Such A Lucky Lady

them again, the man said that Wally could buy an air rifle and kill them himself. So a few weeks later another pair came and decided to nest in the same place. Wally went out and brought an air rifle, and then when it was dark, he went and tried to remove them. He managed to kill one, but the other one flew away. He picked it up and put it in a black bag, then popped it in the dust bin. I told him to place a house brick on top in case it woke up and tried to get out, lucky the dustbin men came the next morning. While cleaning the upstairs windows, I noticed a pigeon on a roof, so I got Wally's rifle out then aimed it out the window and fired only to hear a strange sound I had fired into the window frame, so the pellet ricocheted all around the frame.

A little while later early one morning, I was in the garden when I saw a pigeon on the roof of the house opposite our house, so I went upstairs and loaded the rifle, aimed it at the pigeon and fired. I missed the Pigeon but hit the garden gate, right at the top was a pellet hole. On going upstairs to put the rifle away, I just looked out of the hall window, when I saw what looked like a hole in our neighbour's car window, on the passenger side right by the wing mirror. I started shaking as because of the angle it was obvious it had to have come from our house. I got out Wally's binoculars to have a better look, I was still shaking I found it hard to focus, but when I did. I nearly fell, down the stairs with joy, as it turned out to be a spider's web, and what I thought was the pellet hole was the spider.

Wally has banned me from touching any guns or rifle or even bows and arrows not long after I had to start

Lady Donna Louise Wilder

wearing glasses. Wally was doing the manly thing in the garden one day, like cleaning the guttering out in the garage and the study. I was indoors doing my usual, improving my computer skills, (online shopping). When Wally slipped from the ladder, and the side of the step stuck in his leg. He pulled it out, and his leg started bleeding, a lot. I had heard him fall, so I ran to the hallway, as I was going to the front door to see if Wally was ok. But he came in through the back door, dripping blood everywhere. I had to drive him to the hospital where he was stitched up; I think it was an excuse for me to have to cook him his favourite meal, Shepherd's pie followed by Apple Pie, which's is the way to my man's heart. (I didn't make shepherds pie, I made cottage pie. because I only had minced beef and as for the apple pie, I had an aunt Bessie one in the freezer).

One time I was busy cooking Wally some dinner as he had just come in from work, as I was waiting, for his meal to be ready. I started eating some prawns, then just as I, had finished eating them. I had what I thought was a bit stuck in my throat. I quickly drank a pint glass of water, but it was still there, so I downed another pint straight after. I felt ill, so I went up to the bathroom where Wally was just getting out from the bath, where I was violently sick, with that my voice went funny and I was finding it hard to breathe. Wally rushed me to the hospital; I was, given lots of tablets to take all at once. They discovered; I had become allergic to shellfish. Then about 18 months later, I picked up a tin of white crab meat from the supermarket, went home and made myself a lovely brown bread sandwich. The little boy I

Such A Lucky Lady

was looking after was having a nap, so with feet up and TV on, my delicious sandwich and cup of coffee to hand, I settled down to enjoy. Well, I did enjoy it. It was delicious, and then after I had finished my coffee, I got up to wash my plate and cup up, when I felt that my face felt very strange. I went to look in the mirror, and I couldn't believe what a hideous thing was looking back at me. My face looked like I had been, used as a punching bag, I grabbed the little boy, I was looking after. Then drove to the hospital again. I then was given lots of pills to take and was, once again told that it was a shellfish allergy. And that I was to stay away from shellfish. I phoned Wally, who was at work. He came straight down, saying what do you think you were doing? You know you can't eat shellfish. I hadn't even though that a crab was a fish. Then the last time and hopefully this will be the last, we were at a beautiful family wedding, Wally had drunk one too many, so decided to go back to the car in the car park to sober up. While I stayed and continued having fun,

I walked over to the buffet, still talking as I do. (No not to myself, I'm not that mad yet?). I picked up a couple of things and put them on a plate then I popped two little-breaded things into my mouth. Well just as I had swallowed them, I knew what was happening. So I asked a waitress to walk with me to the car, as I had some Piriton in the car, as we got to the car Wally had locked his self in, so it was a job to wake him up, but I did. I took the Piriton, and it worked. But it took nearly two weeks before I was over it. I went to my doctor who said that I must carry an EpiPen with me at all times, just in

case. Touch wood I haven't had to use it yet fingers crossed I never have to.
The school had asked the children to save any pennies and bring them to school. So I placed a bucket in the den for them to fill up. Then in the summer holidays. I encourage the older ones to organise a fate outside our house. They made posters and put them up around the estate, and posted notes through all the houses on our estate. Inviting them to join in and help them raise money for the school. They, really got into it, they iced and decorated biscuits, made juice drinks, and they even made friendship bracelets. Along with a table set up with some board games, like droughts, snakes and ladders, snap, lucky duck with numbers on the bottom in a paddling pool with ducks from another game, etc. Nail and face painting, they collected toys and books to sell, plus lots more games. We had a two seated rounder about and a bouncy castle that they charged 10p ago. They spent weeks preparing it all, even down to making the bunting. I had told them that half the money was for the school, and the other half they could use to buy something for the den. Wally told them that he would match whatever they made as well. Well, they did a fantastic job, they made enough to buy a children's karaoke machine. And with all the pennies they Had been putting into the bucket they had £100 for the school.

We had a great holiday when we went to Florida with Jo-Ann Tony and her four younger boys. We stayed in a villa with them all for two weeks. Wally was doing jacket potatoes one time for us all, but he accidentally put parmesan cheese on them, the smell was atrocious. See what happens when you let him loose in the kitchen while he has been drinking. He has never lived it down. On our return from Florida at the airport, Jo-Ann and I went to browse the shops, when in one, we came across a chocolate Voodoo doll. We just couldn't resist buying it as both had one person in mind, that we were going to use it on. Our thoughts were running wild with our plans. What we were going to do with it, bite its head off, stick a candle in it and watch it melt, you name it we were going to do it. One day we did get it out with every intention of putting it to good use, but when push comes to shove, we chicken out.

In 2004, We bought a villa at regal palms in Davenport Florida. It had four bedrooms; we bought it to rent out, and for ourselves for our holidays. It was in a gated complex with a lazy river and pool. Then we put a deposit down on a four bedroomed villa with its, own pool, off plan. Then before they started building our villa, the company went into liquidation. So we lost our deposit. Then when we went and stayed in our villa again, someone had broken into our lock off. That was where we placed all our personal things. When we tried to claim from the insurance, that was recommended by the company. They told us; we were, not covered, as the place was, not occupied at the time. So we lost confidence in the rental company and decided to sell up.

We then put a deposit on a new build in Spain; this was on a golf course with an enormous sun terrace on the roof, but once again the company went into liquidation so another loss for us.

It soon dawned on us that we were not supposed to live in a nice warm country. We were to spend all our hard earned money on flights to much warmer climates and to have to stay in hotels If we wanted to have a healthy colour. I persuaded Wally to buy a large sunbed along with a toning table, the one where you lay on it while it moves exercising all of your body. I still have the toning table in our spear room as thinking It may be needed one day if my joints start playing up. But we had to get rid of the sunbed as it took up too much room.

Chapter 32

Through The Pearly Gates

They say things happen in three's well in 2005 we had our three's, first in the January we got the news that my Uncle Roger had passed away.

Then in February we lost My Mother, even though she had always been ill throughout our life, it came as a shock. We were informed. My Mother was in the hospital and that her organs were not functioning properly, by Jo-Ann. Who went to see My Mother first, when we heard we went to see her as well. We were a little shocked at first because she in herself look quite well. But her appearance was none too good, for she had on a dirty nightdress, and her slippers had seen better days. She was sitting in a chair next to her bed when we arrived; we started chatting about this and that. Then My Mother told us that Rebecca was down as her next of kin as she didn't live too far from her home. That at the time seemed to make the most sense. When we left, we said that we will be down to see her very soon. Jo-Ann would go and see My Mother lots of times, as she wasn't far from the hospital. Jo-Ann would even pick Rebecca up, and they would go together sometimes.

One time Jo-Ann was visiting My Mother, when she said that she would like to see My Father, Roy (they both had always had a soft spot for each other). Jo-Ann got in touch with My Father. And they arranged for him, to come and visit My Mother. Well, as he arrived, with Jo-Ann. Rebecca stood at the entrance to My Mother's ward and told the nurses that he wasn't allowed to see her and that My Mother wouldn't want to see him. So they asked him to leave, the next rigmarole, was when My Mother asked Jo-Ann to get her some jelly, and Turkish delight. So to be on the safe side and to be sure she could have it. Jo-Ann went and checked with the nursing staff, who said, if My Mother wants it, then to let her have it. So Jo-Ann got her some and took them in for her it made her happy, but the next time Jo-Ann went to see My Mother, Rebecca mouthed off that Jo-Ann had tried to kill My Mother as My Mother was diabetic.

My Father later told me that, Rebecca had gotten him to rewrite My Mother's Will out, in October before she died. Leaving everything to Rebecca and her children, but nothing was put in her will, saying anything about us being, excluded from her funeral service. In all honesty, if I were given the choice to pick anything from My Mother's estate, to keep as a keepsake, I wouldn't have been able to. As she lost everything that may have been worth keeping in the house fire in Hillingdon, like the family's photos. My Mother had absolutely nothing of any value whatsoever.

One day after our visit to the hospital to see My Mother. I phoned Rebecca, to see how My Mother was doing. As the hospital had said it would be best if one person were, given any updates and they were to pass it on to My Mothers family. But when she answered the phone, she

Such A Lucky Lady

started having a go, saying why do you want to see your Mother, why now. I said I just what to know if My Mother needed anything, and had everything she needed or wanted, i.e. new slippers, nightdress, photos of her family. I said I'm just checking; she has whatever she requires wants or needs, as luck would have it. I was all ready for her to start, so I had turned on a dictator phone, so I was able to record the whole conversation between us. I still have it to this day as proof.

On the day, My Mother passed away 15/02/2005, I phoned the hospital as I had a weird feeling that something wasn't right, but when the nurse answered, she said hasn't your sister phone you yet? I said no. The nurse, then told me, I'm so very sorry, your Mother passed away, very peacefully half an hour ago. With that, Rebecca came to the phone, and within seconds, was shouting down the phone, saying, don't start I've just watched Mother die, in front of me, so don't start. I hadn't had a chance to open my mouth. (I bet that has shocked you all). Well, I just put the phone down on her after telling her, I'll call you later then. I left her to grieve for a few days. I just waited to hear from her. We waited and waited to hear from Rebecca about the funeral arrangements. But when we hadn't heard anything I phoned her, only to be told that My Mother had said that she didn't want me to attend her funeral. She said My Mother had even written it in her will, (Well, knowing this to be entirely untrue). I told her to show it to me then. I knew that she wasn't able to. I phoned and asked Jo-Ann and Richard only to find, that they had both also just been, informed that they were not going to be

Lady Donna Louise Wilder

allowed to go to My Mother's funeral. So we didn't know where it was going to take place. As they wouldn't tell me (this was something so unbelievable I just couldn't' believe it). So I phoned around the local undertakers in Gosport where My Mothers home was. Eventually, one said that they had a Mrs, Daphne Brian but not O'Bryan. When I asked what the arrangement were, they stated that they could only tell me if I had the password? I had, never heard anything so unbelievable in all my life. So a little while after, Jo-Ann phoned them and just said, that she was one of the people from where My Mother had lived. And that they had a collection and would like to know where to send the flowers. They told Jo-Ann that My Mother was going to be, cremated at Portchester Crematorium. When I found out, I told the rest of My Mother's family. Well on the day of My Mother's cremation, some of her family had travelled a very long way. With their flowers and wreaths, that they had made, only when we all turned up, we found that the cremation had been, moved to a different place. It was the most disgusting and despicable thing that anyone could do. My Mother only had a handful of mourners attending; we were all deprived of our rights, to say our good buys to My Mother.

I wrote a letter, and two poems to Rebecca, telling her how we thought that what she had done was so very wrong. And that she will never be forgiven, by us for her evil behaviour. I also said I was sending her these poems, and I was asking her to place them at our, My Mother's resting place. They were all sent back to me in an envelope where my name had been written like this.

Such A Lucky Lady

To Donna Louise Pearce, O'Bryan, Isaac, Farrant, Elliot, Wilder. Our postman said it looks like someone is playing a game with you

Lady Donna Louise Wilder

My Cousins On My Pearce Side

Top Left to right;
(1) Baz Moran, (2) Donna Moran, (3) Tracy Peterson, née Moran,
bottom left to right;
(1) Cara Taylor, née Pearce, (2) Amanda Pearce,

Such A Lucky Lady

The Memory Letter

Could you please find it in your heart of hearts to place these two poems in the garden of remembrance along with our Mothers ashes?
As our Mothers, Children
Donna Jo-Ann and Richard
Her son-in-law's Wally and Tony
Daughter-in-law Caroline and Tina
Her Grandchildren
Michael with Helen
Kerry with Rob
Terry
Melissa with Steve
Gemma
Bradley
Craig
Connor
Mitchell
Shane with Nicola
Haley
Charlotte with Neil
Liam
Annie
Cheryl
Brady
Lisa
Plus, our Mothers Great Grandchildren
Adam
Brendan
Lewis

Lady Donna Louise Wilder

Ethan
Plus her ex Husband Roy
Sister-in –Law, Maureen with Barry
Mother-in-law, Ann
Plus many, more to many to mention who would have liked to have said their goodbyes
But we're not allowed to grace our Mothers service with their presence
In Portchester Crematorium on Friday 25th February at 1:30 pm
We feel that our Mother should have had a much bigger and better service than the little one you, lot arranged for her.
As Roy, our Father, wrote out our Mothers last will, for her when she was in the hospital last October.
At that point, she did not mention anything about us not being allowed to go to her memorial service. If that was her wishes, then don't you think she would have said so in her last will).
So that means it was not her last wish after all
(But yours).
You should have taken the time and trouble to think about what you were doing!
(But wicked people have no conscience do they?).
All you have done is prove that you are so selfish and bitter that you will stoop so low

Even when our Mother is dead, you do not stop
You think that by not letting us go and say our goodbyes to our Mother. That you're only hurting us
But how wrong you all are
She and God will never forgive you

Such A Lucky Lady

There are at least 60 mourners that you lot have stopped from attending our Mothers service.

You may have Our Mother's body. But we have her spirit and soul.
We believe Our Mother should have been laid to rest with all the care and consideration any human being deserves.
So we have arranged our, own private Church service for Our Mother. Were all those that did not get their opportunity to say their personal goodbyes can, and a wake will follow.
Plus, we will have our very own special place where we will lay Our Mothers spirit and soul in peace and harmony, where we will all be able to visit whenever we wish.
We know that in time what you have done will play on your minds, and Will haunt you until your time is up.
But God does not let wicked, evil people like you into Heaven.
So you will not be able to meet Our Mother up there like, we will.
We know that you will not be able to live with your guilt?
But as you know we have nothing to feel guilty for,
So in the typical O'BRYAN style
We wash our hands of you all.

Lady Donna Louise Wilder

Auntie's And Uncles

Left to right;
(1) Maureen Moran, née Pearce, (2) Patricia Stephens, née Stewart, O'Bryan,
(3) Charlie Stewart, (4) Barry Moran, (5) Roger Pearce,
(6) Lorraine Pearce, née Ingleton, (7) Josephine Hone, née O'Bryan, (8) Kingsley Hone,

Such A Lucky Lady

In Memory Of Our Mother Mrs Daphne C. O'Bryan (Pearce)

I Did As You Told Me

When I was just a little girl,
You told me things I didn't know.
But most of all you told me
Something I didn't want to know,

A very special secret
That only you should know.
You made me promise, on your life
To keep it until you go.

For the secret that you told me
So many years ago.
I'll keep your special secret
Until she needs to know,

The time is sadly here now,
The time that I can tell.
But I'll lose your special secret
If I go ahead and tell,

Lady Donna Louise Wilder

I've proved that you could trust me
Your secret I did keep.
But I'll never reveal your secret
To those who long to seek,

But I'll take our special secret
And give it back to you
When we're both in heaven.
It will be just you, and me,

For God has made a heaven
A place we had in mind
Where no one there can harm us
Or judge us for our crimes

From your
Specially Selected
Daughter
Donna
x.x.x

Such A Lucky Lady

In Memory Of Our Mother
Mrs Daphne C, O'Bryan
(Pearce)

God Took You To Rest To Ease Your Pain

Your time on earth is over
A new one, just begun
No pain or tears but laughter
And joy in everyone

In heaven, you can see us
Upon you cloud nine
And see that we miss you
In our, own little minds

We know that you forgave us
In all we said and done,
You know that we're, not perfect
In everything we've done

I'm sorry we weren't with you
When you had to go,
But nobody told us
I know you did not know

Lady Donna Louise Wilder

Your world will be so different
In o so many ways
You will be able to talk to us
And help us on our ways

Today tomorrow our whole lives through
We will always remember you
Too far away for sight or speech
But not too far for our thoughts to reach

Love from your
Daughters Donna and Jo-Ann
Son Rick
Son-in-Law's Wally and Tony
Daughter-in-law's Caroline and Tina
All their Children
Your Great Grandchildren
Plus Roy and Family
x.x.x.x.x

Such A Lucky Lady

Rebecca tried to put the blame on My Auntie Jo, who no doubt had her say, but as far as I am concerned Rebecca could, and should have put her foot down, and told us where and when the service for My Mother was going to be. Even if she did it behind Auntie Jo's back. She has tried many times to speak to Jo-Ann, Richard and me telling us that we should forget it as it was a long time ago, but I don't need someone with so much bitterness and hatred in my life.

Many times I have forgiven, forgave and forgot things Rebecca had done or said like you do with your family, but, this time, she had gone way to far. Now there is no turning back not ever; she will have to wait until hell freezes over and then I will still say never.

Then on Saturday 18th June, we were having a BBQ to celebrate our 21st wedding anniversary, with family and friends. When My Father received a phone call to say that My Nan was in a bad way in the hospital, saying that he needed to get to the hospital very soon. She later passed away; we had been to see her a couple of times at the hospital, the last time we saw her we thought she was doing quite well. She had fallen over a few weeks back. Nothing had been, arranged about a wake for My Nan. everyone was just going to go back to their homes, but then someone suggested that we go and have a drink in her memory. So we landed up in a pub, where we had far too many drinks. So much so that when Wally was just about to have another whisky. That someone very kindly had just brought for him and knowing that he, and I for that matter both knew that he shouldn't, as he was driving. I tried to take it from him while we were sitting at an enormous round table; he held on tight to it, but I wasn't going to let him drink it. So I held on. Well like an arm wrestle match I won. the whisky was tipped onto the table. Then to my horror, he tipped the table up and drank it from the table. (yuck.)

Such A Lucky Lady

Chapter 33

Jet Setting

March 2005 we went to Florida, with my Auntie Maureen, Uncle Barry, Jo-Ann and Tony, Michael and his friend Helen joined us a day later. We had such a laugh with lots of drinking. I have to say the funniest thing I did with Wally was when we were in Florida staying in our villa; Michael had come to join us, he arrived on a different flight. When he arrived, we went to get some more drinks from the local supermarket that was in the complex. As we had got too much drink to carry, Wally decided to take the shopping trolley back with us to the villa. So as we passed the reception office on the compound, I saw a policeman sitting in his police control car; he was working on his computer.

As Wally, and the others were ahead, I went over to the office and asked him if he would go and tell my husband, (the man with the shopping trolley) (Wally). That it is an offence, to remove the shopping carts, from the shops. He just continued working, so I thought he wasn't going to do anything. So I kept walking back with everyone. I was just a few steps behind, when ahead of everyone, a police patrol car came down the road, heading towards us all. With its lights on, and then stopped right by Wally. He stepped out and said "sir, do you know it is a federal offence to remove the shopping carts from the shopping mall". As he was saying this everyone just carried on walking. I, on the other hand, was doubled over in stitches. Wally told the officer; I'm sorry officer, I didn't know I, promise to take it back.

For my 50th birthday, we went for a meal and to see an Abba tribute night, with some family and friends. My sister Jo-Ann came with two gift bags full of lots of individual gifts that she insisted I opened in front of everyone. Well, she got me, some big girl knickers, size 22 inch, Velcro rollers and a hair net, incontinence pads, some steradent, hair dye, vitamins, a trowel to apply my make-up, bib and sipper cup, and many elder people's essentials.
My dear husband gave me some beautiful gifts, along with a few days spent in London in a lovely hotel, with shopping and the theatre to see Phantom of the Opera.

My Auntie Maureen asked Wally where he was going to take me for my 50th birthday. He said he had no idea, so she said, why don't you take her to Goa, well when Wally said it to me, I said if it's good enough for Auntie Maureen then it's good enough for me, he then Said you do know it's India? I didn't know where it was; it just sounded like it was some were exotic. As I heard that Auntie Maureen had said, that she and Uncle Barry were going with their Daughter, (my cousin) Tracy and her boys for Christmas. So I thought why don't we go with them. So we decided to go, so I went ahead and booked it. But first, we had our two week's holiday, to Florida in November. In our villa with my sister Jo-Ann, her husband Tony, my brother Richard, my Auntie Maureen, and Uncle Barry.

Such A Lucky Lady

When we got back from Florida, I started packing for our next holiday to Goa for Christmas, we were going for two weeks, when we arrived on Christmas Eve, a few hours after Auntie Maureen Uncle Barry and my cousin Tracy with her boys Casey and Lewis. Wally wasn't at all impressed with the place and was just about ready to get the next flight back home. I, on the other hand, was willing to give it a go. Wally kept saying this place is such a dump, (words to that effect) well it's not the cleanest of places we have ever been but within a couple of days, we just knew we would definitely be coming back to Goa.

I went to the meeting with the tour operator where I booked two trips one for us to go and spend a night in a sheik's tent on a quiet beach. The second one was a day on a boat trip where we could go fishing, snorkelling and or swimming, and then we would land on a beach and have a BBQ on a private island. Well, when I got back and told Wally. He said no way, am I going camping, I done that with the scouts when I was a kid. I tried telling him that it wasn't anything like scout camp, and anyway, it was for my Birthday, and it was what I wanted to do. Well, the first one was the boat trip, we stopped just short of the island and dropped anchor. I caught a couple of fish with a hook on a line, and that was wrapped around a small bit of old polystyrene so it would float. Wally didn't find any fish. Then as Wally had a bit of a cold, he decided not to go snorkelling. But me as I'm game for anything thought I would get in the water and snorkel with my lifejacket on of course. As I, can't swim well, it wasn't long before I was out of breath. So as I reached a rock that was sticking out of the water, I managed to get on it. But with all the coral that was on it. I got scratched to bits. Once I got my breath back, I backstroked it back, to the boat again. Wally had to help me up into the boat as I was out of breath; we continue to the island where we had a lovely BBQ with fresh fish, not my ones as they were too small, and plenty of alcohol.

Our next trip was camping. Wally was not at all impressed his expression said it all. We arrived by coach at a secluded place, called Montego Bay, right on the beach. The tents were white they had a little porch with two sun chairs, and table outside and a door mat. Leading into a zipped door, on unzipping it and going inside, we had a double bed, wardrobe, side tables, and an electric fan, lights and even an electric mosquito killer. Then there was a zipped doorway at the back when Wally opened it; he said I thought you said we were going camping, this isn't camping as it's got its own En-suite. We spent that evening sitting on the beach watching the sunset it was beautiful,

Then a few days later we were approached to buy a timeshare, we went ahead and signed up for one. We have used it only twice, as after staying and socialising with the locals. We found that it was hard to see them being verbally abused, by some of the residents, that thought they were better than them. We had a fantastic time so much so that when we arrived back home. We booked up to go back eight weeks later, this time, Jo-

Such A Lucky Lady

Ann came with us, she loved it just like we did we all had lots of fun,
One time we had been out for the day, and when we arrived back at our hotel, our intention was for us to have a shower and to get ready to go out for a nice dinner. Well, Jo-Ann went to her room, to get ready. I got into our shower before Wally. While I was in there, I couldn't remember bringing in the camera. I shouted, to Wally, "Darling did I put the camera on the little table" not finding it there he called back No you've gone and left it in the taxi, that's clever of you now we have no camera, and we have lost all those photos that we took. I got out of the shower and said, I will go downstairs to reception and phone the taxi driver as he had given us his card. Wally said you will never get it back, well I grabbed a long flowy dress and slipped my flip flops on, and that was all, I phoned up and yes the taxi driver had just arrived home and found it and was just on his way back to leave it at the hotel reception desk.

Well, I was going back to our room thinking how lucky we were, then as I got to the room, I found Jo-Ann, was already, and so was Wally they were now waiting for me. I grabbed a long flowy skirt, put it on under my dress, lifted my dress off, then put on a top that didn't require you to wear, an upper topper flopper stopper. (bra) And of we went, well as I was getting into the taxi, I remembered that I had forgotten to put on any knickers. Well, like everything I confided in Jo-Ann, (what a big mistake). All evening I was reminded of how drafty it was, and how I was going commando. She even suggested that Wally, should, at least, offer to give me his boxers. At one point Wally did say, did I want him too, I told him that it would be better than nothing. He went off to the men's washroom but came back with a smile on his face saying, no way. As he knew, Jo-Ann would just tell everyone that he didn't have any on. Then Jo-Ann informed me that as soon as I was on the steps of the hotel she was going to lift my skirt up so everyone could see what I had for breakfast; I was a nerves wreck, lucky Wally was with me to protect me as anyone that knows Jo-Ann knows she would. Jo-Ann also got hooked on the place, so we would all go twice a year for two weeks at a time until January 2010.

When we were in Goa with Jo-Ann, we had worked out that the locals believed anything we said to them. So one time we told this lad that parts of a body had been found buried on the beach and that the police were still looking for other parts of the body. Then two days later I took a dummy arm that we had brought with us and buried it at the foot of the sunbed, I was laying on, and then I placed my flip flops on top. I asked the young lad to pass my flip flops. As he did, he saw the hand and fell back in a state of shock.

The best one was when we were in a taxi with Jo-Ann, Wally was in the passenger seat when the driver asked him what his name was Wally replied Charles, as they find it hard to pronounce Wally. But the man couldn't pronounce it, so Jo-Ann tried to help him by saying, you know Charles as in Prince Charles. Well with that he seemed to believe that he had Royal tee in his car. As he said Oh my, you come to our country. So then Jo-Ann

Such A Lucky Lady

piped up and said, you mustn't tell anyone we are here, so no paparazzi no photos don't tell anybody ok. Well as he was driving he noticed a man on the corner of the road with a camera, so he very quickly turned down a side road, when Wally said this isn't the right way. He said a man with a camera no photos. When we arrived at our destination, he got out of his taxi, then as Wally went to pay him, the man went to shake Wally's hand, well then Jo-Ann piped up and said don't touch the prince. Word soon got about so in Goa Wally, and I are known as Prince and Princess in some of the shacks we go to on Baga Beach.

Every time we went to Goa, I would collect things I could take to give to them. I heard about a shop that was closing down, and they sold used football shirts. So I ask the owner what he was going to do with them if he had some left on his last day, The Man told me that he would give them to the local charity shop. So I asked if he would be willing to donate them to the children in Goa. He said go ahead you can have them all, well there was over 150, we only took half of them with us this time, and then the other half the next time we went out to Goa. Along with the mobile phones that I had also managed to collect. Then a lady from the school heard what we were doing and gave us lots of Indian clothes from her daughter and family for the little girls.

On holiday in Goa one time with My Sister Jo-Ann, Paul, and my nephew, Terry. We decided that we would like to book a day trip to an island by boat, spending the day there. We had been talking about it to a lad, we all had got to know by the name of Sam. He told us that he would take us five, plus his friend that way we would have the boat all to ourselves. Sam filled the boat with food and drinks, and off we went, Sam first sailed around the beached ship the Princess that had run aground, and then Sam said as a treat he was going to take us to a very private island. When we arrived there was this concrete walkway that was a bit broken, we all got out of the boat and started to walk, then as we were going higher and higher, I thought it strange that we were walking on what looked like a Tarmac path.

There was a building that looked derelict it had no doors windows or roof, and we still went up higher and higher. We then heard a plane flying over, and it began to circle then when Sam looked out to the Sea he said, he has got to go and see the boat that had just come over, so off he went. By this time, we were all sweltering, so followed him down, as we got down Sam came over and said for us all get into the boat and go over to the other boat, he also told us to say that we had been on the island before. We got into our boat and Sam rowed us over to there's, there were about six uniformed men on the boat, they used a hook and pulled our boat over, and one man said, what are you doing on the island. We said just looking around, he then said did you take any photos, to which we said yes, as we had so he said give me your camera, as the man was looking he said, how much you pay this boy, (Sam). We told the Navy Police that we hadn't paid Sam anything and that we were just friends with him. My sister Jo-Ann said pointing to Sam. Sam, he is my son, I come to Goa a long time ago, get pregnant, have the baby, look at the baby, think yuck, so leave the baby on the beach. We all started laughing; even the man looking at the photos on my camera cracked his face. Then Jo-Ann said you like the pictures, don't we look beautiful. He then said where are your passports? We told him we didn't bring them with us on a boat trip. He then said, that it was a naval island, and we were not, allowed to go on it, he then let us go on our way. Sam was just trying to give us more for our money, as we had always been good to him in the past. He would call us Auntie & Uncle. Our trip before he even spent a lot of money on us buying Wally & Terry a shirt each and Jo-Ann and I a beaded bag when you think that a good day's salary at the time was around £4-£5. When he gave then to us, we said, "Sam, you shouldn't off", he said, "I, have just been to church, where we were praying for our family, and I thought of you". He told us that he thinks of you as his family, so he had to buy a gift for his family we were so touched".

Early in 2007, we went to Spain where we found a lovely place. So we put a deposit on a new build, this house was on a golf course with a huge sun terrace on the roof. But once again the company went into liquidation before they even started building our villa so another loss for us.

My Father in the summer of 2007 was, diagnosed with cancer and was in the hospital in Northampton. Jo-Ann, I went to visit him a few times.

In 2007, we sold our house in Old Stratford and moved to Northampton. After I had a big row, with Wally. I was in our town with a friend one day, when I saw our old next door neighbour from Conniburrow, the woman that caused so much trouble. She was coming out of a shop, as she saw me and just grinned at me, but said hello to my friend, I felt sick, my friend stated that she knew her from work. I didn't tell My friend that I knew her as well. My friend started giving me all the gossip about her, telling me that she was still single, and the women at work would keep well away from her. She had gotten herself a reputation as a marriage wrecker; My Friend said that she had split a couple up and was boasting about how she knows how to get any man.

When Wally came home from work, he didn't know what hit him. I told him that she was still on the lookout, and I wasn't happy that she was so close to our home. So I wanted to move again. He wasn't at all happy about it at first, but after a bit, it made a lot of sense for us to downsize and move on to something smaller, as by now the house prices had gone up a lot, so we had made a tidy little some. Also, we didn't need a four bedroomed house just to our self's we were just rattling around in it.
So like everything once I have decided on something I get stuck into it, so that is what we did.

We rented a house for 6 months until we found a lovely townhouse at 43, Lime Street Rushden Northamptonshire NN10 6DW. I continued to child-mind two girls that I had been already looking after in Stoney Stratford as they lived in Rushden then after a bit word got around at the school, so I was approached to look after more children and Wally would drove to Alpla until we both decided to retire in October 2010.

That Christmas Wally and I were spending Christmas Day with our niece, Tanya and her family, (my Sister-in-law Sheila's Daughter). I had put my handbag in her hall cupboard, so I didn't get the message until we were leaving later that night.

That, My Father, had passed away earlier on in the day. On 25th DECEMBER 2007 in Milton Keynes Hospital from cancer. (That was the day I became an orphan). We let his last three children make all the arrangements, even though I was his eldest child I thought it only right. He had spent their whole life with them. Rebecca told Nikki (Nicola) That My Father's dying wish, was to be, buried with My Mother. She even asked if she could have back the silver chain that she had brought him, even at My Father's funeral, Rebecca tried to start an argument with Jo-Ann and Me. We didn't or wouldn't stoop to her level. My cousin Donna's Son Curtis stepped in and told her this isn't the time or the place.

We celebrated our 25th wedding anniversary in June 2009 by renewing our vows, in a church in Higham Ferrers, just down the road from where we lived, in Lime Street Rushden. We even exchanged new wedding rings. We had decided that it would be nice to do the same as we had done for our first Wedding 25 years earlier. By providing a free bar, with plenty of food. Some of the 12 flower girls we had, were the daughters, of some of our original bridesmaids. Along with some of the little girls,

Lady Donna Louise Wilder

I was child-minding at the time. We even had some of the children that I had looked after over 20 years ago turn up to celebrate with us, and it meant a lot more as we were both much more relaxed, with lots of family & friends old and new. We played three very appropriate songs at the service. First, we walked down the aisle to Through the Years sung by Kenny Rodgers, before our vowels were read out, we played.
You are the love of my life sung by George Benson & Roberta Flack.
Then to finish, we walked out the church to
Hear and now sung by Luther Van Dross

Chapter 34

Early Retirement

We went out to Goa for Wally's 60th Birthday, for three weeks. While we were there, we got talking to some lovely couples, some who told us that they had sold their house back in the UK, and we're living in a static holiday home, down on the coast throughout the summer, then renting an apartment in Goa for the winter time for six months. When we got back home, we went and looked at some holiday homes, but we decided that it would be more beneficial to us to downsize and rent rather than buy. That way we would be able to rent anywhere we liked in the UK. Our first choice was going to be down the coast somewhere, so we started planning, first was getting our heads around the fact we wouldn't have any income until Wally got his pension, some five years later.

Our plan was to do and go wherever we wanted to for the next 5 Years, spending some quality time with each other while we were both fit and able. (Like so many people we have known have waited until they retired only to pass away soon after). We needed to de-clutter all the toys from the playroom, so we packed most of the Toys up, and my dear sister Jo-Ann allowed us to store them in her large shower room downstairs. We put the house on the market and made our plans to go and rent in Goa for five months; we found an apartment through one of the couples we had met. I wasn't sure how I would cope with living in a rundown place, but after a while, you just adapt to your surroundings. It wasn't long before I realised that material things just don't matter. As you can't take them with you when your number is up. I, like most people had fallen into the I must have its syndrome.

Wally found and brought his retirement car a sovereign Jaguar; then a buyer was found for our house. But as house prices had dropped a great deal since we had brought we were going to be losing a big fat £70,000 on the sale. We had to make the choice do we wait till the price goes up, or do we just count our losses and go with the flow, so to speak. Our gut feeling was to, let's just do it; life is far too short to hang around. So on the 11th October 2010, we sold up and put all our belongings into storage. We stayed with my sister Jo-Ann in her house in Gosport, till the beginning of November, when we went out to Goa for five whole months. It was fantastic we didn't have a care in the world we had no bills to worry about we were in fact, homeless.

Every day the sun was shining, the sky was blue, and we met more and more long-timers who have become such lovely friends to this day.

We had decided we would arrange a party for the street children, so we paid the fruit lady to cook for us 100 portions of vegetable rice. So each child was given a tinfoil container with veg rice with a spoon, a cup of fizzy drink, Coke or Fanta, banana, a packet of crisps and a packet of biscuits sweets and a wrapped up TY beanie bear as a gift, and a blown up balloon. They took forever for us to blow up. We provide cricket bats, balls, hula hoops, skipping ropes, Frisbees, footballs, etc. The children came and played for hours. It was such a lovely feeling, seeing them play and having so much fun. Then a few days after, we gave 50 party boxes away to some of the children we had got to know from the beach; Inside was a packet of crisps biscuits sweets and another TY Bear. Then we filled up 20 carrier bags. That Asda had kindly donated to us. With 10 x packets of chips, 10 x packets of biscuits, some powdered drinks that they just had to add water to and a six pack of Maggi noodles that the children loved to eat.

We then gave out pieces of paper that I had put a number on, for 1-20. That I gave to the children that I had come to know, who came from large families. I told them that they had to give the ticket to their mum. And tell her to come and see me at 4 pm on the beach with the number. Where I would give them a bag as a gift, we wanted to give it as a little hamper for their family.

We picked a lot of brains out in Goa, but still found our plans suited us. So we had a look on the Internet at the Right Move site, for somewhere to rent. We knew we would have to get something with a garage and a large place. As we had to downsize all our belongings that were in storage. We were thinking of the South Coast first, as it was quite central to the rest of the coastal resorts. We found a three-bed townhouse with a garage that was in Gosport. So after looking at the photos, we decided it was much better than the apartment we were staying in at the moment in Goa, and we had managed quite well with the changes. We got back to the UK at the beginning of April, we first went and agreed to rent the house, that was found, on Right move, but had to wait for two weeks before we could move into it. So as we had an invite to a friend's party in Bunbury, we travelled to visit My sister-in-law Sheila's, where we were going to stay for a few days. I took with me the new epilator, a gift Wally had kindly bought me before we left for Goa, (I found it a bit painful to use at first but bearable).

I went into Shelia's Bathroom and started to get ready with my epilator. I first used it on one leg, and then I put that leg down and continue with my other leg then putting that foot down, I noticed lots of blood on the bathroom floor, both my legs were bleeding a lot, it just wouldn't stop. What had happened is that the epilator pulls each hair out, so as my body hadn't adjusted from the long haul flight. So everywhere that hair had been pulled out from began to bleed I was a bit scared at first as it took ages for it to stop. Wally just wrapped a towel around both my legs until it stopped, luckily, I had some dark trousers to wear as we were going out.

Within two weeks from coming back from Goa, we had moved into 4, The Mews Trinity Green Gosport Hampshire PO12 1EZ. We filled the garage to the top, and the spare rooms. Then was the mammoth task of downsizing, we done a couple of car boots and got a dealer to buy lots of things at ridiculous prices.

Such A Lucky Lady

We have also prepaid for our funeral as we don't want to be a burden on our family. We have decided that whichever one is, called for first. Will be buried in a Double plot. With a headstone and kerb memorial that shouldn't need any looking after, and with only one flower vase as we're not expecting many visitors.

I am planning on, being buried in my fur coat. Wally had bought it for me back in 1984 for Christmas, it cost over £1000.00 at the time, and he even had my initials DLW stitched on the inside. We first would send it to Harrods in London as it had to be, stored in a cold volt during the summertime. I haven't been able to sell it, as it's not popular to own one, so it only seems fitting to buried it along with me, I do intend to have a dress and underwear on as well. (as I don't want to be, known as Donna, fur coat and no knickers).

We were all settled in and having a great time; we had booked to go back to Goa for another five months from November 2011 to April. We started renting a beautiful villa, with all the mod cons (well for Goa they were Modern). In the garden lived a lovely old lady and her family, she would sleep under our window right by the steps. She looked very, old. And would be up at the crack of dawn sweeping the loose dust that was on the solid ground. Then filling any vessel with water from the well, that she drew on her own. One day Wally had gone around to the little shop to get a few bits for us, like milk eggs. etc. When he got to the shop the old lady was just being served with her shopping Wally told the shop lady that he would pay for the old lady's shopping. She was very great full and looked up at the sky and nodded, and even blew him a kiss. When Wally came back to the villa, he said well that backfired on me. He said I just offered to buy the old lady's shopping, it was a carry a bag full, So I said that was sweet love. He then told me it cost him 20p. Yes, that's right 20 pence, hey big spender.

On Christmas Eve. I placed a gift under her cover while she was sleeping, so that when she woke up she had a gift on Christmas Day. It was two saris. Like the ones that she was wearing, but her ones were all torn and made from scraps of material. Then in the morning, we gave her a box of groceries for her family. We went away one time early as we were going to stay in a beach hut on another beach for the night; again we had a lovely time. But on our return to the villa the old lady (who I might add couldn't speak any English., and we couldn't understand her at all). Started waving her arms about saying something and coaxing us to go around the back of the villa with her. When we got there, she showed us that we had left the back door open. Wally had forgotten to lock it; her daughter-in-law told us that the old lady had stayed on guard at the bottom of the steps all day and night until we returned. Love her.

We have stayed there three times in total each for five months, from November to April until 2014. That was our last visit to Goa. (so far). It wouldn't be fair to go until, Wally doesn't have to wear the compression socks, as we both enjoy spending a lot of time on the beach, he would be so uncomfortable. But we hope to visit again sometime soon.

Such A Lucky Lady

After spending so much time in Goa, it has helped me tremendously. I can now remove items from the tumble dryer and fold them up without ironing them, but I have to put them away immediately before I get a chance to think about it.

In August 2011, Wally's Mum (My Mother-in-law) had a fall and broke her hip, so she had to be taken to the hospital. Unfortunately, she passed away. Vera was a lovely lady, who lived for her children. She had 11 children, and we have lost count on how many grandchildren, great-grandchildren, and even great, great, grandchildren she has. But it most definitely runs into a very lot. The family did her proud, and she was laid to rest with her husband, who had passed away way back in 1967. I got on very well with My Mother-in-law, it wasn't long before she could see that I was right for her beloved son Wally. As I made him happy and that is all a mother wants for their children, to be happy.

Lady Donna Louise Wilder

My Sister-In-Law's

Large photo left to right back row; Vera Whelan, née O'Conner, Wilder, Jackie Wilder, Bottom row left to right; Sylvia Shaw, née Wilder, Christine McCullough, née Westerman, Wilder, Vera Wilder, née Hook, (Mother-in-law). Sheila Hogan, née Earl, Wilder, Mandy Gittings, née Wilder, Middle row; (1) Elizabeth Wilder, née Atkins, (2) Dot Wilder, née Briggs, (3) Diane Wilder, née Sutherland, (4) Brenda Wilder, née Deacon, Bottom row; (1) Caroline O'Bryan, née Stutz, (2) Vicky O'Bryan, née Baker, (3) Tina Staunton, née O'Bryan, née Bagwell, (4) Thi Bich Van O'Bryan, née Tran

Chapter 35

Family Meeting

As my cousin Mandy was going to be over in the UK. from Los Angeles, at the same time as we were going to be arriving back home from Goa in 2012. The arrangements had been made for us long before we even left for Goa for our five month's holiday, with Mandy via Facebook we had already booked our hotel for when we arrived back. We would stay in a hotel the night we landed so we could meet up the next day. We hadn't seen each other for over 30 years. Jo-Ann and Richard were also going to meet up as well with us.

But a few days before we left Goa to fly back home to England. Mandy text to me to say that Rebecca wanted to meet up at the same time. Mandy told me that she had spoken to Jo-Ann and Richard who both had stated that they didn't want to meet up if Rebecca was going to be there, and It was up to me if I did. I said that as Rebecca wasn't working she could off come anytime in the two weeks that Mandy had been over in the UK. I told Mandy that I wouldn't meet her then. But after a bit, Mandy text back to say that her daughter had told her that she should keep to our original arrangements. Well, they had all been made such a long while back.

So, the new arrangements were that we meet in the morning up until 1 pm. then she would meet up with

Rebecca after. So that is what we did. It was great seeing her again, we got on well, and we were invited to go and visit them in Los Angeles later that year, we went to stay for three weeks it was fantastic, Mandy showed us to our room it was lovely and cosy. By the bed was some shelves, and on them, I noticed an ornament of an old lady holding some balloons. I went to pick it up to see the maker, saying to Wally this, is made by Royal Doulton it's called the old lady balloon seller. I couldn't pick it up; it had been stuck down. My heart sank I said to Wally "they have only stuck things down so I can't pinch anything". Wally said don't be so silly when I finished unpacking; I went into see Mandy and asked her about the ornaments. She just laughed and said it's because we have earthquake sometimes; I said, I thought it was because of Auntie Pat's ring that I took when I was 17 years old. We met all Mandy's family, and some of her friends, my cousin Stephen and 2nd cousin Mikala, plus my Auntie Jo. I wasn't expecting Auntie Jo to have changed her mind about what she thought of me.

Well, our meeting with Auntie Jo went very well. She was very civil to me, and we talked a bit, and when we left, she said see you again. We had such a brilliant time and we were made to feel so very welcome. On our last day, we were out for dinner with Mandy and her family. When my Auntie Jo phoned Mandy to ask if we had left yet, as she had something that she wanted to give to me. Mandy drove us over to see her when we got to her house, Auntie Jo, handed me a little ring box saying I've never given you much before, I'll like you to have this, her eyes were watering a bit, my heart sank.

Such A Lucky Lady

I thought to myself please God not that b----y ring from Auntie Pat's. But when I opened it there was a lovely old gold necklace inside, I said thank you so much it means a lot.

We were invited back to Los Angeles again the next year. This time, to join in the celebrations off my cousin Mandy's second daughter Jade's wedding, to Grieg. The location was stunning. But I must say it was a privilege to be a part of a very special day. I got to meet Judy and Sue, again the last time I saw them was at Judy's wedding to Jack when Mandy and I were bridesmaids. We were all staying at Auntie Jo and Stephen's house this time. When it was time for Sue and Judy to go home, Stephen took them to the airport. Then when he got back Auntie Jo said, "where were those two ladies and who were they", Stephen told her but she didn't remember that they were her sister-in-law's, then she said to him when is that other lady going he can stay but she can go, meaning Wally and me.

Well, the next day when we were leaving I said thank you for letting us stay to which she told me you're welcome to stay anytime. What with he forgetting people and going out and getting lost plus forgetting to eat, it wasn't long after that it was discovered that poor Auntie Jo had dementia. That would explain the strange story's she had previously told us, about how she was at Buckingham Palace one day when Princess Diana drove passed and told her to come over and get in the car with her. and that how she didn't like it when she went to Australia (somewhere she had never been to), along with the episode we had with her the first time we took her out. I had offered to take Auntie Jo with her favourite Yorkshire Terrier Reggie to the local park. She told me that she often goes for a walk on her own with him. Well, the park is on the opposite side of the road to her house, which means you have to cross a very wide main road. To cross there are traffic lights at the crossways when the lights turn red there is a hand sign, and you have to wait till the sign turns to white, with a person walking, and then it is safe to go. Well, we reached the crossroads, and I pressed the button, before I had time to turn around, My Auntie Jo, had started walking across the road. She had reached half way. (how I don't know). Luckily the car drivers obviously not in any hurry, were kind enough to slow down for her; she was completely unaware of what she was doing. My stomach was turning I felt sick, just thinking how do I explain to My cousin that I hadn't looked after there Mum properly. Wally and I did manage to get Auntie Jo home safely, then not long after Auntie Jo had a fall at home when Stephen was at work so poor Auntie Jo was laying on the floor for hours, as by now Auntie Jo had dementia as many a time she had gone out and got lost,

Mandy and Stephen spent a long time hunting for a suitable caring and comfortable place for their Mum to go and live, they eventually found one that suited her needs. Luckily it is not too far so they can visit and she comes to any events, or family party's that they hold. (How I wish we had been close with my cousins when we decided to purchase our holiday Home in Florida. As that would never have happened, we definitely would have brought in Los Angeles).

When we got back, we had my lovely Sister Jo-Ann's Wedding to help out with all the finishing touches. I made the order of service booklets and the wedding invitations for My Sister Jo-Ann and Paul's Wedding, I even sent, an invitation to Her Majesty the Queen. Inviting her to the wedding, well we are related, and would you believe my sister got a reply back?

I made up a private Facebook page as a joke for, A Liz Queen. Where I invited her along with everyone else on the event page on Facebook, I replied on behalf of Liz Queen saying. I would be delighted to attend your very special day, how wonderful of you to invite me to a very special event what is the dress code, as one would not want to upstage the bride. So looking forward to the 24th August this will be a day to remember. One is overjoyed. Unfortunately, her Majesty was unable to attend on the day. Jo-Ann became Mrs Paul Davies as she remarried in Trinity Church Gosport. On Saturday 23/08/2013. I was honoured to be her matron of honour on her very special day.

While we were in Goa the last time, just after January 2014. I just happen to have a look at our lottery results as we do it online. I hadn't checked them for some time, when I noticed that we had won, not once but twice. Being me and not keeping secrets from anyone. I put on Facebook that we had won, well everyone that knows me knew it wasn't going to be the big win, apart from one very nosey person who couldn't wait to ask how much. When she asked, I said I don't discuss my finances with anyone. Thinking that was it. Then down the beach, the next day she tried a different tactic, telling me, my friend has asked me to ask you how much have you won. I couldn't believe what I was hearing. So I said when your friend comes over, I will ask her how much she has in her bank. To which the woman said, she won't like that. Then not wanting to leave it at that, later that afternoon she said, I don't think you should advertise it on Facebook. As someone could try to break into the villa and steal it. (if we had won the money it wouldn't be in Goa).

Well a couple of nights later, we were out having a great time with some of our lovely friends, we were all talking about what we would do if it had been the big one. Well, I don't know what came over me, I just saw a lovely picture of us all celebrating with a bottle of champagne. So I asked the owner of the bar if he could let us borrow, 12 champagne glasses and have them filled with soda water, (well in photos it does look like the real thing) so we could take a photo. He said I can lend you a bottle if you like for your photo, but don't open it unless you're going to pay for it. So we all posed for the photo, and then I uploaded it to Facebook, still it was eating away at the woman. She said the next day if you keep spending your money like that it will soon run out. (if only).

When we landed back in the UK, we were greeted with the cold and wind that we call home. Poor Wally came down with the sniffles, He was coughing all night long,

Such A Lucky Lady

he said to me, am I keeping you awake darling, I said don't worry, he then said, if I am you can always go and sleep, in the other room (cheeky sod). As he was suffering from a bad cold, he decided to put on a polo neck jumper before going up the town one day. He tucked it into his trousers then put a jumper on top along with his coat hat and scarf; his gold chain was around his neck under all of this. When Wally got up the next morning and went to put his chain on, he couldn't find it. (Wally is a creature of habit he keeps his chain and signet ring in the same place). We both came to the same conclusion that he must have lost it downtown,

Wally retracted his tracks and asked in all the places that he had been, but with no luck. It just didn't make any sense, as we both agreed, that it should have fallen inside his polo neck jumper. Well, weeks and months went by, and then one day as I had decided to sort out the chest of drawers, where Wally used to keep his chain. In the top draw was his chain. I put it on and calmly walked into the lounge with it on. (trying to keep a straight face). I began talking to Wally, and then he noticed it on me, he said that's my chain, with a great big grin on his face. I think It was my fault as I must have dropped it into the top draw when I was polishing the sides.

My cousin Stephen in Los Angeles asked if we would like to house/dog sit for a couple of weeks. As he needed to go and work away in Hawaii on a TV show, the wheel of fortune. And as My cousin Elaine and her Daughter Julie, who I haven't seen for over 40 years, were coming over to Los Angeles for Elaine's 60th Birthday. We decided we had to make it a longer holiday. So we booked to go for just over two months. Then two weeks before we were due to fly out. Wally developed deep vein thrombosis. DVT. after checking many times with lots of doctors at the hospital. It was decided that he would be okay to fly, as he was taking thinner blood tablets and wearing compression socks.

So we went and had another fantastic holiday. We met up with My second cousin Mikala and her partner Steve at their apartment in Marina Del Rey. They took us out for the day on his lovely yacht, sailing around Santa Monica. And we made another trip to Las Vegas, where we went to see some lovely shows. Then before we left to come home My cousin Mandy, arranged a lovely BBQ for my Birthday where I met some lovely friends.

Such A Lucky Lady

Chapter 36

Living The High Life

Where we are living now in Gosport. We are right opposite Gunwharf-Quays. When they have fireworks we go one floor up to the observatory so we are 16 floors up, which gives us fantastic parametric views. We can see the Isle of White, and Southampton, from up there. We had a great sighting from our window of the Theodore Roosevelt aircraft carrier; that was moored out in Stokes Bay in March 2015. Much better than when we went down to the beach to see it, plus the grounded cargo ship The Hoegh Osaka.

We bought a yearly ticket for the Portsmouth Historic Dockyard. Where they have lots of attractions, like The HMS Victory, HMS Warrior 1860, HMS M.33. We go on the Harbour tours, The Mary Rose Museum, we can also go to the Royal Navy Submarine Museum, Royal Marines Museum, and the Explosion Museum of Naval Firepower, this entitles us to visit all year round. It's great value for money. We also booked to go to the Victorian Festival of Christmas at the Dockyard I would highly recommend it as we had a great time; unfortunately, we will miss it this year. As were be away in Los Angeles.

We didn't enjoy staying home for Christmas last year, as we were on our own. You see we had gotten used to spending it on the beach or with children around, so it was just like any other day for us. So this year should make up for it as we will be with Family in Los Angles We will be there for Thanksgiving, Christmas and the New Year. Who knows, where we will be next Christmas. It looks like now that Michael and Kelly live much closer it could be with them? Wally's was only on Rivaroxaban Xarelto (Anticoagulant) the Blood thinning tablets for six months, but has to wear the compression socks for a total of two years, so he only has six months left to have to wear them.

Out with My Auntie Maureen and Uncle Barry one day, I for a joke looked at my phone and pretended that there was some news, saying that the government has decided that anyone with a spare room will have to take in homeless people. They would be, paid £25 per person and each single room can house six people, and a double room can accommodate ten people. As I was saying this, I was in stitches, as Uncle was nearly foaming at the mouth. I tried to make it sound a bit better by telling him that the government will not expect you to provide bathroom facilities as they would place a porter loo in your back garden,

Auntie knew it was all a joke but poor Uncle began to think it was for real, he actually said he would s..t on their beds so that they wouldn't want to stay. He spent most of the evening pondering about it, and then the next day we went to see a friend of his who had a farm. Then as we were sitting in the farmer's kitchen having a lovely cup of coffee, when suddenly Uncle said to his mate

Such A Lucky Lady

"have you heard of what the government are going to do". My heart sank, I thought oh no what have I done but I just couldn't confess, I just let him tell him, his mate said well no way I'm having any of them living here, I'll just dig a big hole and bury them, obviously only joking. when we got back Auntie cooked us a lovely meal then we all sat down for an evening of drinking that starts at exactly 9 pm in their house, after just one drink Uncle said, he was going round to tell his friend about the government's idea. I then thought it was my time to confess, I told Uncle it was a joke, and he called me a few choice words in jest, he then offered me some olives he went out into the kitchen to get them. I hadn't even noticed that he had been gone longer than was usual. Then when he came back, he gave me mine, and he had some for himself. I ate them, but I didn't notice anything different about them, Auntie said what have you done, as he had a big grin on his face, it turned out he had given me some olives that were stuffed with chilly, but he had put extra chilly in one of them for me. I obviously like stuffed olives as I didn't even notice,

Strange as when My Father took me to the American Air Base in Ruislip, once when I had run away one time he got me a pizza, I had never had one before so as usual my Father ordered the best one. As it had these black things on it and I had never seen or had them before. I asked My Father what they were, he said "to try one first, and then I will tell you", well I did but didn't like it, he stated that they were olives he said that when I was grown up, I would probably like them, he was right.

Lady Donna Louise Wilder

My Brother Richard met and married his second wife Van in Vietnam. He met her while visiting Vietnam, where he had gone to watch Arsenal, we have to wait until she can get her visa to meet her, and her son, my Brother Rick has just told me their good news, they are expecting a baby boy in April, I'm so happy for them.

Not really wanting or needing anything for our thirty-first wedding anniversary this year. We decided to buy ourselves a little bit of Land in Scotland. So we are now the proud owners of two plots of land in Bonny Scotland. (One square foot each). At Highland Estate in Glencoe Wood. So from this date forward 16/06/2015, we are now to be known as Lord Charles Walter Wilder and Lady Donna Louise Wilder.

What a laugh we had, when it came to visiting our Bank. Well, when we went to see our Bank so we could change our Titles as now that we own land in Scotland we are entitled to change our titles to Lord and Lady. You see, by purchasing a personal souvenir plot of land in Scotland, we can choose to take the title of Lord or Lady of Glencoe, as we have a Master Title Deed. Well, first the bank manager straight away said no we can't do that for you, to which I tried to tell him it is a legal document, but he just said it is not the bank's policy. I said that other family members had brought land, and they had no problem with their Banks, but he still said no, so we went back home,

I phoned up the head office. Where I spoke to a lady, who told me that they could see no problem. Because we had bought, Land in Scotland. She then said that they would phone the bank. To find out what was his problem and get back to me. Well, they didn't. so the next day I phoned up again and was told the same. So waited for the phone call back, but it didn't come. So later that day. I phoned up once again. After going over my complaint. I then was told that they would give me some compensation for the bad service. £50 then, £10 towards my phone calls plus £5 for my travel to the bank. Then the lady said here is your complaint number to take to the bank, telling them that they can change our titles. Well, off we went with a smile on our face. First, we checked our account. And sure enough, £65 had been paid straight into our bank. Then I told the assistant bank manager that I had spoken to his head office and that I had a complaint reference number. He still said he couldn't do it. I said but your head office has said that it can be done. He told me to phone them and he will tell them that he can't. I started to call the head office again while he walked off. Once I got through I, had to give my account number, then my sorting code, followed by my three digits from the back of my bank card. All this was done in the foyer right by the reception area, with customers all around. I felt very uncomfortable, as I am aware that my information is private.

Once I got through, I asked if the lady I had spoken to was available. As she wasn't, I had to give a brief rundown on the situation, obviously my notes were on his screen so he said is the bank manager there now. Please let me talk to him. I then handed my phone to the assistant Bank manager. Then when he started talking he noticed my phone was on speaker, so he proceeded to turn it off. Wally said hey, what are you doing. We want to hear what is being said. His reply was that he doesn't have conversations with his colleagues on speaker. He then proceeded to walk away with my phone, so Wally said oh! where are you going you can't just walk off with my wife's phone (as it happens my bank cards, etc. are with my phone). He then said right that's it this conversation is over and handed my phone back to Wally. (he walked off and started a conversation about us with three of his colleagues, we believe this to be true as they were looking at us through the glass door that divided us) I took my phone and told the man at the other end of the line what had happened; he told me to ask the assistant manager to come back to the phone. Where he told him once again that it could be done. Then the assistant manager said, well the manager is away and that he can't override his first decision. He was told then that he needed to make us an appointment to see the manager. He gave me my phone back and said I'll give you an appointment to speak to the manager.

Just as he was saying this, a colleague came out and said, she has the head office on the phone. And they would like to talk to me. At this point, we were all still in the public foyer, so all the customers had seen or heard all this. Then we were led into a side office (this should have happened at the very beginning). On the phone, the lady said I'm very sorry but we cannot change a title that you have bought, I told her that we haven't purchased a title. We have bought land in Scotland that gives us the right to do so, as we have a Master Deed Poll. She then said Oh I see. It was left that she was going to put in another complaint on our behalf, and we should hear about it within 48 hours, so it was left that we were going to see the manager with our appointment, but we were never given it. We went home and had a drink as one does under these circumstances.

Well, the next day I did get a phone call, to say that, unfortunately, their policy was that they will only change our titles if I can prove that I had bequeathed the land. As I had bought the land, they were not prepared to accept my Master Title Deed Poll. Well, as I had been given the wrong information from them. I was given some more compensation again a total of £50 plus £20 for my phone calls. (as we use an app on my phone called WQ4U, we didn't pay anything for the phone calls). The lady on the other end of the phone said she will take my complaint to her next meeting as I told her that some branches of Lloyds do change the titles, but this one doesn't and that it should be their policy right across every branch. So the first thing the next day I went and opened a new account with Barclays Bank, who were only too willing to call me a Lady.

My Son Michael, his Wife Kelly and Son Ben, moved to Gosport on Friday 10/07/2015. One day before their first wedding anniversary. As we knew, they wouldn't have had time to arrange anything special. We invited them over to ours, where we cooked and served them a three-course meal. Their favourite lamb shank, as Michael is still suffering from nerve damage from the fight in the pub. And Kelly has Chronic Fatigue Syndrome (CFS), also known as ME (Myalgic Encephalomyelitis) This means that they are now classed as Disabled. We went round as much as possible to help them move in by placing items in the attic, while I was up the ladder as I was the only fit one at the time, what with Wally's DVT. As well, I fell from the ladder and slide down the wall luckily, so I sat still for a little while contemplating my injuries. I could move all my limbs and I wasn't bleeding apart from a couple of my natural nails that had broken off. I was just shaken. I didn't move for a little while. I just sat on the landing. So I told Michael just to get me a cup of coffee. Wally was concerned but just kept saying are you alright. When Michael passed me my coffee and I took it, my hand started shaking uncontrollably. The shock had set in, after about 20 minutes I got up and continued my task of filling the attic. Then when I had finished, I came down the ladder very carefully and slowly as now I was beginning to feel some pain in my right leg. When I got downstairs and sat down in the front room, I pulled my leggings up to view my leg. As by now I had a rather large lump on the inside of my leg just below my knee, there was no bruising at first for a few days but then when it came out it stayed for over six weeks, the lump did go down a lot but not completely.

Michael bought a gas BBQ. So anytime the sun decides, to show its lovely face, which isn't that often. We can light up the BBQ, and enjoy ourselves. It's lovely having them live closer to us.

Another one of my pranks I did on Wally, I asked everyone on my Facebook friends list, to send Wally a card, note or letter, through the post. Just saying Hi, saying that he was disappointed, that no one bothers to send post these days, as we are all just saying happy birthday on Facebook instead of sending a card. etc. So a few days later the first few came. The very first one was a postcard with a picture of a camel on the front, and then on the back, it said Hi Wally hope you're having a good day, from Di & John. Then the next one was a card with a gorilla, that one just said, Hi Wally. The third one was an envelope with an A4 sheet of paper with the words, Have Nice Day. In big print. That was it he was baffled. He quickly worked out that someone was playing a joke on him, so when he said is it, you? I said I thought you would think it was me, he took that as it wasn't. So, when the next post came the next day. He received some more, birthday cards, handmade cards, notes, letters the lot, all just saying hello, or Hi. Some, saying a little birdie tells me you're missing postal communications and have a lovely day. Nothing was giving him any clue as to what it was all about he was even discussing them with me and analysing each and everyone. Wondering why anyone and everyone, were sending such stupid post to him.

Well, this went on for nearly two weeks. There was the post from America, Australia, New Zealand, the lot. Then to spice it up a bit I asked people on my Facebook to write on his Facebook page, saying just Hi, he worked out that some of the posts were from my friends, who were not on his Facebook, but he still couldn't understand why him and not me. I must admit it was very hard to keep a straight face for so long, as by now he was thinking that he was being hacked. He had numbered all the cards and envelopes as they arrived, in case he needed to report it at a later date. I would bring it up to everyone we saw, so Wally had to talk to them about it, not one of them let on it was me. Then we were around our Son Mike and Kelly's, having a little BBQ and drinks when the conversation came up yet again. I backed down a had to confess what I had done. I was called all the names under the sun, in a very loving way, I must say. He said he wasn't surprised in fact. He found it quite amusing when I told him that even our neighbours knew about it, in fact, everyone except him.

Michael Kelly and Ben invited Wally and Me round for a lovely dinner for my birthday, and Wally brought me a lovely new warm coat along with some nice clothes, perfume some new boots and shoes.

Chapter 37

America Christmas

Well, it's now November 2015 were all packed and ready for our trip to Los Angeles on the 17th November until the 5th January. (That's after the cases had been, packed and unpacked three times). As we had only got 23kg each, and we had brought some gifts to take with us for some of the family. That meant we weren't going to be able to take any for our self's, not that we needed anything. It's just nice to open a present or two on the day.

So as we were not going to be at home for Christmas and the New year, we booked to have a lovely Sunday roast at the Castle Tavern on 15th November, with our son Mike, daughter-in-law Kelly and step-grandson Ben. We had a change of heart when we saw that they had Lamb on the menu expect Wally and Ben, Wally went for, the Turkey while Ben went for the Gammon. Mike drove us to the Thistle hotel on Monday where we spent the evening relaxing.

(By the way, the Thistle Hotel used to be called the Crest Hotel so always brings back fond memories for us both).

We are so looking forward to spending our first Thanksgiving, Christmas and New Year with My family. not forgetting our newest family member Charlee Rae, who as we were Airborne has not made her entrance to the world. We thought we would buy something for ourselves at the airport, apart from some perfume and aftershave, there wasn't anything to get each other. I don't think the four bottles of duty-free Famous Grouse will last till Christmas Day? We kept checking what gate we were going to be leaving from many times. I had plugged my phone into one of the charging stations that were there. Then as Wally had another look to check our gate number, it came up with gate 19. So we gathered our bags and headed for gate 19. By this time, we had 2 flight bags on wheels, one large handbag, one bag containing both our phones, iPads, and camera, then four bags from duty-free, not forgetting our 4 bottles of whisky. So of we went on a long hike to our departure gate 19, as they are making some improvements, we had a long way to go.

On arriving at the final door, we checked in and sat down waiting to board the plane. Lucky for me, I realised I had left my phone on charged back in duty-free. As you can imagine I was in a panic; it was like losing my right arm. (Wally was none to pleased with me) I ran and I mean ran back to discover my poor phone was still waiting for me. (I think it has to be the longest time that we had been apart).

As they say, it was sods law that as soon as I left they started to call for us to board the plane. Well after that everything went well with our journey, we arrived at LAX airport and boarded the Flyaway bus to Woodley,

where Mandy picked us up and took us to Stephens, where we stayed for seven wonderful weeks.
A few days later our diary was full of lots of invitations. First both Wally and I had been, invited to a coffee morning at a lovely couple's house, Margaret and Terry. We had met them the year before at my birthday party that Mandy had arranged for me in her garden. Well, I can tell you they don't do there, coffee mornings like we do back home in the UK. As they had champagne at there's, we got to see Annie and Cookie again before they jetted off back home to live in the UK. Along with some more lovely people.

My cousin Mandy took us to see my Auntie Jo in her care home, as they were laying on a Thanksgiving party for them, plus two members of their family, as we were visiting Mandy asked if we could come along as well. They put on a lovely spread, a full three course, starting off with a creamy mushroom soup with crackers, a full roast dinner with all the American trimmings, and then a piece of pumpkin pie, all washed down with apple cider. Well, Mandy and Wally said that they didn't want any, so as that would have left Auntie Jo eating on her own, I thought it would be nicer for her if I joined her. So I sat next to her encouraging her to eat it, I think it worked as very soon she had cleared her plate. I for one could have done without it. The staff in the care home call Auntie Jo, the Queen. Which suits her just fine.

After we had finished, I pushed Auntie Jo, back to her room. But on our way there was this poor man, in his wheelchair, he was trying to move along the corridor by pulling himself along by the bars on the walls. He got in our way a little a few times but I just waited patiently, as I didn't think Auntie Jo was in any hurry, maybe she was, as Auntie Jo shouted to him saying, you deliberately done that. Poor chap, we got her to her room and said our goodbyes, leaving her talking to her black and white cat, a soft toy, that she takes everywhere with her.

On Thanksgiving, we went to Carley and Brady's house. I have to say I have never seen, so much food laid on in anyone's home before. My goodness, it was all so delicious. We had brought a lot of Cadburys chocolate over for everyone and had divided it all up into Christmas gift bags for them all. Stephen had left his on the table not too far away from his Mum, Well Auntie Jo took a liking for it and removed a lot of Stephens and placed it in her bag, along with all the wrappers. It's a wonder she wasn't sick with the amount she had eaten.

Our next appointment was to Kennedys 10th Birthday were we enjoyed some of her lovely birthday cake. Carley asked if we minded watching Kingsley in a few days' time as they were going out for dinner and they were going to take Kennedy with them, naturally we said we would love to. Then when we arrived, Kennedy decided she would like to stay with us, which was nice. We had great fun making videos on my phone to Father Christmas.

Wally and I having plenty of time on our hands volunteered to help Mandy and Carley wrap all their Christmas presents up, well believe me; they had loads.

Such A Lucky Lady

We felt it was the least we could do after being invited to join them to celebrate the holiday season with them all.

The next gathering was round Stephen's we helped him put on a lovely spread, Mandy and Ray's Grandchildren loved all their Uncle Stephen's Hallmark decorations. He has hundreds of them, Star Wars, Star Trek, the Wizard of Oz, to name but a few. He had his Christmas tree all done up in a Star Wars theme.

To help Stephen keep a count of what Hallmark items he has, I spent time listing them all for him.

Then we all spent another lovely evening round Carley and Brady's, where we had another delicious feast, well, one thing I will say about this beautiful family they sure know how to fatten us up.

Mandy took us to Aunties Jo place again as we had, been invited to the Christmas party, they were doing for all the residents, so that meant another Christmas dinner for me again!!!! While we were all sitting at the table with Auntie Jo, when some of the staff caught her eye, they would wave at her, but she would wave back at them followed by sticking her finger up at them laughing as she was doing it. Something that shocked Mandy.
They had a man doing karaoke; that seemed to be going down well with everyone. He was going around with his microphone and encouraging people to sing, when he came to Auntie Jo (who was already singing without the microphone) well, it was the first time I had heard her sing, she has a beautiful voice.

Lady Donna Louise Wilder

Christmas Eve, we all spent at Jade and Grieg's house. (where we had been informed that we had to wear Pyjamas. Luckily we had been given some notice. So we had to buy some along with the ugly jumpers, that, we had been told we had to wear on Christmas day). It was a lovely time getting to know dear baby Charlee-Rae. Christmas day was, spent at Mandy and Rays, Stephen had gone to pick up Auntie Jo, and Ray was in the kitchen making the Yorkshire puddings, Mandy, was told, about a better way to cook them. It was by adding cooking oil into the first compartments in a muffin tin and then tipping it down so that the oil runs into all the rest of the chambers. Then heat it up in the oven Well, this was done, and Ray topped each one of the compartments with his Yorkshire pudding mix and placed it in the hot oven. A little while later Wally noticed smoke pouring out of the top of the cooker. Ray went into the kitchen along with Wally Mandy me. Ray tried to open the oven trying to save his Yorkshire puddings, but it just ignited it, so he quickly closed it up. What had happened was, the mixture had risen nicely, but as there was too much oil in the pan, it had pushed some of it over the sides of the pan, and onto the bottom of the oven. Mandy had placed a sheet of cooking foil to catch any mess, being a gas oven; the flames caught, the oil so it was on fire.

Wally got a tea towel and after getting it wet wrung it out. So that he could put it on the flames, to dampen them down. When Ray opened the oven, this time, he got hold of the foil and pulled it to the front of the oven then onto the oven door, as Wally was putting the damp tea towel over the flaming oil, some went onto his shoes and burnt the leather. I could be heard saying No, No. As I was afraid, the flames from his shoe would ignite his trousers. My hero put out the fire. And no one was hurt. Apart from the Yorkshire puddings but Ray, not one to give up that easily proceeded to make some more. (This time without so much oil) And what a great success they turned out to be. Auntie Jo arrived, and we all had a wonderful Christmas Day together. Later when it was time to take Auntie Jo back, Mandy said to me to get the new purple jacket, she had brought he mum, out of the bag that Auntie Jo had placed it in along with all her gifts. I rummaged through all her bags to find it. Only to find the Mug that I had given Auntie Jo her tea in, a set of salt and pepper pots from the table, along with a bunch of keys we later found out belonged to Jade, who had earlier gone home in here husband's car.

Boxing Day Stephen, who works at CBS. Said that he needed to go into work just for an hour or two, so we said if he dropped us at the Grove, we could have a look about and see the Christmas Decorations that he had been telling us about, he had told us they were the best. Much better than the ones in The Village That had recently opened by Topanga Canyon. Well after we spent a very long time like five hours as Stephen had to wait for a delivery that was late arriving, we went to Shavahn's where She and Monica had made a lovely tasty batch of bubble and squeak along with other delicious goodies.
Also, I might add this family know how to pour a mean drink

Lady Donna Louise Wilder

My Brother-In-Law's

Big photo left to right back row;
Ronnie Wilder, Stanley Wilder,
Front row;
Stephen Wilder, Mother-in-law Vera Wilder, née Hook, Charles Wilder, (Wally) Kenneth Wilder,
Middle row;
(1) Peter Shaw, (2) Herbie McCullough, (3) Len Whelan, (4) Brenden Hogan,
Bottom row; (1) Robert Gittings, (2) Tony Rigg, (3) Paul Davies, (4) John Webster

Chapter 38

A Great Discovery

I have managed to trace a lot of my family thanks to modern technology mostly Facebook. One day I received a message from a lady called Lynda Kelly on Facebook, informing me that she was my 3rd cousin removed, it turns out that we both have the same Great Grandparents Minnie and James Gardner. We have since met up a few times.

On our visits to Los Angeles staying with My cousins Mandy Church, née Hone and Stephen Hone so far in 2012 I have met up with My Auntie Josephine Hone, née O'Bryan. Mikala Ackerman, who I had never met before, her mother is My cousin Mikala Ackerman, née Baker, Hone, who I met in 2013 along with Paul Hone and his son Christopher Hone. Sue Thomas née Hone, who lives in Dorset, plus her sister Judy Hanf, née Hone, who lives in Nebraska. Last time I saw them both was at Judy's wedding way back in the 70sWhen she married Jack. Then in 2014, My cousin Elaine Davis née Mountford, Stewart and daughter Julie Toll née Drake, Mountford, who I hadn't seen for over 40 years they had come over, from Australia to visit Mandy and Stephen.

On our visit in 2015, we got to meet Mandy's new addition to the family beautiful Charlee-Ray Carlson born 19th November 2015. To Jade Carlson née Church

Lady Donna Louise Wilder

Then I met up with some more family, this time, descent cousin's, on my O'Bryan side of my family. Marie, Ray and Connie, who I knew nothing off.

While helping my cousins Stephen, declutter some cupboards, he came across a large box containing loads and loads of birth marriage and death certificates along with some old family photos and paperwork. All to do with the family that my Auntie Jo was trying to piece together with the help of one of her cousins called Audrey Shanksy. I have now got in touch with, and she has very kindly sent me some more information, so I along with what I have gathered am going to spend some time with Lynda Kelly trying to piece it all together. You see dear Lynda, is very much, hooked on doing the family tree on Ancestry, and she will be able to pass on anything new to the online family tree that is on the website www.jacobstree.co.uk

I am so thankful that I joined Facebook and even more great full that I had the confidence to be able to work out how to get around the Internet.

Chapter 39

My Claim to Fame

I hold an unusual talent it is that whenever I get the hiccups, I, have noticed that 9/10 times, that as soon as I'm aware that I have them. If I acknowledge to someone and say excuse me, I've got hiccups they stop. I thought you would like to know this useless information.

My claims to fame are that I appeared on TV 4 times. In one instance in the local news, back in 1972, when I was seen laying my coat out at Reading Pop Festival. Then on GMTV back in 1994 when we were in Benidorm with Anthea Turner and Mr Motivator. They were asking about stress on holiday. So I volunteered to go on there show it was just a bit of fun really, they were filming it on the beach.

Twice in 2014 on Deal or no Deal with Noel Edmonds in the audience and then 2015 on the Jack Dee show in the audience yet again.

Then of course not forgetting my appearance on page 3 no less (no, not in the Sun newspaper) it was our local paper in Rushden when I was asking for donations of mobile phones, plus a couple of times in the Market Trader paper, when we opened the market and our cross stitch stool.

But I'm most famous for my singing in Goa I took it up after a lot of persuading. From friends to have a go at karaoke, good for a laugh I gave in and had a go my first attempt at karaoke was,

These boots are made for Walking by Nancy Sinatra. Followed by Gypsies, Tramps and Thieves by Cher Then I found a song that I liked (Funny as this was the number one song on the day that I was born) So I started singing that one Lay Down Your Arms by Anne Shelton.

And finally for writing this book.

A Massive Thank You

I would like to thank each and every one of you for taking the time and trouble to reach this far; I hope you have enjoyed my life story to date?

If along the way you have found that I have repeated myself, or misspelt any words, and I'm sure the educated ones of you out there will have come across many missed punctuations. Please accept my humble apologies. I can only put it down to being uneducated and the onset of old age.

Well, this has to be the hardest thing I have done so far in my lifetime. As much as it has been fun and a big challenge for me.

I do hope that I have many years left in me to enjoy the remainder of my life. My plans for my future apart from the obvious one that is to be healthy? Is to live to a ripe old age along with my loving and caring husband, in our cosy two bed flat, with our excellent views across the Solent. To keep fit, warm-hearted and loving, to keep smiling, happy and jolly, and to be kind to all mankind. Plus, not forgetting to have plenty of laughter along the way. I thank God for each person along my life's journey that has prompted me to be me....

Lady Donna Louise Wilder

Just Me

Holidays party's and days out.

Such A Lucky Lady

And Finally

On 13th February I got to meet up with my cousin Mechelle, whom I haven't seen since 1974, she came to visit with her husband, Alastair. We had a lovely meal cooked by my one and only naked chef. Looking forward to meeting the rest of my Auntie Pat family sometime soon.
We are going on the 6th March to my niece Charlotte's daughter Keeley's Christening. Then we have a dinner date on the 20th March for my sister Jo-Ann's Birthday at the Water Margin at Gunwharf.

Hopefully, we are going to find some spear time to visit Lynda Kelly to go through the mountain of certificates We are looking forward to meeting up with the Goa gang in Leister on the 29th April where we are all going to see Our Fred in person,

We have been kindly invited to our Ex daughter-in-law's son Vinnie's 1st Holy Communion on the 29th May Then to the wedding of the year Kimberley and Andrew on 2nd July.

That's without anything else that pops up before our holiday. It's all booked we go out to Los Angeles at the end of August till the beginning of October.
Plus, we are planning to have another trip to Las Vegas for my 60th Birthday treat. We have to be back for the Victorian Christmas at the Dockyard. It is looking like we will be in the UK this Christmas but you never know what is round the corner do you.

Lady Donna Louise Wilder

Just The Two Of Us

Charles Walter Wilder, Donna Louise Wilder

Such A Lucky Lady

Lady Donna Louise Wilder

Printed in Great Britain
by Amazon